COAST-TO-COAST PRAISE FOR

METROPOLIS

"CHARMING, WITTY, INTERESTING!"
Ed Koch, Mayor of New York

"A STORY THAT WILL MAKE NEW YORKERS
PROUD TO LIVE THERE AND MAKE THE REST OF
US ENVIOUS THAT WE DON'T" *Boston Globe*

"ONE OF THE BEST BOOKS ON NEW YORK
I HAVE READ" Norman Mailer

"WONDERFUL, SHARP, FUNNY...PURE PLEASURE"
Judith Rossner, author of *Looking for Mr. Goodbar*

"A NATIVE SON'S JAZZY HYMN OF PRAISE TO
NEW YORK CITY" *Newsday*

"SCINTILLATING!" *Booklist*

"DELIGHTFULLY WACKY" *Publishers Weekly*

"BRILLIANT, IMAGINATIVE!" *Sacramento Bee*

and for

JEROME CHARYN

"FAST AND FUNNY AND BRILLIANT"
Philadelphia Inquirer

"MAGIC-MAKING WITH AN ABSOLUTELY
SINGULAR AND PIERCING VOICE"
Herbert Gold, *Los Angeles Times Book Review*

"HIS LANGUAGE SINGS!"
The New York Times Book Review

METROPOLIS

NEW YORK AS MYTH, MARKETPLACE, AND Magical Land

JEROME CHARYN

AVON
PUBLISHERS OF BARD, CAMELOT, DISCUS AND FLARE BOOKS

The lines from "The Patients and the Doctors" by Julian Schnabel are reprinted by permission of *Artforum International Magazine*, February 1984 pp. 54-59, copyright *Artforum*.

AVON BOOKS
A division of
The Hearst Corporation
105 Madison Avenue
New York, New York 10016

Designed by Mary Jane DiMassi

The Putnam edition contains the following Library of Congress Cataloging in Publication Data:

Charyn, Jerome.
  Metropolis : New York as myth, marketplace, and magical land.

  Bibliography.
  Includes index.
  1. Charyn, Jerome—Homes and haunts—New York (N.Y.) 2. New York (N.Y.)—Social life and customs. 3. Novelists, American—20th century—Biography. I. Title.
PS3553.H33Z464   1986   813'.54   85-30752

First Avon Books Trade Printing: September 1987

For Henry Stern and Hugh Mo

CONTENTS

—METROPOLIS—

one

ELLIS: AN INTRODUCTION

[1]

Bronx boy, I grew up in a poor man's pile of streets, a ghetto called Morrisania, which had its own Black Belt on Boston Road and a strip of bodegas under the tracks of Southern Boulevard, a wall of Irish surrounding Crotona Park, and a heartland of Italians and Jews, poor as hell, except for a handful of furriers, accountants, lonely physicists, and our congressman, who lived on Crotona Park East, something of a golden corridor, with courtyards facing a long stitch of green. This congressman was supposed to have an idiot son who'd seen *The Mark of Zorro* too many times and haunted his own building with cape and sword, coming out from behind the banisters to challenge housewives and delivery boys to a duel. It could have been an apocryphal tale. But one of the delivery boys was a friend of mine. I didn't invent the scar on his face. He'd been touched by Zorro. But it's the nature of politics that our congressman's son was never carted off to an asylum. The corridors and the stairwell were his particular paradise. Perhaps it wasn't corruption on the part of Congress, or even political pull. Just simple neighborliness that allowed Zorro to lumber in the halls. Golden corridor or not, it was still a ghetto, and the ghetto protected its own. Naturally, these were romantic times (circa 1948), before there was ever a South Bronx.

The Bronx I remember consisted of east and west. The official demarcation line was Jerome Avenue. But Jerome Avenue was so far to the west that most of the Bronx remained in some deep pit, an endless east that was like a continent. And so we made our own geographer's rules. The Bronx's Champs Élysées, known as the Grand Concourse, became our magic marker. Everything near the Concourse was considered west. When you arrived at the bottom of Claremont Park, you were in no-man's-land, that hazy border where the East Bronx began. By the time you got to Third Avenue, there was no longer any doubt: you'd entered the borough's eastern heart, land of the lower middle class.

Morrisania was where Ed Koch was born. And if our mayor seems rambunctious, it's nothing more than the heritage of Crotona Park. If he moved to Jersey by the time he was eight, so what? Eight's an old man. Ed Koch was formed by Crotona Park and Boston Road. He was always a street kid, a kind of Bronx savage. And he runs our city with a savage's code of honor. "I'm not the type to get ulcers. I give them," he says. He's Ivan the Terrible with a Bronx lisp. A wild child, like me.

That's where the resemblance ends. I'm the one with ulcers. I was something of a thief. I swiped polo shirts and pink erasers. I hustled chess on the rooftops and in the streets, shoving pawns down my sleeve when an opponent's eye would stray. I twitched a lot, like some casualty of a long-forgotten war. I walked the streets like a city wolf, eyeing, eyeing everything. My father rarely worked. He existed in a state of psychic grief. I couldn't grasp his syllables when he talked. There was some horrible un-declared war between us.

I was a guerrilla in my father's house. I lived under siege in the room I shared with my brother. But I wasn't Maxim Gorky or Kerouac. I couldn't take to the road. I wore my swaddling clothes a terribly long time. Illiterate as I was, without a dictionary at home, I became a Tal-mudic scholar, seeking revenge on my father with words. The only library in Morrisania was on the black side of Boston Road. I crossed into that ghetto, the lone white wolf, to borrow a child's life of Spinoza. That little glass grinder was a revelation to me. He defied all the Jewish patriarchs of old Amsterdam to declare that the universe was outside Jehovah's jurisdiction. He compared it to a giant clock, subject to musical and mathematical laws. Spi-noza ground his glass in isolation, and I suffered over his story, a child in the new Amsterdam of the Bronx. But I wasn't so successful with my dad. I belittled him in Spi-noza's voice, talked of clockworks in the sky (I was twelve), and he beat me with a broom.

That was thirty-six years ago, and I've developed am-nesia about my dad. Had to or I couldn't have survived. But I never really rubbed away that relentless look of anger in his eye, as if my existence were an affront to him, an outrage he had to endure. That's how my twitch be-gan. It was like an electrical scream running through my body, my own musical clock, filled with fury. I was Spi-noza's planet of storms. I've buried that twitch some-where, but how do you find the right cost accounting to compensate for the anger of your own dad? He's seventy-five. His hair is blacker than mine. I still can't understand his syllables. He speaks a language of wounds. His new Amsterdam wasn't very kind to him. A Polish boy, he'd come to America all by himself. His mother had left him behind in the Old World because he suffered from con-junctivitis. He lived with an aunt near Warsaw until his pinkeye was cured. Ah, but was it ever cured? My father carried it with him to America, like a mark on the brain. I never once saw him smile at his mother or his father,

who'd arrived earliest of all and sold apples in sweatshops
and on the streets. That was my grandfather's single success: apples for every season of the year. No spectacular
rise. No great drama. Just a railroad flat on Henry Street
in Manhattan and a history of apples.

I sought prouder tales, like *The Rise of David Levinsky,*
the metamorphosis of my grandfather into a merchant
prince. Or a bit of a gangster maybe. Couldn't he have
cornered the market on apples, parceled out the supply,
like cocaine? It would have given me pleasure to brag of
my grandfather as the Lower East Side's apple king. But
that's infantile romance. My grandfather was an apple
peddler with yellow teeth and no English in his skull. At
least my father graduated to a sewing machine. He had a
talent for building fur coats. That talent wasn't much
prized after World War II. A recession hit the country,
my father went into business for himself, bought a car. It
almost seemed as if he'd solved the riddle of the United
States, becoming the owner of a Plymouth and an entrepreneur. The car was my security blanket. I can still recall
the emblem on its hood, that silver reproduction of a
ship, the *Mayflower's* little shining masts. My father had
produced his own Plymouth Rock. He was a Polish Pilgrim with a fur cutter's knife.

I dreamt of my father's Plymouth, green and silver,
with wood paneling and straw upholstery, my dad and me
both at the wheel, sailing over Crotona Park into the out-
lands of Riverdale, like a long creamy ride to the moon.
But that Plymouth never got us out of the East Bronx. It
sat in its garage most of the time. My father never learned
to drive. His business failed. He sold the car and sank into
debt. His Pilgrim days were over. We landed in poverty
and were anchored there. It terrified me. From the day I
entered high school I was never sure we'd have enough to
eat. My father would go down to the fur market and sit
behind a machine for a month or two. His work was as
seasonal as selling apples in the street.

I buried my nose in report cards. I was the Talmudic
prince, too involved in academics to find a part-time job. I
could always defeat my father by grabbing A's and B's. I

wondered why he never abandoned us, left to start another life. His rage seemed so incredibly large. But he was stuck in some seesaw battle with himself, a battle I couldn't understand. He'd remained my mother's child, angry from the minute he woke to the minute he started to snore.

I went on to college, but I still lived at home. Became a substitute teacher in the City's school system, like a wandering minstrel, going from school to school with Spinoza's bag of tricks. I talked about the universe—the possibility of planets like our own, with a duplicate Bronx and ghettos of green men. I was adored by most of my students, Mr. C., the "sub" who softened Shakespeare with science fiction.

I got married, moved to California. The marriage didn't last. I was caught in the middle of a war zone I'd created. I was still that savage from Crotona Park, a golem who'd been building my own feet of clay, without a magical rabbi to protect me, as the original golem had—some medieval man who might give me lessons in diplomacy and manners. I drifted from relationship to relationship, unable to settle in long enough to have a child. Golems aren't such terrific mates. We're too busy sucking clay.

I was haunted, like that congressman's son, old Zorro, but I didn't attack people in apartment houses. I had a much more reasonable career. I taught college, I wrote books, but I was still a golem, cradled in some unreasonable fear.

And then, by luck, I happened to start a novel about a Polish gangster who'd gone through Ellis in 1900, and I wanted to see what that island was all about. Bought a ticket at Battery Park, climbed aboard a little ferry with a bundle of tourists, and we landed on the corroded docks of the old immigrant station. The station looked like a Polish castle lost in the weeds. The roofs had bite marks in them, as if they'd been under attack from some prehistoric bird.

A U.S. ranger took us on a guided trip through the main building. That ranger knew her facts. She was a

woman of twenty-five or -six, with trousers, a military
buckle, and a ranger's hat. She talked of the baggage
room, where immigrants had to store their belongings
when they got to Ellis, the Isle of Tears. She didn't lecture
in a condescending way. She showed us the dining room,
where immigrants could eat for less than a dime in 1910.
The walls were cracked. The floor had begun to buckle.
Nothing was tarted up for us. No fancy paint or an added
bench. The whole bloody island was in disrepair. The
station had been closed for a long time. The U.S. couldn't
seem to get rid of it. There'd been some talk of turning it
into a gambling casino. But Lyndon Johnson, who was
president when that rumor hit, wouldn't donate Ellis Island to a syndicate of gamblers. That's what the ranger
told us.

She took us step by step through an immigrant's day,
and for me it was like going through the Stations of the
Cross, rituals of suffering every five or ten feet. Immigrants had to climb a flight of stairs while doctors looked
at them and chalked up their clothes with secret signs, a
cabalistic code that recorded whether they had tuber-
culosis, suffered from pinkeye, or had suspicious lumps. I
imagined myself being plucked by foreign hands and
shouted at in a language that must have sounded like all
the babble of the world. I was thrilled and scared, a voyeur passing through my mother and father's primal journey to America.

We arrived at the Great Hall, the enormous registry
room where immigrants were processed and tagged. It
was a tall cave with a barreled roof. It had a bridge along
the sides where relatives might wait, or some chief inspector could look down at the proceedings. Nothing had
prepared me for the deep well of that room, the accumulation of so much emptied space. Great pendulous chandeliers with missing globes lent a kind of sadness to the
room. But they couldn't mask the awfulness of that place,
like some Roman arena for horses to prance, horses and
slaves.

No one could have felt secure in a room like that, big as
America. I would have crapped in my pants. Not from

fear of the processing station. But the hopelessness of a room where you could no longer define yourself. Grandfathers, pregnant women, criminals could only have shivered and behaved like a child.

Seventeen million people went through that station. My father was only one man. But I understood his pathology for the first time. He'd never quite recovered from Ellis Island. Yes, yes, he'd been damaged before all that. No pathology can begin in some registry room. But I'd swear the island had stunned him, chalked my father for life. An odd case? Perhaps. Others got through it, went on to brilliant careers. But I wonder if Ellis Island didn't leave some invisible tag.

It's dangerous to impose one person's psychic dilemma upon the history of a whole town. The Big Apple had been around over two hundred and fifty years before that station was ever built. But I still believe that *modern* New York comes right out of Ellis Island.

That argument may be the prejudice of an immigrant boy, but it's also a perfect hook to comprehend a city that's so varied, so dense, that contradicts itself minute by minute, the most European of all American cities and the most American of any city in the world. In 1975 people thought New York would become another Atlantis and disappear into the ocean. The City had to beg money to keep alive from day to day. It couldn't meet its enormous payroll. Our mayor, a five-foot-three accountant who'd come from the Brooklyn machine, was ignored by almost everyone. The wounded hippopotamus of New York stumbled around old Abraham Beame. Abe had to fire people. But the wounded hippo couldn't even tell how many people were on its payroll. Companies scattered across the river. An investment banker, Felix Rohatyn, formed a kind of shadow government. He was our Cromwell, saving us and reducing us, like an animal doctor who can heal a hippopotamus. Rohatyn ran New York. He brokered for every group, obliged our unions to swallow the City's "paper," bonds that no one wanted to buy. The City had to decimate its services. Teachers, firemen, and cops were let go. Playgrounds became shadowlands. Cen-

tral Park grew dirty and wild. The Bronx was burning.
Most construction had stopped. Manhattan was beginning to look like a phantom village.

Ten years later New York is the acknowledged capital
of the world. The hippo has come out of its own big sleep.
Henry Kissinger lives here now. We have Trump Tower
and Philip Johnson's AT&T. We have a whole city-within-
a-city being built near Battery Park. You can see blue
pyramids rising out of the rock piles. Manhattan is becoming a fairyland of new construction. It has its own
ramblas on Columbus Avenue, where mannequins look
like real people, and customers in restaurants and ice-
cream parlors remind you of dummies in a window. The
Bronx has stopped burning. We have ranch houses in the
rubble of Charlotte Street, and the Grand Concourse is
being rehabbed, block by block. Brownsville is still Berlin,
but Bed-Stuy is beginning to look like Greenwich Village.
The Big Apple has become a boomtown under Ed Koch.
Traveling with him one afternoon, I watched his gray
eyes peer at a houseboat moored to a City dock. "I don't
know who owns this houseboat," he said, "but I'm sure
they're paying rent. With me you gotta pay rent."

You have to pay the piper, Ed Koch. The City's coffers
are high again. That Brooklyn accountant, Abe Beame, is
long gone from City Hall, and a king rules there now, a
street king who loves eggplant and garlic sauce and brings
his own brown bag to Italian restaurants. We come from
similar clay, but I'm prepared to argue all his policies,
while I sit in the mayor's limousine. His own adviser, Dan
Wolf, had invited me to have lunch with the street king.

"Mr. Mayor . . ."

His gray eyes swiveled out. "Call me Ed."

"We went to the same school. We're practically citizens
of Crotona Park. Only what about . . . ?"

"The death penalty," he says, like a wizard who can
anticipate my words. "Capital punishment is not extreme.
Torture would be extreme."

The wizard has disarmed me before I could declare my
case.

The lunch turns into an endless picnic because Koch

lets me follow him around for the rest of the day. It's June '85, and the mayor has declared a moratorium on politics. He basks in golden silence. Koch won't campaign, except for his flurry of press conferences, often twice a day. Everybody knows that he'll win the primary with a whisper or two.

The Irish were becoming his most loyal constituency. He had eighty-one percent of the Irish vote. The Italians were next in line, with almost eighty percent.

"What about the Jews?" I asked.

A bit of gray went out of his eyes. "Seventy-three percent," he said, as if he'd been mugged in Gracie Mansion. Then he laughed, and his eyes broke into their usual color. "Gives me an opportunity to say the Jews are a little crazy."

We didn't have to talk about the Protestant vote. The WASPs were like some forgotten country in New York politics. In spite of its sudden renaissance, New York still hadn't climbed out of the melting pot. The yuppies might rule on Columbus Avenue, but the Irish and Italians would deliver the vote. There were over three million Catholics in the City of New York.

I rode in a helicopter with Koch to Riverdale. Our heliport was near the wonderful old fire station in Battery Park. "It will be turned into a restaurant," the mayor told me. He put on metal earmuffs. "I have a problem with my ears."

The chopper lifted off the ground, close to the Statue of Liberty and her latticed truss, all that scaffolding to prepare for her hundredth birthday in America. I watched the blue curl of the water under our feet. Ellis Island looked like a bit of candied grass and stone. It couldn't have traumatized a horsefly from up here. But I wasn't fooled by a helicopter's slanting run. That station still stood in the ruined grass, a reminder of who we were and where we'd come from, even if it hadn't housed immigrants in over forty years. We landed in a baseball field, the police chopper bumping down onto the grass. The neighborhood kids were in awe of Ed Koch, a king who'd come out of the sky, and I was the king's apprentice. The kids waved to all of Koch's retinue, bodyguards and advance men. He was going to deliver the commencement address at the Riverdale Country School. He'd slept on the chopper, glanced at the notes of his speech. Koch is notorious for inventing his own speeches. He's as quick as Lenny Bruce, but this street king has an instinct for survival. He's the greatest stand-up comic City Hall has ever had.

But the mayor decided not to be funny in Riverdale. I stood behind the podium with the mayor's bodyguards, amid a fairyland of clean white faces. The bodyguards laughed among themselves. One of them was black. "They charge a special rate for blacks," he said. "It's twice as expensive for blacks to get in."

Public service was "the noblest of professions" for Ed Koch. He'd written a bestseller, diminishing presidents, governors, and a few mayors, but that gave him no "psychic satisfaction," he said. "I love my job. Everybody knows that. If you don't, I'm telling you now." The street king isn't descended from a royal line of mayors. He's a mongrel, like the rest of us. "My parents were immigrants from Poland," he said. And the Apple was unique because "sons and daughters of immigrants could rise so high and so quickly . . . there are very few places where that is so."

As we left the grounds of the school, a student approached Koch. He didn't look like a wacko. The bodyguards let him through. He had a curious picture for the mayor to sign. He'd once been photographed with Koch, but the photographer had "lost" him and captured only his hand. The student wanted Koch to sign that disembodied hand in the photograph. This encounter could have been a piece of fiction, a parable out of Kafka, but the mayor didn't hesitate for a moment. He scribbled his name over the hand and we returned to the helicopter.

There was an ambulance on either side of the chopper. The mayor winked. "One ambulance for each of us." The dust spread around us as we walked to the chopper, climbed a tiny stool, sat down, belted ourselves in at the back of the machine, the mayor giving his thumbs-up sign to a crowd of kids near the ball field, that magical king who had dropped down into their territory in an iron bird, and rose up out of their lives. I congratulated him on his speech.

"Ah," he said. "I was bored. My heart wasn't in it."

But he'd told my tale, an immigrant story. He was just another Polish boy, riding into the wind. It didn't matter that all the property around him was his. It was on loan to him as mayor. In New York only a public servant could become king. Donald Trump had his name in gold on a building; he could even construct a castle with a moat on Lexington or Third, but he'd never preside over Gracie Mansion, no matter how many millions he had. Koch wasn't king for life; it was only a borrowed mansion. But he'd made New York his by the force of his personality; he'd imposed himself upon the town.

The streets of Riverdale looked like cardboard cutouts. We rode back into the City's heart; the Manhattan skyline was like an ugly toyland of similar cluttered boxes, rescued only by the Chrysler Building and its eccentric silver top. We climbed down toward the piers and bounced onto the heliport's floor. The mayor removed his metal earmuffs and we ran to his car. He was already late for his next speech.

[2]

My day with Koch felt like a tapestry off the rotting walls of Ellis Island. The sons of immigrants out on a ride. But it was more than that. The mayor had no dinner plans, and he invited me back to Gracie Mansion after one of his marathon town hall meetings. He'd fielded questions for an hour and a half. It was brutal work. Everyone in the audience seemed to have a grievance against New York. Koch didn't shirk. He had no slick answers. He'd involved himself in some intimate dance with the audience. If soccer players were pissing outside a woman's window, Koch guaranteed that they would no longer piss. One old man complained, "I've been mugged so often, if I'm not mugged, I feel the muggers are angry at me."

The mayor didn't rattle off crime statistics to that old man or try to snow him with facts and figures. He conferred with the deputy police commissioner at his side and told the man, "We'll follow it up. Let me tell you."

He created "marriages" at this meeting, putting people together with his commissioners, having the commissioners promise to look at local problems out on the street. A certain Mrs. Moskowitz could hardly believe it when Koch invited a deputy sanitation commissioner to sit down with her the next day and examine the garbage problems on her block. "I'll have coffee with you," she told the commissioner.

The mayor said, "I'll be back," and I followed him out of the auditorium with his bodyguards. We took the chopper back to Manhattan. I was becoming a sky cowboy: four helicopter rides in one day. We landed at a Pan Am heliport on the East River, and I rode with the mayor to his mansion.

Koch was beat. His schedule would break an ordinary man. He was on the go from six in the morning to midnight. He had "opened" City Hall at seven-thirty and now I sat with him in his living room at Gracie Mansion, eating pasta and lamb chops and drinking red wine.

We both had our dinner off a tray, watched *Reilly, Ace of Spies* and then the news, which told of a construction crew chief who earned four hundred thousand dollars a year. "I work twenty-four hours a day," the crew chief said. "I'm always on call."

"A gonif," Koch said, biting into his strawberry tart.

It was time for me to go. I thanked the mayor. It was my first meal as a guest of the City. Koch dialed his chauffeur. "I have a customer for you," he said.

The mayor accompanied me to the door, slouching a little at six feet one. Who knows how many phone calls he had to make? He might be up in the sky again within the hour if one of his policemen was shot in some corner of Brooklyn. He was the watchman of New York. There'd been no other mayor like him before.

Ed Koch is the golem mayor. His clay was formed on Ellis Island. His fierceness and his humor come from the Big Apple's odd split: New York has taken on a kind of schizophrenia in the twentieth century, a curious, biting wound that has little to do with the gap between rich and poor. That gap was there three hundred years ago.

Maybe we ought to examine our preschizophrenic past. The Apple's industry began with the Dutch, merchants who wouldn't allow religion to wreck a good deal. Peter Stuyvesant hated the Jews and wanted to rid them from New Amsterdam. He was the City's first anti-Semite. But the Dutch West India Company wouldn't let Peter have his way. Some of the Jews prospered, others remained poor, while New Amsterdam developed into a mercantile town.

Then the English came along, and the Dutch surrendered New Amsterdam to a tiny fleet of warships on September 8, 1664. A curious amnesia settled in for over a hundred years. How many schoolboys can recall the name of a single English governor? It's almost as if history stopped after the congenial Dutch. But we can always remember the two Peters, Stuyvesant and Minuit. Stuyvesant was a tyrannical son of a bitch. Yet the City has a plaque where Stuyvesant's pear tree once stood. That tree outlived Stuyvesant by two hundred years.

But the English couldn't engender a single myth. It's part of our stubbornness. We've held on to our Dutch beginnings and shed our English skin.

The City seems to recapture its memory around the time of the Revolution and the English occupation of New York. It was seven years of shame, but not because of the British troops garrisoned here. The population began to swell with loyalists. New York was Tory town, the king's own capital of the New World. The City prospered. With so many Tories, merchants, and soldiers, New York suffered its first housing shortage. Quick fortunes were made. Prices jumped over the moon. Some people had to live in tents. The town was overrun with whores, who serviced King George's Hessian and British troops, while captured American soldiers lay starving in prison ships.

Then the English lost the war and fifteen thousand Tories suddenly disappeared from sight. The City's brokers had been trading under a buttonwood tree near 68 Wall Street, but New York became the banking capital of America after this stock exchange moved indoors. Alexander Hamilton and Aaron Burr started their own banks. Hamilton was my first hero. Short, dark, with wooly hair, he was the bastard son of a Jewish merchant, Lavein or Levine. His real dad was a highborn drifter, James Hamilton. His mother, Rachel Lavein, was a bit of a whore. I always had a suspicion that other fathers were involved. Rachel Lavein had a closetful of beaux in the West Indies, where she lived. For me, young Hamilton was black *and* Jewish. He fought a duel with Aaron Burr, who wanted to become emperor of the United States, and Hamilton got himself killed. Burr became a pariah after the duel. He died in a rooming house.

He'd also been a sachem of Tammany Hall. Tammany was a narrow club of American patriots, with little regard for the Irish or any other immigrants until these native sons scratched their heads and discovered that the common tribe of landless white males suddenly had the vote. Then Tammany kissed the Irish, who'd been treated like dogs up to then, and a unique kind of politics began. Tammany helped the Irish become citizens and counted on their vote. It was the party of the rabble. And the Irish, who were used by the Tammany pols as their own donkey force, soon took over Tammany itself, and that was the beginning of modern New York because it was the first time that a foreign rabble had competed with the "nativists" and won. "There were sixty or seventy years when the Irish were everywhere," Daniel Patrick Moynihan tells us in *Beyond the Melting Pot.* "The Irish came to run the police force *and* the underworld; they were the reformers and the hoodlums; employers and employed."

I hated the Irish as a boy. They ringed Crotona Park

and wouldn't allow a little kike to enter their zones. But we all owe an enormous debt to the Irish. They helped create the character of New York, its reputation as an immigrant town. They lived in the worst rookeries when they arrived. They were exploited, beaten, forced to grub, these shanty Irish who'd grown wild and coarse under English rule and developed their own wild English, a crusty tongue that was almost like an act of vengeance upon their rulers.

The Irish came here and discovered another ruling class. Politicians, bankers, and grocers. The natives clamored to send them back to Ireland, organizing into secret societies like the Order of the Star-spangled Banner and other Know-Nothings, who were a kind of northern Klan. The Know-Nothings didn't want these wild men around, a dirty, stinking folk that never washed or combed their ruddy hair. They multiplied like rats in their stinking warrens. An Irish woman wasn't satisfied until she was delivered of thirteen sons, the Know-Nothings said. The Irish were nothing more than Negroes with white skin. They had to live among the blacks. A decent landlord wouldn't take them in. But the Know-Nothings couldn't destroy the Irish, who kept to their rookeries. The worst gangs New York has ever had were formed in the Irish slums of Mulberry Bend.

The gangs worked for Tammany, getting votes and building bonfires on election eve. The Irish legitimized themselves through their finagling and their own brute force, capturing a third of the City vote by 1855, with their ruddy hair and dirty faces.

And when the Italians and the Jews began to arrive from Eastern Europe after 1880, they were no more dirty than the Irish had been. Other nativists opposed this "eastern horde." But the Italians and Jews moved into the old Irish rookeries on the Lower East Side. And my granddad, who couldn't howl a word of English, became a citizen through Irish auspices. He peddled his apples and voted the Tammany line. I ought to know. I'd never have gotten born without the Irish. My dad arrived after the National Origins Act of 1924 cut off immigration from

Eastern Europe. He couldn't have landed in America if
his own dad hadn't become a "cousin" of Tammany Hall.
And Ellis Island wouldn't have been the birthplace that
bloomed in my head.

[4]

Ellis was an island that no one seemed to want. It had its
particular ghosts. The Dutch called it Little Oyster Island,
but they wouldn't start a settlement there. The English
considered using it as a "pesthouse" for victims of the
plague. But even such victims couldn't get onto the island.
It was turned into a "hospital" for pirates who were hung
in Washington Market, then rowed out to the island and
chained to a gibbet. These dead men were the island's
chief inhabitants for most of the eighteenth century. It
fell into the hands of someone named Samuel Ellis, but he
couldn't dispose of the island. In 1794 Ellis's island was
given to the state of New York, and a fort was put up to
house a company of soldiers. But these men began to
desert. They couldn't tolerate the loneliness of that island. New York offered it to the United States, and the
island took a melancholy turn, holding British prisoners
during the War of 1812. It was soon deserted again, except for an occasional hanging. Ellis couldn't seem to get
away from the dead. It was a ghostly fort, staffed from
time to time by the army and the navy. The navy built a
powder magazine there in 1835. But that magazine wasn't
much of a success. In 1861 the island had a population of
five people.

Local pols began to worry about the munitions dump.
One Jersey congressman calculated that if lightning ever
struck the island, Hoboken, Jersey City, "and parts of
New York" would disappear. But nothing happened. The
dump remained on Ellis Island.

In 1882 Congress passed a bill forbidding lunatics,
paupers, and convicts from entering the United States.
Until then the states themselves "determined the desir-

ability of immigrants," according to Thomas Dunne in his text on Ellis Island. "Beginning in the 1880's . . . recurrent newspaper and magazine stories told of degenerate aliens being cast out of European and Asian alms houses, insane asylums and prisons, and dumped on the shores of America."

Congress had to choose between Ellis and Bedloe's Island (home of the Statue of Liberty) as the headquarters of a permanent screening station, but the press imagined immigrants who might leak out of the station and bother people visiting the statue and its little park. So that former gibbet, an island of pirates and ghosts, hardly ever occupied for two hundred and fifty years, was filled with "hundreds of workmen" in 1891, laboring "at a large, three story reception center, a hospital for ill and quarantined immigrants, a laundry, boiler house and electric generating plant," made of Georgia pine.

Ellis Island opened on the very first day of 1892. *Harper's Weekly* likened it to "a latter-day watering place hotel," a hotel that could process ten thousand immigrants in a single afternoon. But *Harper's* "water palace" burned down in 1897.

Immigrants were shunted to Castle Clinton, an older depot at the Battery, until Ellis Island was rebuilt as an elaborate fireproof dormitory, designed by the young architectural firm of Boring & Tilton. It was a Beaux Arts assembly modeled after the Gare Montparnasse—immigrant house as railroad station, with a great hall of Guastavino tile. Once again the praise was considerable. Immigrants would enter the United States in a kind of secular church with high, vaulted ceilings and almost religious sunlight. The new Ellis Island was a brick-and-tile palace-church that could offer "lavish hospitality." Because in spite of its "nativists," America itself had become a receiving station. It was a country that had no rational order of population. It was created by other people's drifts: Dutch, French, English, Irish. . . .

In 1900 the nation's crucible was New York. Whether immigrants moved on to Milwaukee or Kalamazoo, for the vast majority of them their initial point of entry was the station at Ellis Island. The processing usually took about four hours. *Four hours,* and I've become the bard of trouble, singing about lifetime wounds. Battle scars, victimization. I'm not searching for a sentimental paradigm of failure, a bleeding heart. Most of the immigrants came through Ellis and went on to form their own character. Their fate wasn't determined by Ellis Island unless they were ill or were "troublemakers" sent back to Europe on the "anarchists' boat." Indeed, there were three thousand suicides on Ellis Island, sometimes more than six a month. Most of these weren't the result of that simple march up the stairs to the registry room. The men, women, and children who committed suicide were detainees, those who were kept on the island and weren't allowed "in." But I'm talking about that *investment* each immigrant must have made, fathers, mothers, bachelor women and men thrusting themselves into the New World; the hallucinatory image they held in their minds during days of steerage, *land of gold, land of gold,* and the residual fear that America wouldn't take them, no matter how healthy they were *or* unpolitical. The fear must have passed: only two percent didn't make it, the lungers and the anarchists, midgets and known murderers.

And the others? Seventeen million souls. I'd be willing to bet my life that most of them didn't *lose* Ellis Island, that in some piece of their psyche they were always "five minutes out of steerage." Ellis was still a ghost island. The babble they'd heard went deep. That didn't prevent them from becoming farmers in Wisconsin or gravitating to the Lower East Side, an infinite ghetto land that could swallow greenhorns looking for patches of Europe on Grand Street, particularly if those greenhorns were Italians and Jews. Peasants for the most part, they'd felt betrayed by all the czars and kings that ruled them. They didn't take kindly to governments. The Sicilians who came here were considered savages by the rest of Italy, "black Italians." And the Russian and Polish Jews, with their beards and wigs and funny hats, were a planet apart from the uptown German Jews, those who'd arrived long before Ellis and had established themselves as brokers and department-store tycoons, and prayed in temples that were the closest thing to a Protestant church.

The downtown Jews clung to their ghettos, sold apples like my granddad or grew much more ambitious. Some became tycoons like the uptown templegoers. But they had the authentic stink of the street. And a sadness. It wasn't simply a conflict of the Old World and the New, the shedding of phylacteries for a button-down collar. It was the sheer explosion of their lives, the replication upon replication of immigrant tales, like looking at your double in the window, a double with dark lines on his or her face. The Jews had fled from Czar Nicholas and his thirty-year induction policy that made a soldier out of you from kindergarten to the grave. Grand Street had no pogroms. But it was futile to consider yourself part of a black-coated colony. This was New York, a town that had just swallowed up four other boroughs, absorbed Coney Island and Forest Hills.

In 1880, twenty years before the appearance of Ellis Island's brick church, there were less than one hundred thousand Jews in New York, a quiet population that had no criminal class. Hardly a single murder had ever been committed by a Jew in the United States, from the time of the Dutch through the English rule and a hundred years of independence. There'd even been a banker-patriot, Haym Salomon, a refugee from Poland, who'd helped finance the Revolutionary War. I ought to know. Haym Salomon haunted my childhood. He'd come to my public school in a film featuring Claude Rains. He was a pious man, singing in a prayer shawl and doing undercover work for the Sons of Liberty. But Claude Rains was also the Phantom of the Opera, a devil with an acid-eaten face who lived in the scaffolding above *La Bohème* and murdered opera people. That's the misfortune of movies. Actors never stick to one role. Haym Salomon was the Phantom of the Opera and Claude Rains. That Phantom terrorized me. I couldn't go to the toilet in peace. And in my own immature mind, an evil man in a black hat had saved the Revolution and started the United States.

But Haym Salomon died long before the mass immigration of Jews. In 1900 there were six hundred thousand of us in New York, packed into the Lower East Side, which had become a Jewish Calcutta. Those with a little more wealth or wanderlust had already gone up to Harlem or established colonies in the new borough of Brooklyn. By 1910 the Jewish population had doubled to twelve hundred thousand and Brownsville was a second Lower East Side. There was also a considerable cadre of Jewish whores and thieves. In *World of Our Fathers* Irving Howe dismisses this cadre as a kind of growing pain, some simple disorder of the dispossessed: ". . . crime was a marginal phenomenon," he tells us, "a pathology discoloring the process of collective assertion and adjustment."

I can guarantee Irving Howe that the assertion wasn't so collective in the Bronx. And this was forty years after 1910. In the lower depths of Morrisania, at the edges of Charlotte Street, Jewish gangs flourished with their Italian counterparts long before that great blitz of the 1970s, when even the rats were organized into gangs, because the burnt-out buildings had thrown them onto the rubble with wild dogs.

But there were no wild dogs in 1950. Humans could still venture into Crotona Park, sit around Indian Lake, which hadn't grown into a rotting swamp. But we were the poorest Jews in creation. Progress had passed us by. Our fathers hadn't gone to City College, that Harvard of Harlem Heights, which was supposed to be ninety percent Jewish. City College graduates didn't come to Morrisania. We were the lumpen, lumpen proletariat, Jews that were left behind.

We still had one foot on Ellis Island, though I couldn't have known that as a boy. We were the underside of that Jewish success story—the leap from Ellis Island to dentistry school in one lousy generation. There were enough Jewish dentists around to pack the Polo Grounds. But what did that mean to us? My father never had a checking account. I knew what checks were. I'd read Theodore Dreiser. But I had a savings booklet, like my dad. It was my wife who introduced me to the magic of scribbling checks.

I was a greenhorn without ever realizing it. Morrisania was one big registry room. My brother Harvey's a greenhorn too. Took him fifty years to feel comfortable riding in a plane. He was a terrific puncher as a kid. The Irish would have owned all of Crotona Park if it hadn't been for my brother Harvey. He's a homicide detective and I'd swear he doesn't have a checking account. Talk to me about the "lightning leap" of Jews. Harvey's son is a cop, like him. And if I had a son he'd be an apple peddler.

And my dad? He's still caught in the daze of Ellis Island. A ghost without a gibbet tree. He's been enduring this country like a complicated dream. I wouldn't have uncovered his muteness in America without my own research trip to that island. Ellis was his teacher, Ellis showed him how to talk. He had a wolf's call, a howling that passed for English. I'd taught myself to grasp the lines in his face, not the words but the little puckers of need. My father wasn't a frigging cryptogram. If I'd had his pinkeye and was kept in Warsaw with an aunt, I'd have stood under the Guastavino vaults and howled a song that held to no continent but was a general closing down, a shutting off of the engine. It didn't matter. I'd inherited my father's muteness: the very act of writing is only a mute's revenge on a talkative world.

That's modern New York, a mixture of silence and screams. It's a city with no sound barriers. Noises echo everywhere and boom back into silence. We golems have imposed ourselves upon the contours of New York. Pathology has a way of seeming normal in this town. Think of Yannick Noah, tennis champion and former refugee from France. After he won the French Open in 1983, Noah fell apart. Paris became his personal blitz. People wouldn't leave him alone. Interview followed interview, until his insides ripped. He walked Paris like a zombie in the middle of the night and considered suicide. But Noah didn't jump off any bridge.

He landed in New York. He could chew on a bagel in

SoHo without reporters sitting near his knee. Noah was anonymous in New York. "I can wear what I want to wear, be however I want to be, feel free in the middle of people. You can even scream, and nobody cares because everybody is screaming."

That's what New York is, a howling in the head, a great babble of voices, like a siren's song, the screams of Ellis Island. This is the one city in the world where communities explode and die with such regularity, they aren't noticed at all. I dare anyone to track the path of Russian and Polish Jews in New York and discover a rational line. It's almost as if a flight mechanism is built into our bones. The Grand Concourse was *our* boulevard, the most ordered, stable Jewish society, all through the 1950s; by 1978 it was almost a Mayan ruin. Apologists will say that sons and daughters ran to the suburbs and that the old were frightened of a "black invasion" from the East Bronx. But it was much more than that, a kind of cultural schizophrenia, that terror of always being "five minutes out of steerage." The German Jews created a fabulous design for themselves, but New York was never their city. Their desire was to blend, to assimilate, to reproduce their own version of an American aristocracy. They had culture, these Jewish WASPs. They didn't turn their backs on the Russian and Polish Jews; they considered them at least partial brethren and formed societies to "uplift" them and relieve despair, but there was always a rivalry between them. Uptown and downtown. Culture and the wild beards. The wild beards won.

If New York was once an Irish town, it became Jewish and Italian during the first half of this century. The Irish watched their lines of support disappear. They held on to their political machine as long as they could, but even that was taken from them. They just couldn't fight off the rampant energy of Russian Jews. Those wild beards coupled themselves with the Sicilians in a curious way. I'm not talking about Murder, Inc. That's another story. The Italians preserved their sense of a village, forging neighborhoods in Manhattan, Brooklyn, Staten Island, the Bronx, and Queens, neighborhoods that policed themselves with their own families of crime. They wouldn't give up their Sicilian ways, a slow, delicious life, where you could linger over a cup of bitter coffee with a bead of milk on top, while the Jews swarmed around them, going off to college like Yankee Doodle, building vast schemes or sinking into despair, characters out of their own Russian novel.

The Russian Jews were like Krazy Kat, who stands longingly in some eternal present while the landscape keeps shifting around him and he looks for his "dahlink," Ignatz Mouse. George Herriman's "Krazy Kat" is probably the most perverse presentation of the immigrant in any art form. It continues to plague my head forty years after the Kat disappeared (Herriman died in 1944). Krazy was a mysterious creature, male *and* female, a city Kat who could never quite assimilate. He lived in a universe that was near anarchy. The Kat is mortally in love with Ignatz Mouse, who hates his guts. Ignatz's whole constitution is absorbed in the idea of braining the Kat with a brick. The Kat doesn't run. He "waits every moment like a bride for the expected ecstasy, the blow always new and always the same. . . ." That Irisher, Offissa Pup, feels sorry for the Kat and protects him as much as he can. He's eloquent on the subject of Krazy Kat. The Kat's life is "warped with fancy, woofed with dreams."

Woofed with dreams. That's what the wild beards were all about. Krazy is a constant child: obsessive, adoring, brilliant, dumb. He can never graduate to anything. Only the decor around him can change. Not the Kat. He's frozen in his love. And Ignatz is like some enchanted dream of America, that underside of the immigrant's own self: irrational, shrewd, unadoring. Ignatz will never love Krazy back. Only bricks can materialize from a dream mouse. Bricks for Krazy's head.

The wild beards didn't need Murder, Inc., when they had Krazy Kat and Krazy's secret pals, the Marx brothers, who were much deeper into "crime" than Dutch Schultz or Abe Relis. The Marx brothers weren't restrained by Offissa Pup and his fanciful English. And they wouldn't have been amused by Ignatz Mouse. Harpo and Groucho distrusted everything: governments, children, themselves. They tore the twentieth century down with their antics. They weren't actual greenhorns, but they grew out of the cunning and hysteria of immigrant New York.

The wild beards didn't invent humor, or shouting. It just came natural to them. Lowlife immigrants, they discovered that self-mockery was a wonderful defense. It confused your enemies. You could smother them with a laugh. It was David and Goliath all over again, but in the New World, David's slingshot was strung with a howling laugh. Underneath that howl was the terror of isolation, the dread of losing still another country, the fear of that czar who was just around the corner, the czar who would shackle you with his latest subscription service: some dreaded army or an oven.

I'm ethnocentric, I guess. Harlem was once as powerful as the Lower East Side. But until World War II, blacks were invisible to most whites. Harlem was only one more Chinatown, an exotic place to visit; there were rent parties and the great black clubs, but you couldn't find a black man in Central Park. Harlem itself was born out of Ellis Island, built to encourage an immigrant boom. But it was overbuilt, and when landlords couldn't get their high prices, they rented to blacks, who had little choice of living space and had to pay through the nose. Harlem's boxed-in energy fueled the schizophrenia of this town, the deep split within its own psychic landscape.

New York wasn't a simple tale of two cities. It had always been rich and poor, black and white, ever since the Dutch, who didn't know what to do about their slaves and freed a number of them. But in this century, blacks developed their own institutions that echoed the whites in a sad, bitter way. When the Negro Giants borrowed the Yankee Stadium for their own World Series, it was obvious to whatever white men were around that these Giants could have knocked the pants off most professional white teams. And when Joe Louis came to town, heavyweight champion of the world, he had to room in a Harlem hotel. I'd swear New York is a little less racist than most other cities, but it happened to be the Negro capital of America. With so much ability cooped up, so much psychic wealth, it's no wonder that a craziness abounded in New York, the old lie that the Negro was a "natural child," that he loved to play and would never learn how to spell or keep his money. The blacks, in order to survive, danced to the lie, pretended to be that natural man and woman the whites were looking for. And the whole relationship between blacks and whites became an illness for both parties.

The blacks don't even have Harlem anymore. It's nobody's playland. It's a remembrance, like the Lower East Side. Boulevards have been renamed, but so what? I didn't see much black pride, or anything else, on Adam Clayton Powell Boulevard. It's not even a war zone now. It has its own heroes, like the Reverend Calvin Butts, who's trying to rebuild the politics of Harlem and is also saving lives at the Abyssinian Baptist Church. But Harlem is a ruined village. It's had to give way to Bedford-Stuyvesant, which holds four hundred thousand of Brooklyn's 723,000 blacks and has been a much more considerable seat of power. Bed-Stuy is being rebuilt, block by block. It has a *mean* political leader, Assemblyman Al Vann, an ex–public school teacher who often tilts with Ed Koch, Ronald Reagan's "friend" in New York.

That's the irony of this metropolis. Our golem mayor appeals to as many Republicans as Democrats. It's the texture of his clay. "I hate radicals," the mayor had told me at lunch. "They have no sense of humor. They're holders of the holy grail. They think of everybody else as shit."

Ah, I shut my mouth and didn't admit to Ed that I was something of a radical, an anarchist with a sense of humor. Krazy Kat. I felt a closeness to Ed Koch. We were an endangered species, the last sons of Ellis Island. That old mother of an island is now a national monument, and few people will experience that vertigo I felt in the old, crudded registry room, and they really ought to shiver. Shivering is what Ellis is all about.

The main building won't be dolled up in time for the Statue of Liberty's hundredth year. It'll take a while. The roofs will be coppered again. The Guastavino vaults will be scrubbed. The island will have a new canopy like the one under which the greenhorns traveled from the dock to the station's front door. The station itself will be an elaborate theme park: a palace of immigrant folklore. It will have a computer bank equipped to trace an immigrant's family tree. I'm willing to confront that machine. I might find a Tartar prince somewhere in my blood, or a lot more Polish apple peddlers. I worry about its arrival. With all the remodeling, Ellis will become just another museum.

The ghosts will be gone, and the terror of the place will be put to sleep with slide shows and other attractions. It won't be a haunted castle. The walls and windows will never scream. Ellis will become a slick affair, like the South Street Seaport. I don't want nostalgia. I want the real thing.

Ellis Island crystallized the terror that most immigrants must have felt upon their arrival. First that symbol of America, a copper lady on Bedloe's Island, with her welcoming torch, and then the rude fact: a cattle station disguised as a church, where you were chalked and shunted from bench to bench. Forget the fits of madness and depression some of the greenhorns suffered. Forget the three thousand suicides.

Suicides can occur on the most enchanted island. But they do register the pain that must have been endured. The separation from loved ones and language. The bitter days of steerage. Greenhorns who could afford to travel first class didn't have to stop at Ellis Island. Ellis is where the poor landed, speaking no English at all.

Irving Howe can tell us about the tales of assimilation. Fabulous success stories. Immigrants who built their fortunes on the Lower East Side and moved into the heartland with their American families. Night-school wonders who went to Harvard. Their children's children are now senators and novelists, as American as Milky Way bars. But what about the madness suffered in almost every family, like some chrysalis that absorbed the pain surrounding itself, took the pain inside and fell silent? And the rest of us, who absorbed pieces of shock and became assimilated bandits, cooperative by day but bearing some crazy cultural wound that shoves in and out of our dreams.

Commandos, possessed by the dark side of the moon, we don't submit easily to anyone's rule. We're like Ed Koch, who's more of an anarchist than he thinks. Growls at everyone, makes people cry. He lives right inside the City's skin. Golem mayor in a golem town.

two

LAND OF THE SPIDER LADY

[1]

In 1961 Jane Jacobs, a forty-five-year-old editor at
Architectural Forum, published her first book, *The Death and
Life of Great American Cities,* and our sense of the city has
never been the same. Until Jane Jacobs, we had Lewis
Mumford, a graduate of Stuyvesant High School, who'd
been predicting the death of New York since 1938. "Each
great capital sits like a spider in the midst of its transpor-
tation web," Mumford told us. New York had little more
to give than "shapeless giantism" and "megalopolitan
growth." It was "a Plutonian world, in which living forms
became frozen into metal." Mumford offered us an entire
schema, "A Brief Outline of Hell," from the birth of cities
through their decline as Parasitopolis and Patholopolis
until their final state as "Nekropolis, city of the dead."
It was a schema that many people subscribed to. Over-

crowding. Dirty streets. "The tear and noise" would stran-
gle us all. Mumford believed in the virtues of village life.
He was the Natty Bumppo of urban planners. Natural
was best.

The flight to the suburbs that began after World War II
was almost like an accompanying song to Mumford's *The
Culture of Cities.* We'd entered the age of shopping malls.
Whites started a slow, cautious search for their dream
house in the suburbs, while blacks and Latinos moved
into the cities. And for the first time we had *two* migra-
tions, like opposing cribs of people, an out-migration of
whites and a continuous *in*-migration of Southern blacks
and Puerto Ricans. But it wasn't only a white exodus.
Middle-class blacks were also moving to the suburbs. And
it was in the fifties that Harlem began to die. Patholopolis
had arrived in New York. It was the Eisenhower era.
Mumford planned garden cities and industrial parks.
And there were few dissenters until Jane Jacobs came
along. "I like dense cities best and care about them most,"
she said.

She debunked the myth of urban renewal, that desire
of planners to waylay Patholopolis by turning each ghetto
into a model of a suburban mall. Malls required people,
and Jacobs found "promenades that go from no place to
nowhere and have no promenaders." The neatness that
most planners craved was the real Patholopolis. "There is
a quality even meaner than outright ugliness or disorder,
and this meaner quality is the dishonest mask of pretended order."

Most planners had never lived in the ghetto. They saw
pathology everywhere and no sense of fabric among the
poor. They couldn't "read" cities. They had rectangles
and garden boxes in their brains, bulldozers and great
iron balls. Contemptuous of anything old, their one reason for existence was to tear down and build on top of the
rubble. And so we have huge bunker cities in East Harlem
and on the Upper West Side, cities without sidewalks and
neighborhood stores, and nothing for the eye to feast
upon, and we scratch our heads and wonder where
graffiti came from: graffiti began on bunker walls, out of

anger and that primitive love of design. *Look at me. Here I am. Ghost Boy of East 108.*

But Jane Jacobs's most important contribution wasn't her attack upon Mumford and other decentrists who decried the "bad old city" and craved order and a paradise of green. She wasn't a cultural anthropologist. She was a woman who cared about great cities, particularly her own. She lived on Hudson Street at the time, and she managed to characterize her neighborhood with the poetry of profound love. She revealed New York the way no one had ever revealed it before. She had the eyes of a taxidermist and the heart of a crab. She was stingy with her revelations, and because of that, the first part of her book, "The Peculiar Nature of Large Cities," is a wondrous guide to New York.

Strangers, she tells us, cities are "full of strangers." It's as if Odysseus had come to town, and that town were a huge market fair of faces and goods. Odysseus could feed his curiosity in such a town, feel protected on the streets by his own anonymity. A town is where you come to look, and a successful street always has something to see. Stores, a constant traffic of faces, a kind of electric excitement that's rarely found in any mall because a mall has no definable street. Consider that open prairie at the World Trade Center. Odysseus would have suffered on that prairie, without vendors near him or a face that he could search up and down.

Not all strangers are good. There might be a thief behind Odysseus's back. But that's not to say most of us would prefer to live in an armed camp or a mausoleum. The street has to defend us "against predatory strangers" but it must also "protect the many, many . . . peaceable strangers." Without that sense of the street as a constant treasure of faces, city life has little meaning. Odysseus might just as well run home to his wife.

But *The Death and Life of Great American Cities* is twenty-five years old. Jane Jacobs has left Hudson Street. She lives in Toronto now. *Stranger* is no longer a cherished word. It reminds us of muggings and serial murders. The Grand Concourse flourished when Jane Jacobs was around. The Bronx hadn't started to burn. Now we have whole villas rising out of the sludge near Battery Park. The City is becoming a land of artificial inventories, a builder's paradise. We have a reconstructed seaport, our Disneyland near the water, a tableau of "Old New York" for every kind of tourist. It's not a place where locals can go for a cup of coffee. It's much too charged with its own significance. The same firm that helped "restore" South Street, Beyer Blinder Belle, is also reconstructing Ellis Island. Ah, I shudder a bit. Beyer Blinder Belle. It sounds like a witch's call, some incantation, the magic of rebuilt arenas. But there's very little of old New York at the South Street Seaport. It doesn't even have the authenticity of a bad dream. It's the rudest sort of commerce. History in the form of a dollar bill.

Now there's a new restoration afoot, a plot to reclaim Times Square for all the decent citizens of New York. In fact, Times Square may soon be a forgotten dinosaur, one more field of rubble in our cityscape, another chunk of the moon, but a costly chunk, because those thirteen acres that are scheduled to be destroyed might become the most expensive piece of real estate in the world. That's the nature of Manhattan. From sex shops and "action" movie theaters to four office towers, a 560-room hotel, and a merchandise mart before we have the chance to blink. I wonder why that dumb and dirty corner can't be "landmarked" like Greenwich Village, because it's part of our psyche, as valuable to us as the lions at the Public Library. But who will listen to an anarchist like me, when Philip Johnson, the pharaoh of modern architects, is involved? He's designed four office towers of limestone and red granite, with mansard roofs of glass and iron crowns. Four eloquent mausoleums, with their sense of absolute order and grace, in the most irascible and lawless territory of the United States. Not even Lewis Mumford could have predicted such a ponderous and undignified death for a pack of streets.

The Times Square redevelopment plan smells of the same old predictable feud between order and chaos. But there's an added twist. Times Square has tumbled in the past quarter century. It's become a playland of the poor, a black and brown park in the midst of a white city. And if the builders have their way, that playland will be gone. What the hell is Times Square, and why is it so important that it be smothered in roofs with iron crowns?

[2]

Once upon a time it was Long Acre Square, a triangle really, at Seventh Avenue and Broadway. This was 1900, the year Ellis Island reopened as a fireproof castle, and Long Acre was in the middle of a building boom. It was a district of carriage-repair shops named after a section in London devoted to a similar kind of shop. New York was coming out of its insular web and longed for a "style" that might accompany its commercial success. It was the most powerful city of the New World, but its artists and writers had fled to England and France; power couldn't bring New York a sense of fashion. And so it assumed a bit of an English map. New York had its own Brighton and Chelsea and Long Acre Square. But the rich wouldn't venture above the carriage shops of Broadway.

Eighth Avenue was where the smelly zones began. That was Hell's Kitchen, the home of Irish, German, and Italian gangs. Billy the Kid was born there. Hell's Kitchen was worse than the Wild West. But its gangs held to Eleventh Avenue and rarely bothered with the carriage crowd. It was the polite insularity of American hoodlums in 1900. They preferred to kill themselves.

Meanwhile, a tower arrived on Long Acre Square. The *New York Times* had moved uptown. It was trying to compete with Herald Square, which had Macy's new department store and the Sixth Avenue el. When New York's first subway was opened in 1904, its station at Forty-second Street was called "Times Square." And Herald Square was eclipsed as the crossroads of Manhattan.

But how did all the hullabaloo begin, the New Year's Eve festivals that could draw a million souls? Blame it on the *New York Times*.

On December 31, 1904, the *Times* celebrated its new terra-cotta tower with a midnight fireworks show, and New Year's Eve at the Times Tower became an annual event. Soon fireworks weren't enough. In 1908, the *Times* began to lower a lit ball down the length of its tower needle until the ball arrived at the needle's base at midnight on New Year's Eve. But it wasn't only the magic of a darkening ball that drew people to the tower once a year. The old Long Acre district had become the theater capital of America, Times Square, crammed with electric signs; a 1916 zoning rule started the era of enormous billboards. The whole district was electrified. Times Square became a second Coney Island, with shooting galleries and penny arcades, freak shows and belly dancers. There was no steeplechase, but it was the new Dreamland, an electric city, the great white road of Broadway. When the movie palaces arrived, and the old legitimate theaters were pushed to the side streets, a mythical culture began, *Broadway*, the land of ups and downs.

It was a universe unto itself, with its own argot, a language of clowns and bums, a kind of half-Yiddish tough-guy talk, chronicled by Damon Runyon, the vicar of Broadway. Runyon caught the particular music of midnight cafés, delicatessens, loan sharks, and whores. It was sentimentalized, like Broadway itself, where every miserable character was on stage and there was nothing between a whisper and a shout. Broadway had no middle ground. It was where all the bandits went, actors, strippers, and comedians who existed a little outside the law. They stuffed their mouths with cheesecake from Lindy's, the "Jewish" cafeteria, and left a lot of crumbs.

"Broadway reads better than it lives," Runyon once said. Like all *colorful* places, it existed as a kind of newspaperman-and-novelist's dream. Runyon's gangsters never killed. They hardly ventured away from the Stem, as insiders called their precious zone of Broadway. Times Square was a slightly wounded Oz, a nighttime village in a daytime town. There were witches beneath the lights, a dim and dark side to the Great White Way. Runyon himself was a lonely man. He lived like an extravagant gypsy in the penthouse of a Times Square hotel. It was almost as if he were a creature of his own invention, more Runyonesque than any of his Guys and Dolls. He wasn't a native, after all. He was born in Manhattan, Kansas. And when he died of throat cancer in 1946, "after 36 years of chain-smoking and drinking 60 cups of coffee a day," his ashes, according to his own request, "were scattered over Broadway from an airplane piloted by Eddie Rickenbacker."

Runyon's own era might have died with those ashes, but Times Square didn't go away. It was a playground for the ghettos long before blacks and Latinos inherited the turf. Times Square was a walker's paradise, the cheapest form of entertainment in town. My single memory of Manhattan until the age of twelve was Times Square. I'd never heard of Helen Hayes. And Eugene O'Neill sounded like someone's Irish brother. But I was a hairy ape at public school and I had my own extortion racket. Started shaving in the fifth grade and I offered my services to the other kids in my class. For a dime a month I made sure no one harmed them. It wasn't a bad deal. I had an explosion of dimes in my pocket in the days when a nickel could get you anywhere in New York. Not the nickels they have now, with Monticello on one side and Thomas Jefferson on the other, that guy who wrote the Declaration of Independence. I'm talking about the buffalo nickel, because there was no other piece of change like it in the world. When you dropped it into the turnstile at the Freeman Street station, you could watch it grow in the turnstile's glass intestine. It was like some great optical trick, because the buffalo in its yellowing glass berth was as big as a human head. That's how a subway ride began in 1946.

I wasn't afraid to enter the belly of Forty-second Street, that endless underground with gyps selling their pencils beneath the arcades. You could discover Times Square without ever going above ground. No other stop on the

IRT had such a maze of platforms, corridors, and stairs. The whole metropolis seemed to converge at that gloomy point. It was dangerous for a boy with so many dimes in his pants because there were pickpockets even in the good old days.

I didn't linger. Climbed up the stairs of the Seventh Avenue exit and it wasn't estrangement I felt. It was like coming home. I hadn't learned about Lindy's cheesecake. It was the *Times* ribbon I loved, the constant news story that traveled across the tower, letters blinking on and off, like a perfect vocabulary. It was the only landscape I trusted as a kid. You could always believe the messages on that tower wall.

It wasn't only that. There was a glorious parting of the streets at Seventh, Broadway spreading out like a golden wedge, with billboards over your brains that seemed to advertise half the world . . . and Hollywood. Esther Williams's body descending from a waterfall, Rex Harrison wearing a jeweled hat out of *Anna and the King of Siam*, Gregory Peck's cheekbones, large as a cave, on a sign that dared you to miss *Duel in the Sun*.

I went to the Stanley, where all the Russian newsreels played. Stalin was a hero in 1946. The Russian newsreels always had Uncle Joe building steel mills with his knuckles or pulling on his mustache. He was much more exotic than Harry Truman and his daughter, who couldn't stop playing the piano. Stalin had eyes like Eddie Cantor. I imagined how it would be to have him as a dad. Stalin would have solved the intricacies of a steering wheel and he'd never have sold my father's Plymouth. He was no greenhorn. He didn't have to spend his life looking for a job.

After the newsreels, I headed for carnival country, that strip of arcades and freak shows beside the Stanley. I had enough dimes on me to blow the month away. It was ten cents to watch the bearded lady, who seemed bored with her own munificence, and the illustrated man, with his green-and-blue skin. He had a page of the Bible on his left arm and Solomon's head on his shoulder. There wasn't a part of him without a story to tell. He was nar-

rative from head to toe. The illustrated man could give
any novelist a kick in the ass. I discovered Bathsheba on
his back. But I couldn't concentrate on his skin for more
than half an hour. I'd wander in those lit caves until it got
dark. And then I'd step outside onto Forty-second Street
and into the anarchy of Times Square.

I felt safest here, among all the geeks. There was a flow,
an essential kind of movement, almost like a rubbing kiss
that you could find nowhere else in New York. It was the
quality of being anonymous in an absolute way, without
the ordinary identifying marks of city life. Business suits
meant nothing near the Stem. We were all essential
strangers, women, men, and fifth-graders with a beard.

Times Square was an anarchist's Ellis Island. These immigrants weren't refugees from the czar's territorial Pale.
The Stem was the first landing point for strangers from
the country's interior. It was a nation of cheap hotels,
where you could rest your head without the bother of a
real address. Close enough to all the bus terminals, it was
a beehive for the lost, for those who could sniff their own
transience.

I wasn't the only immigrant's son who flocked there. It
was a powerful dream song for all of us who were hysterical about our roots: half American and who knows
what? My whole sense of clan came from a single apple
peddler. What neighborhood was mine? Not the lower
depths of Charlotte Street, an area that took on the stink
of immigrants who sought respectability without much
success. A whirlwind ripped through Charlotte Street. It
sank into its own rubble in less than twenty-five years.

There were no whirlwinds in the "sweet districts" of the
Upper East Side. The geographic heart of the Social Register has shifted only a few blocks since 1939, from Sixty-
eighth and Madison to Seventy-second and Park. That's
not much of a migration. The stability this suggests may
even be part of some greenhorn's tale. Who knows how
many immigrant sons and daughters married their way
into "society country"?

But Times Square is like a shadowland to the Social
Register, a hint of New York's underbelly. And it always

was. Sitting at the border of Hell's Kitchen, it started as a
row of carriage-repair shops for the rich. Then the theaters came, with their lights and sense of marginality,
because nothing was more transient than an actor's life.
After the actors, the *Times* moved in, the subway stations,
the big and little hotels. The fable began. Broadway imagined itself as a permanent landscape of drift: the nighttime city, with its own peculiar clientele. Runyon. Walter
Winchell. "Good evening, Mr. and Mrs. America . . ."

The fable worked for fifty years. Broadway was an um-
bilical cord and cocoon for show-business people. Its min-
strels could defy conventional rules. They preferred
these lights to anywhere else. And then Jolson and Fanny
Brice moved to the suburbs. Rothstein, the gambler, was
shot down like a dog. Jimmy Walker, Broadway's own
man, lost his crown as mayor of New York and the um-
bilical cord started to tear. The movie palaces became big
tombs after the arrival of TV. Broadway went out of fashion. All that was left was its own anomie, laced with legitimate theaters. So that a kind of war zone developed
between the theater crowd of "tourists" and the drifting
populations. There was one more ingredient. The drifters were becoming Latino and black.

We don't need Mandrake the Magician to tell us what
happened. Harlem had had its own Great White Way on
125th Street. But its theaters began to die. Black musicians moved downtown or to Hollywood. Harlem lost its
Strivers Row, the fabric of a middle class. It couldn't support the lights of 125th Street. Its poor had to find another playland. That playland was Times Square.

Meanwhile, in the seventies, Hollywood went fishing
for a new black audience. It created a series of black
"exploitation" films, with Richard Roundtree as a bad-ass
detective and Pam Grier as a sexual spider lady. And
Times Square grew more and more black. The spider
lady's gorgeous legs are gone and Richard Roundtree has
drifted into lesser roles, but the black audience is still
around Times Square.

In fact, Times Square has grown with this black and

brown migration. It's pushed west to Ninth Avenue and is chewing up the borders of Hell's Kitchen, known as Clinton now. It's gone south as far as Penn Station, north to Forty-ninth, and its eastern edges aren't so easily defined. It snakes in and out of Sixth Avenue, and at Forty-second, it's come down to the hump of the Library at Bryant Park. Half the midtown core has a population of drifters, three-card monte players, black chess champions with their sidewalk tables and chess clocks, black and white whores and pimps, drug merchants, shopping-bag ladies and men, geeks of all description, wandering tribes of young gangs, the mad, the lonely, and the forlorn. It's not that the drifters have taken over the streets, except for their private sanctuary (Forty-second, between Seventh and Eighth), it's that they seem ubiquitous. They have their corners, their own ritualistic dance in the midst of tourist hotels and businessmen's roosts. Seventh Avenue has its ordered, old-line dairy cafeterias and its anarchistic orange-juice stands.

But the most obvious example of Times Square's burgeoning roots is the decline of Herald Square. In 1947, when *Miracle on 34th Street* appeared, Macy's was the most popular department store in the world. It's no surprise that Santa, played by Edmund Gwenn, should want to become a citizen of Herald Square. The film used the old, honorable rivalry between Macy's and Gimbel's as a strategic point. Macy's and Gimbel's were as much of an archetype as Santa himself. But they're not archetypes anymore. Macy's can't even win a sturgeon war with Zabar's, that mad, old appetizing market on the Upper West Side.

If Santa comes down again, it won't be to visit Macy's or Zabar's pickle barrel. He'll come to Bloomingdale's, where the "guppies" (groups of young urban professionals) go to shop and find husbands and wives. There's no desolation or anomie. Even the bag ladies at Bloomingdale's have their own charge cards.

The whole thrust behind the Times Square Redevelopment Corporation, a creature of the City and the state, is to bring a "Bloomingdale's atmosphere" to Forty-second Street. The corporation is hoping for a ripple effect. Once the stinking heart of Times Square is bulldozed, the drifters will lose ground to yuppies, tourists, and out-of-town buyers. William J. Stern, chairman of the state's Urban Development Corporation, has said the following about Times Square's pornography merchants: "Scattering them is the first shot. We fire the first cannonball which scatters them and then we hunt them out."

Stern has come up with his own fable: "The proposal will help to bring back the days of George M. Cohan, when Broadway was truly the Great White Way." It's a George M. Cohan of his dreams. The landscape he's proposing—mansard roofs, a merchandise mart, and nine "revitalized" theaters—has nothing at all to do with the old mix of Times Square. It will become Rockefeller Center without a skating rink.

Stern's Times Square sounds like the heart of darkness to me. A universe of granite bunkers crowned with glass. I'm not the only "anarchist" who distrusts the absolute order of that design. Philip Johnson's Xanadu has failed to enchant a number of people. Thomas Bender, who teaches urban history at New York University, believes that Philip Johnson and the developer George Klein "may have devised the only conceivable plan that could make the Times Square and 42nd Street area more threatening than it is at present. . . . The Klein-Johnson plan rejects any notion . . . of the street as a significant public place. Instead, it proposes four massive buildings whose sheer granite walls will dwarf the street."

Urban strategist William H. Whyte also wonders what will happen to the street, which can't be choreographed by architects and builders or simply stuffed with people. Times Square is a streetscape that's been gathering for eighty years. It's developed stratagems and retreats, pockets, and very particular turfs. But it's still "the national cesspool, so bad, New Yorkers can take perverse pride in it, overflowing with pimps, whores, transvestites, male prostitutes, and the like." Whyte would prefer that the cesspool go away, magically, if possible, or by a re-development plan that protects the streetscape and covets the pedestrians' point of view. A people's Times Square, rather than Xanadu.

[3]

I understand Whyte's dilemma. Caught between male prostitutes and an architect's vision of concrete and glass. I'm curious if we'll ever find a "proper" environment for Times Square. And so I decided to take a long stroll into our "national cesspool." Not as an innocent abroad. It wasn't 1946. I couldn't rediscover my illustrated man, with his blue complexion, stories tucked between the veins of his arm. But I still had a love of anomie, Times Square's disregard for the rest of the planet. I'd walked that wild side, who hadn't? I'd written about the screaming men and women in the mad hotels. I'd seen the monte players, lost twenty-dollar bills to the artistry of their hands. I'd felt disgust at the pimps, rage at the roving gangs who'd jostle me with murder in their eye. But I'd never anatomized Times Square.

I started in Jane Jacobs country, on Hudson Street, before the wildness begins. But I didn't have far to travel. It was in the little triangular park in front of 2 Horatio Street, known as Jackson Square. The park had become a hobo jungle, a haven for black, white, and Latino drifters. Children never play here, even though the park has a bit of a garden at its northern edge and a strange monkey bar in the middle. As I walked past, two policemen had come into the park and scowled at the hobos in a half-hearted way. I sensed the folly of their situation. These were the park's habitual users, winos and their wives who occupied a triangle of benches and made this their address. It was a mini Times Square. A patch of unrespectable people holding on to their turf. But if it hadn't been such a small island, who would have noticed the bums?

I crossed Fourteenth and had come to Chelsea. Hudson Street was gone. The City had turned black and brown on the far side of a street lamp. Chelsea is the lower limb of Hell's Kitchen, half gentrified, half slum. There was an exciting mix on the street, a feel of cultures rubbing together, gourmet shops and Latino grocers. It didn't have a solid wall of boutiques. Thank God there were no ice-cream parlors, the first sign of an invasion: speculators in chocolate chip, betting the neighborhood will go white.

Eighth Avenue becomes a buffer zone in the low Twenties, a nondescript circus until Times Square South, the area of cheap hotels bordering Penn Station. Three men stood outside the Vigilant Hotel on West Twenty-ninth, like a chorus of dirty cuffs. And then I shoved over the line, into the crazed, scratchy fabric of Penn Station itself. Two of the doors were broken at the Eighth Avenue exit and had been replaced with wooden slabs. Those doors looked like coffins. There'd been a sniper around the year before, shooting up platforms and people. I wondered what point that sniper had wanted to make. Getting to know you with a bullet? The quickest kind of communication.

Young black men were standing beside the Felt Forum's concrete pots. I recognized a buzz in their voices, a weaving of the shoulders, a determined slouch, the insane business of having nothing to do.

They weren't the only loiterers around. A few stranded people were sitting on the great long stairs of the General Post Office. The only other place with a similar sweep of stairs is the Metropolitan Museum of Art. But the stairs of the Met are a meeting ground, a lively land of lookers and vendors, a fixed environment where the "players" themselves change all the time, just like the Yankees' batting order. Most of these players are white, and they can afford to loiter. They have an income in their pockets. But there wasn't much of an environment on the Post Office steps; a few dusty souls, without vendors or moving traffic. It had all the ennui of the wild side, that rootlessness of the poor without prospects.

Had to go visit one of the sex supermarkets William J.

Stern wanted to scatter with the state's cannonballs. I knew they'd disappear before Stern fired the first shot. It was a lucky piece of research because, ghetto boy or not, I was too chickenhearted to walk inside without the pressure of writing a book. Yes, the bearded lady had seemed erotic to me when I was a fifth-grader. But I wasn't frightened of the freak show. Now I had visions of being knifed in the dark. *Stern's right, Stern's right,* I muttered in a moment of panic. *Feed them the cannonball.* And then I wandered into the porn mill on the west side of the street, with its promise of a "Live Nude Review." I felt like a greenhorn. I put my dollar down and was handed four tokens by a girl behind a booth. Climbed up the stairs and entered a gallery of rooms with a barker stationed in the middle. He wore a red tuxedo under the gawdy light. "Fucking, sucking," he said with a nimble dance. "Check it out."

There were tiny closets on one side of the gallery with girls in front of them. Some wore polo shirts and panties. Others wore thin black nightgowns or peekaboo vests. The girls assumed different attitudes. They ignored you in the coldest manner or clucked their tongues, inviting you near a particular closet. But you needed a little more bounty with them. A two-dollar token. And I wasn't prepared to part with two dollars for some girl in a polo shirt.

I climbed another step to the quarter-token booths. There were two areas, one for live sex shows, the other for nudie films. I couldn't tell which was which. Men were milling about. They weren't as white and middle class as I'd gathered from the *Times.* This was supposed to be a territory of anonymous white businessmen, sales engineers and such from New Jersey. There were plenty of blacks and Latinos, a couple of Koreans, and lowlifes like me on the supermarket's second floor. I stumbled into a booth with an "A" and a "B" slot. I tried "B" and a film started up on a screen in back of the door, a one-minute treatise on the art of masturbation. Men and women sat around on a couch, playing with each other and themselves. It was too much activity in too little time. I was sentenced to "A" or "B" in random booths, and I didn't like it. Then I discovered the booths' magic formula: there were plot summaries of every film attached to the door. I could drift through an alphabet of sex, from anal to oral and back again. But I wasn't any more satisfied when I knew the plot lines. The films couldn't deliver. They could barely tease. They were like bad trailers in a legitimate movie house.

I walked to the other side, put my token in the slot, and watched the peep show. A man and woman were on a mattress in a circular room, with the woman on top. It was like a gym class. The woman arched her back and cooed with half her mouth. There she was, in a circular fish tank, condemned to constant performance.

I scribbled furiously in my little notebook until the window went down over the fish tank. I'd spent my last token and decided to leave. But I had to pass those closets of girls again. It was like Brecht's Berlin. The girls clucked with absolutely nothing in their eyes. They were frozen in, their smiles as distant as the China Sea. And then I found a black girl with spidery legs. My own Pam Grier. At some spooky level she was actually looking at me. She was younger than the other closet girls, newer perhaps. I got my two-dollar token and returned to her closet.

But she wouldn't let me in. She laughed at the greenhorn, but she wasn't unkind. There was a separate closet for me. The closet had a phone. I should have figured out the general plan. It was like *Paris, Texas,* where Harry Dean Stanton talks to Nastassja Kinski on the telephone, with a wall of glass between them. Picked up the phone, but nothing happened. The wall wouldn't turn to glass. "Hello?" I said.

The spider lady laughed. "This your first time? You forgot the big token." I dropped the token in, wishing it was a buffalo nickel and I could go through a turnstile and into the spider lady's closet. It was the ghetto's fault. The ghetto hadn't equipped me with middle-class notions. It was either magic or complete isolation. The wall disappeared and I had my magic glass. The spider lady sat on a chair and started to undress. Wouldn't have bothered me if she removed her garter belt a hundred times a day. It was still two people talking on a telephone. Her voice cut through the distance between a nudie girl and her closet trick. "Do you like it?" she asked.

The spider lady showed me her legs and started to touch herself. Ah, it didn't matter how practiced she was. I fell right into her fantasy.

[4]

Dear Mr. Stern and Mayor Koch, When you tear down your thirteen acres and remove all the funny people, could you please spare one little closet at the porno circus on Eighth Avenue between Forty-second and Forty-third? Because there's a certain young black woman, name unknown, who doesn't come under the category of nuisance and pest. That's my spider lady.

Went down Forty-third. Paused in front of the infamous Hotel Carter, where Delmore Schwartz had died, maddened, all alone, when the Carter was called the Hotel Dixie. Schwartz believed that Nelson Rockefeller had stolen his wife. He talked to T. S. Eliot in his dreams, disappeared from Syracuse University in 1965, and was found dead at the Dixie. "Dogs are Shakespearean, children are strangers," he once wrote. He was a profoundly suspicious man. When an old friend discovered him on the street during the last year of his life, Delmore said, "You didn't recognize me because the whole shape of my head has changed."

Damon Runyon wouldn't have known what to do with Delmore Schwartz. Delmore's madness didn't have much of a romantic mold. But by 1966, most of Runyon's Great White Way was gone. And Delmore sank into Times Square, one more anonymous soul, with his shoelaces untied and his shirt torn at the elbows. But the Dixie doesn't house poets anymore. It has welfare children and rats in its renaissance as the Hotel Carter.

The old Plantation Lounge, where Delmore drank his whiskey, doesn't exist. The Carter has the Rose Saigon Nightclub attached to its ground floor. The name seems right somehow because Times Square *is* Saigon, or at least the ghost of a city that fell in 1975. It's as if Saigon had been replanted here, along the spine of Forty-second Street, with its honky-tonk and endless drift.

The Marriott Marquis was going up on Broadway. It looked like a pharaoh's tomb. I preferred the Carter, with all its rats, to this complicated castle. The Marquis was a premonition of the new Times Square. Castles and tombs where people would have to fit, without the feel of a living street.

I saw the Times Tower, its beautiful terra-cotta brick masked in such peculiar marble, it resembled an oilcloth checkerboard. The saddest thing was that the *Times* ribbon still wrapped itself around the fourth floor. But it didn't have those blinking lights with which a boy could teach himself to spell and learn what was going down in Arabia. The ribbon was now a bleak line. A skeleton that couldn't summon up the news. More than anything else, the ribbon had evoked Times Square. More than the lights. More than Eddie Cantor's eyes. That ribbon was like a navigator's needle. It gave a boy his bearings in the world.

I trundled down Seventh Avenue with a golem's gray heart. Then, at Thirty-ninth, I discovered a crowd, and I gave up my melancholy to that gathering of hot faces. I'd come upon an outdoor commodities market. Money was changing hands. A monte player had set up his own sidewalk office. Like any entrepreneur, he had his cash, his tools, and a collapsible table of two cardboard boxes. The monte man and most of his customers were black. He had an old Hawaiian shirt and parrot-green pants. He had a goatee and shoes without heels. He had incredibly long hands. The cards he twisted back and forth had developed cracked spines. I saw a nine of clubs, a queen of diamonds, and a black seven.

He got into an argument with a customer who claimed the monte man had cheated him out of a hundred dollars. "I don't cheat, I don't beat," the monte man said. He swayed in his green pants and offered the customer a chance to recoup his hundred. He'd flip the cards, show you the red queen, then lie them facedown on top of the cardboard. "Pick the diamond lady. I dare you, man."

We all looked for the red lady. The monte man shuffled again, showed us the queen, then buried it among the other two cards. That customer spilled out his history the more indecisive he grew. His name was Al. He was a runner on Wall Street, he said. Half-time. "I'm bonded, baby. I got millions behind my ass. I don't need no monte man." He owned one-fifth of a sailboat. He had a fiancée. But he couldn't bet on the queen. The monte man had stolen his assurance with those long bony hands.

"Who'll bet fifty?" the monte man said. "Who'll bet a hundred?"

He kept showing us the queen. He was like a snake charmer with his hands, daring us, letting us win whenever he wanted, to prove that his hands, and only his, were in control. He was the monte man, with his three humpbacked cards and portmanteau of boxes, and we were suckers in his alley. I saw the red queen. Bet twenty dollars. Won. Marveling at my ability to follow the wizard's hands until I started dropping twenties all over the table. And then another man came along. A light-skinned Negro, cautious, tall, with horn-rimmed glasses. He watched the play, then covered a card with a hundred-dollar bill. Old Hawkeye had found the diamond lady.

I assumed the monte man was suckering him with that hundred dollars. "Sweet man," he said. "Sweet man." But Hawkeye stayed out of the next few deals. Then he found the red queen again. Al was bewildered and hopelessly behind and Hawkeye came up with the red queen on every third shuffle. He'd cracked the monte man's system, the lures, the spiels, the swaying of the parrot-green pants. He was like some avenger on Seventh Avenue.

The monte man tore the last six dollars from his shirt and touched his goatee. "Did you ever hear a monte player getting broke?"

He stroked the cards with the same infinite calm, and I wondered if he was going to sucker Hawkeye with the six dollars and build his boodle again. But Hawkeye tapped the red queen and took the six dollars away. I expected the monte man to carry his portmanteau to another location. But he kicked the boxes, and his office came apart. He left his cards on the ground and ran to Forty-second Street.

Al was disgruntled. "That mother cheated me." And he took off after the monte man, whose parrot-green pants had already become camouflage on the street. I turned to look at Hawkeye count his money, but Hawkeye was gone.

three

HAUNCH PAUNCH
AND JOWL

[1]

The bones of a city are often inscribed on a people's back. Particularly in an immigrant town like New York, where whole populations arrived in phantom boats, passed through a brick church while their clothes were chalked and their scalps inspected for lice, and if the country let them in, they toiled to earn their keep, made children, money, and died in the crush to become American. Both the sadness and the vitality of New York come from the same engine: the greenhorn's desire to transform himself into some magical thing, man of the New World. But the New World was as much of a phantom as the Old one because no city could match that vision the greenhorns had of a land where they wouldn't be lonely, where the czar would love them like his very own child. No czar, American or Russian, ever loved a greenhorn.

And it's the frightening distance between the green-horn's invented idea of America and what he finally met that provided the fabric of New York. But it's a fabric with a strange and brutal skin. Because New York is the city that reproduces itself according to the ideals of each generation. It has no continuous line. Everything is possible because its past is only the future turned upside down. New York's history is what happened tomorrow. The Dutch planned it that way. They built a replica of Amsterdam at the foot of Manhattan, a phantom city with windmills and all. And the practical Dutch pretended they were still at home. They weren't *colonists;* they didn't want a New World. They closed their eyes and had their "fabricated motherland." It's no wonder the English took New Amsterdam without a shot. The Dutch were crazy. They thought these gutters and gardens were in some old town. Why should they fight the British for a territory that was as familiar as their own finger? They were Dutch. This had to be Amsterdam. And the English could go to hell.

The Britishers succumbed to that vision. New York remained "new" Amsterdam. The English presence in New York was so illusory because it never took hold. That's why I'd suffered amnesia about the British. They were ruled by Peter Stuyvesant's ghost. And after the redcoats were gone, we still had a Dutch colony, even with the Declaration of Independence. New York was practical and insane. It continued to trade like the Dutch and build on that phantom city. It decided to grow along a grid, ignoring bumps, ditches, and heights, and the particular bend of its rivers. It would be a phantom grid of 2028 blocks, where anything that was built upon them could be removed at will. So we have the Empire State Building dug into the old cradle of the Waldorf-Astoria. And the Waldorf is shoved onto another grid. We have a Madison Square Garden on Madison Square and then the Garden starts to float, like a gondola on the grid. It reappears uptown, caters to circuses and rodeos, the Rangers and the Knicks, becomes a parking lot, and the Garden is born again over the new Penn Station. It's an ugly glass tank, but who cares? Nothing is sacred except the grid. And the grid doesn't allow for memory and remorse. It's part of a phantom town built onto a Dutch vision of Amsterdam in America, which happens to be called New York.

And so we have a city of perpetual greenhorns. First the Dutch, then those temporary Englishmen, then the Irish, the Germans, the Italians, the Jews, then another wave: Jamaicans, Puerto Ricans, the anti-Castro Cuban middle class, Dominicans, Russian refuseniks, the "black" Cubans out of Mariel harbor, Vietnamese boat people, Koreans, ethnic Chinese from everywhere on the planet, and this country's *internal* immigrants, our pilgrim slaves, the blacks, who are much older than the Revolution and have a deeper pedigree in America than most of our granddads.

I'd swear on my life that New York became the center of black and Jewish culture partly because of the Dutch. The blacks and the Jews had their own phantom villages, Harlem and the Lower East Side. Slavery was disagreeable to the Dutch. And so was anti-Semitism, in spite of old Peter. And like the Dutch town of New York, Harlem and the Lower East Side sank into their own future, and who can really say what kind of past will emerge?

Narrowed down, New York is nothing but Dutch fathers, the grid, and all the unremembered dead. Sometimes the dead rise up in peculiar ways, and the records they've kept of their lives, their own night songs, begin to haunt us because those songs are often dreams of the City itself. Herman Melville, our greatest fiction writer, had to "die" twice. Once when he stopped publishing stories and novels and became an obscure inspector of the docks. And then when he gave up his own personal ghost in 1891. But Melville was really a twentieth-century writer. It took a time of explosive immigration to rediscover Melville, that man of Dutch and English descent. The nineteenth century, with its absolute faith in the entrepreneur, wouldn't listen to Melville's dark narrative webs. Bartleby the Scrivener haunts our city as no other character in American fiction has ever done. He's like a wicked Dutch ancestor saying no to America's fantastic growth.

He's the underside of New York's mercurial energy, city
dweller turned into a cocoon.

Bartleby went mad in New York, like the black com-
poser Scott Joplin, who was confined to Manhattan State
Hospital after his opera *Treemonisha* failed, and he died
there in 1917, brooding over America's loss of interest in
ragtime. Joplin was "lost" for fifty years, until his rags
were used in *The Sting* (1973), a film that was almost a
benign version of Melville's *The Confidence Man,* so much
does it depend on thieves tricking other thieves who trick
themselves. And in the background are Joplin's syncopa-
tions, which are a wonderful counterpoint to all the thiev-
ery going on.

There's also Henry Roth, who published *Call It Sleep* in
1934, a Joycean novel of Jewish life in Brownsville at the
beginning of the century, and then disappeared. The
novel wasn't unnoticed, but there are apocryphal tales
about what happened next. Roth was researching a novel
on American communism when he was hit over the head
near the docks. Roth retreated to the country, where he
became a Jewish chicken farmer and a Latin coach at a
nearby reform school. He was plucked out of obscurity in
1964, when *Call It Sleep* was reprinted in a paperback
edition and reached a million readers. Not even this resurrection could draw him away from his farm. He was
still the local chicken slaughterer. But there is nothing in
all of Jewish-American literature that compares with
Roth's imagination of an immigrant boy in the New
World:

> Standing before the kitchen sink and regarding the bright
> brass faucets that gleamed so far away, each with a bead of
> water at its nose, slowly swelling, falling, David again be-
> came aware that this world had been created without
> thought of him.

And what about those who aren't remembered, who
toiled, scratched around, and remained in obscurity: architects, plumbers, bandits, writers, and such, who either
fell from grace or never captured a public at all. Samuel

Ornitz is a particular example. His novel *Haunch Paunch and Jowl*, published in 1923 as "An Anonymous Autobiography," has more to tell about the relationship between Jews, politics, and crime than any other work of fiction *or* nonfiction. The novel reads like a sociological song. Irving Howe condemns Samuel Ornitz to half a paragraph in *World of Our Fathers* and calls the writing "crude," while he praises *The Rise of David Levinsky*, a much more primitive tale of "success" in the New World, a book written in plodding, clumsy English, full of wistfulness and sentimental meat, with none of Ornitz's raw power. Levinsky is a Jewish-American Everyman, as recognizable as your own grandpa, unless he happens to be an apple peddler.

Ornitz's bibliographer, Gabriel Miller, agrees with Irving Howe. The book feels awkward to him, deficient in form and structure. Miller sees Ornitz's nervous, impressionistic style as no style at all. He's wrong. *Haunch Paunch and Jowl* is a "road" novel about the streets of New York. Miller calls Ornitz's hero, Meyer Hirsch, "one of the vilest characters in American-Jewish literature." Hirsch is lacking in the "Jewish quality" of remorse. Unlike David Levinsky, he has no deep longing for a kinder past. Hirsch *is* monstrous. He's an authentic child of the New World, a golem without regret.

He's called *ziegelle,* the little goat, for good reason. A goat was his wet nurse. A goat saved his life. He was born in a ship's manger, three days out of Hamburg, because his dad was running from the czar's military service. His mother had no milk for the baby, ". . . and there was no milk on board." Until a miracle happened. The ship's pet, Hirsch's mother tells Hirsch, "a she-goat with udders plump with milk, escaped from her quarters and came wandering in the steerage . . . and the she-goat suckled my baby and he lived to see the promised land. . . . And so here you are, *mein ziegelle.* . . ."

This goat boy, this child of the New World, is also a child without a country. He's no greenhorn, because he never saw Europe. A goat is his second mother, and his cradle is the sea. He comes to the New World without a single prejudice. Meyer Hirsch has no history. But he does have all the instincts of a goat:

> A goat manages to get along where any other creature would perish. Stubble, twigs, anything is food and nourishment for him. He is a sidestepper, can walk a narrow ledge or a fence, if need be. He is for himself; unfeeling, and befriends no one. An unlikable, ugly thing with a most unreasonable smell. And I have noticed that a goat is the only thing ridicule can't kill.

And that's how Meyer Hirsch made his way in the New World. He's the "fourteenth leader" of the Ludlow Street Gang, the last one in line. But Hirsch risks nothing. He's much too clever to steal with his own hands. "I am the cover guy. In other words, I distract the owner and screen the thief." Hirsch gives nothing and always gets. Yet he's pulled into the romance of his gang, "our sweet, lawless, personal, high-colored life," which covers over "the shabbiness, foreignness and crudities of our folks and homes."

Hirsch lives at home with his mother, father, and Uncle Philip, the family philosopher who despises his bosses, the German-Jewish clothing manufacturers. There isn't enough crockery to go around. Hirsch and Uncle Philip have to eat from the same soup plate.

Philip understands the greenhorn's dilemma. There are no proud grandpas in his line. There's only dust and dead bones. He advises Hirsch: "Meyer, we've got nothing to look back to. It's up to us to be ancestors." Philip starts his own shop and marries into the tribe of German Jews and dies of stomach cancer.

Hirsch sticks to his own kind. He becomes a runner for the local Tammany boss and uses his gang to destroy Republican and Socialist rallies. He goes to law school, builds up an elaborate system of fraud in "that hurly-burly time of New York's nineties," when lawyers, hoodlums, cops, and judges slept in the same "public crib."

Hirsch acquires a mistress, Gretel, a "buxom greenhorn just off the ship," and brings her home as his family's servant. He's crazy about Gretel, but she isn't the kind of girl a pol like him can marry. Hirsch is on the rise. He understands the laws of politics. "Control. Organization. Cash." But he suffers his first defeat when three of his gang members rob and kill a ticket collector on the Second Avenue el and Hirsch can't get them off. They die in the electric chair, but not before one of the gang members reminds Hirsch of "'the potatoes we used to bake in our street bonfires. Do you remember how good they tasted, Meyer; do you remember?' . . . And they escorted him through the little green door."

That moment is much more powerful than anything in *The Rise of David Levinsky*. Because Ornitz gives us the rude, dreadful facts without Hirsch's response. Levinsky would have mourned for two paragraphs and evoked half a million potatoes. And we're left with the horror of a little green door.

Meanwhile, Hirsch grows fat. He's the honorable Haunch Paunch and Jowl. He blackmails the Republicans into appointing him a justice of the Supreme Criminal Court. But Gretel has studied his ways. She obliges Hirsch to marry her, and his career is ruined.

By now Hirsch has become "a hulking pachyderm" living on Riverside Drive, Allrightniks Row. He's conquered the New World. Haunch Paunch and Jowl. But all his grasping has gotten him nowhere. He's still that *ziegelle*, sucking on a goat's teat.

Ornitz provides no sentimental choices. Hirsch is nothing more or less than a child caught in the "hurly-burly" of his time. His destiny is to grow fat and never stop feeding. Golem and goat boy, he's now his own ancestor, Haunch Paunch and Jowl.

The novel seemed so accurate and "real" that its publisher, Horace Liveright, decided to present it as the memoir of an actual judge. And Ornitz disappeared from the book. He "introduced" the judge's story and became the anonymous servant of his own fiction. But Liveright couldn't have been so wrong. The book went into seven printings and sold a hundred thousand copies.

And Ornitz himself? He never had another *Haunch Paunch and Jowl*, no matter what name he used. He wasn't a goat boy, like Meyer Hirsch, and he didn't come off a phantom boat. He was born on the Lower East Side in 1890, the son of Polish immigrants. But he didn't have to share a soup plate with some fictitious uncle. His parents weren't poor. And he wasn't the "fourteenth leader" of any gang. He was an altogether different kind of bandit. A studious little bugger, with glasses on his nose and a writer's bitter heart, like Isaac Babel. He pulled stories out of men and women in the street. *Haunch Paunch and Jowl* wasn't Ornitz's private tale. He was writing about a time that was even more primitive than his own. The book has the urgency of myth. The ghetto itself is born out of goat's milk. Ornitz's greenhorns are like ghosts looking furiously for their own flesh. The ghetto is cluttered with Bartlebys and fat men.

And if Irving Howe sees Ornitz's novel as a marginal text that doesn't admit to the collective assertion of the Jews, I see a different story. There was banditry in that world of sweatshops, and a bitterness that belies the fable of hardworking pioneers on a rough road to success. "Crime," says Irving Howe, "was a source of shame, a sign that much was distraught and some diseased on the East Side; but it was never at the center of Jewish immigrant life."

Crime was also a source of income; it linked politics to the poor. The ghetto was an enormous marketplace, and the potted breast that Hirsch feeds on at the end of *Haunch Paunch and Jowl* is almost like a sacrament; he's devouring the ghetto's blood.

Ornitz understood that the Jewish gangs didn't simply go away as members outgrew their lawlessness. That lawlessness was needed to collect the vote. "The Yiddish gangster is . . . full of business."

Ornitz's own career was typical of a writer with one successful book. He went out to Hollywood, and from 1929 to 1945 he worked on such film classics as *King of the Newsboys, Army Girl, Chinatown Nights, Secrets of the French Police, The Man Who Reclaimed His Head, Portia on Trial,* and *Little Devils.* He lived a kind of double life, scratching

out mediocre scripts and becoming an anti-Fascist orga-
nizer.

He was forgotten as a novelist, but notoriety came to
him when he was called before the House Committee on
Un-American Activities and refused to testify. He spent
nine months in prison at Springfield, Missouri, as one of
the Hollywood Ten. At Springfield he completed a book
that was almost a metaphoric sequel to Meyer Hirsch's
life. Called *Bride of the Sabbath,* it reads like a bitter report
card about the whole idea of assimilation. It doesn't have
the bite of *Haunch Paunch and Jowl,* that mixture of politics
and myth, that marvelous sense of Once Upon a Time.

Ornitz died of a cerebral hemorrhage in 1957, an ex-
con with a sad tale of America behind him. He couldn't
grow fat like Haunch Paunch and Jowl. He didn't have
Hirsch's capacity to rush into the darkness and seize a
profit for himself. He was only one more deracinated
Jew, like the rest of us, "more American than the Americans," without a stinking root.

[2]

I'd love to revisit Hirsch's primitive time and look into the
romance of Jewish pioneers coming to terms with America. Assimilation broke an awful lot of backs. Jews and
Italians were crowded into rookeries that the Irish had
just left. In those "hurly-burly" years, the Lower East Side
was the meanest part of the world. Nothing compared to
the slums of New York. For the uptowners, the "Jewish
Street" was an exotic, smelly place, where only animals
would live. There was one ferocious preacher, the Reverend Doctor Parkhurst, with his Society for the Prevention
of Vice, who blitzed the Allen Street brothels, chasing out
whores and all their customers and cadets. But it wasn't
until 1894 that the Lexow Committee, appointed by the
state senate, "studied" the Lower East Side with Parkhurst's help and exposed all the rich variety of Jewish

prostitutes and their helpmates at the Essex Market Court, "lawyers, policemen, and bail bondsmen" who could have been disciples of Meyer Hirsch. The whole East Side was Haunch Paunch and Jowl.

Other committees followed, other investigations. But the whores stuck to Allen Street. There were too many greenhorns around, lonely men with their wives in the Polish Pale. And also customers from uptown, drawn to those red lamps in the windows and the girls who clucked at them from the halls, until Allen Street became the "international" side of the ghetto, a primitive Times Square. It wasn't a street of Talmud Torahs. You could have Russian tea with a lump of dark sugar that cracked in your mouth and go upstairs with an Allen Street girl.

Prostitution was no isolated "disease." It was big business, protected by Tammany pols and the police, in spite of reformers like Parkhurst. But business alone couldn't have created the aura of Allen Street. Allen Street arrived with a profound wish. The greenhorns desired a private place between the downtown sweatshops and communal toilets and the uptown world they feared. "The only thing that interested Jews in Central Park," said the *Daily Forward* in 1905, "was the zoo. They were afraid to venture further into the park lest they get lost." And so the greenhorns discovered that dark and dank strip under the el. Allen Street. Landlords made a fortune renting the bottom floors to whores. There was nothing odd about those "greenie girls," who were as isolated as the men. Some had rebelled against arranged marriages, running to Allen Street from Ellis Island, where they'd met their husbands for the first time. Some of them had been charmed by a cadet. Others preferred lying down with strangers to being sentenced to a sewing machine. And others were industrious girls who saved their money and moved to Prospect Park. There might have been a hundred reasons, but most of the girls were caught between pathology and good sense.

In *Haunch Paunch and Jowl,* Hirsch tells the story of the rabbi, "a thousand years behind the times," who comes to the Grodno Synagogue and learns that the richest mem-

bers of his congregation own property on Allen Street
and "that certain tenants paid ten times as much as ordinary tenants."

The rabbi runs to Allen Street, preaches in the middle
of that dark road about "dung upon the Shield of David,"
and is struck on the head with a blackjack. Hirsch isn't
surprised. A rebbe has no business here in the land of red
midnight.

But Allen Street wasn't short on piety. The most proper
madams wore religious wigs. Allen Street grew into the
twentieth century, swollen with greenhorns from Ellis Island. The Jews controlled the gigantic garment industry.
Heads were broken during strikes. Polish and Russian
Jews became proficient at the art of poisoning horses. It
was almost like the Moldavanka district of Odessa that
Isaac Babel wrote about. But the Lower East Side didn't
have Benya Krik, that romantic hoodlum in raspberry
pants, who could fall in love and set fire to a police station
in a single instant.

Yes, there was collective assertion on the "Jewish
Street." The greenhorns grew less green. They solved the
puzzle of Central Park and learned to mingle with uptown Jews. They opened banks on the East Side. Some of
them became tycoons. They muttered softly about Jewish
crime, as if it existed in a parallel universe, a place they
didn't have to touch, although the uptown German Jews
weren't quite so blind. The wild beards distressed them,
and the German Jews acted out of shame, guilt, or
charity, God knows. They began settlement houses and
societies to help Jewish prisoners. They grabbed greenhorns coming off the boat, taught them how to dress,
exploited them in the shops they owned, and also raised
them up. It was all a complicated dance. Love. Hate. Rivalry. It might have continued for years. But something
intervened.

In 1908, Theodore Bingham, the police commissioner
of New York, wrote in the *North American Review* that half
the City's criminals were Jews. Bingham didn't care much
for the Italians either. He called them scoundrels and
jailbirds. But he had a particular distaste for the "Russian

Hebrews," who, because they were not "physically fit for hard labor," had turned to crime. "They are burglars, firebugs, pickpockets and highway robbers—when they have the courage. . . ."

Suddenly the German Jews and those wild beards downtown weren't rivals anymore. They had a common enemy, Theodore Bingham. Uptown and downtown leaders sat in the same room and formed the Kehillah, a watchdog agency that could unite *all* Jews and become their voice among the gentiles of New York. Bingham apologized, and the Kehillah gathered statistics to prove that the ghetto wasn't a "nursery in crime." But no matter how hard the Kehillah juggled, it couldn't turn Jewish crime into a disappearing act. The Jews were a quarter of the City's population and committed a quarter of the City's crimes. The Kehillah shouldn't have been surprised. The Jews needed gangs, just like the goyim.

The Italians and those "Russian Hebrews" were the City's latest underclass. But the Kehillah wouldn't rest. It started its own police force, the Bureau of Social Morals, and from 1912 to 1917, the Kehillah's detectives roamed the East Side, collecting data on Jewish crime. The Kehillah closed down a hundred brothels, with the help of the City police. Jewish criminals fled from Abe Schoenfeld, the Kehillah's boss of detectives. "Whenever we walked into an underworld dive, they'd say 'Zechs,' which meant 'Stop talking, the Kehillah's here.'" But the Kehillah itself closed down in 1917. And Schoenfeld's stories began to sound like romantic fiction. Jews were still a quarter of the criminal class.

It was the restrictive immigration laws of the 1920s that weakened the "phenomenon" of Jewish street crime. The nativists had finally won. The National Origins Act of 1924 put an absolute quota on the number of Italians, Slavs, and Jews that could enter the United States: it adhered to the census of 1890, before the "new wave" began, and stopped the flow of immigrants from eastern and southern Europe.

But America lost as much as the greenhorns did because the explosion of immigrants at the start of the twentieth century had vitalized America, turned it into a culture of cities. The cities had existed long before the greenhorns arrived; but they were never quite the same after 1900. The greenhorns transformed Chicago, Cleveland, Philadelphia, Boston, Pittsburgh, Baltimore, San Francisco, New York, and Detroit. Suddenly they were "port" cities again, frontier towns, with upheavals of entire populations, bringing creativity and crime.

Crime didn't end with the National Origins Act. But America closed in upon itself, sat in isolation until World War II. It's almost as if the jazz age began with the winding down of Ellis Island. America had gone to war in 1917, soaked up Europe's culture and "sin," and then cut Europe out of its vocabulary. The "flappers" were native American girls. Without the push of new immigrants, the ghetto shrank, and the greenhorns imitated Yankee Doodle. I have pictures of my mom and dad wearing strange American clothes of the 1920s. They look like mannequins, dolls in the service of America. My dad couldn't whistle a word of English, but he looked like John Barrymore's brother.

[3]

Jewish delinquency was down. Allen was just another dark street under the el. Ghetto gangsters, like Dopey Benny Fein, were gone. The few skinny whores that couldn't find a husband fled uptown. Jenna Weissman Joselit speaks of the "embourgeoisment of New York Jewry" between the wars. That's a wonderful word, *embourgeoisment.* Like a diorama of Balzac's "La Comédie humaine," the movement of nogoodniks into the great society. "Somehow," she says, "a Jewish prostitute or a Jewish pimp did not fit in with the happily bourgeois mothers pushing their baby carriages on Ocean Parkway or with the dapper lawyers and garment manufacturers breaking bread at Garfield's, the 'cafeteria of refinement.'"

There were plenty of thugs at Garfield's, between the lawyers and the garment manufacturers. In fact, the thugs looked more dapper than the lawyers themselves. Crime moved out of the ghetto, as the ghetto broke—and even while the ghetto was still that crazy flower of sewing machines, prayer shawls, and a whore's red lamp. Think of Arnold Rothstein, who was mythologized in *The Great Gatsby* as Meyer Wolfsheim, the man who fixed the World Series of 1919. For Scott Fitzgerald he was a "small, flat-nosed Jew" with a large head and "two fine growths of hair which luxuriated in either nostril." Wolfsheim speaks of Jay Gatsby as an "Oggsford man" and asks Nick Carraway if he's looking "for a business gonnegtion." No matter how we chip at the legend, Arnold Rothstein will always be Meyer Wolfsheim. That's the power of Fitzgerald's novel.

Wolfsheim talks like a greenhorn. But Rothstein was born in Manhattan in 1883, the son of a prosperous cotton-goods merchant from Bessarabia, an Orthodox Jew known as Abe the Just. Rothstein's emergence as the czar of crime is something of a mystery. There's so much fiction surrounding "A.R." that not even Meyer Wolfsheim's nostrils can contain all of him. Like Gatsby, he was a man who invented himself. And like Gatsby, he was also shy. While others talked and cursed, "he clicked his teeth and uttered at most a monosyllable."

But A.R. could also curse, and this Bessarabian prince from Manhattan's Upper West Side, with his silken touch, always carried a gun. He had a beautiful blond mistress and a beautiful blond wife. And he died just as mysteriously as he lived. Shot in the groin by a fellow gambler, A.R. was found "crumpled against the wall" at the servants' entrance of the Park Central Hotel and was rushed to the Polyclinic Hospital, where he died without disclosing who his murderer was.

A.R. was a notorious "chiseler," and he might have been killed on account of a gambling debt. But if one can believe an old Broadway legend, the "A" and the "R" of the Park Central sign wouldn't light up on the day Rothstein died. Even if it sounds like a bit of Runyon talk, the whole Times Square colony mourned its moneylending czar, with or without two dead letters on an electric lightboard.

Just "another Jewish boy who had made good," says Irving Howe. After all, A.R. was buried as an Orthodox Jew, "in accordance with the American requirement that, no matter how brutal their lives, gangsters retain a tie of sentiment with the faith of their fathers." Thus the story of A.R. is glamorized to fit the Jewish tradition and Howe's own song of the prodigal son's return to orthodoxy. But Howe neglects to tell us that A.R. had nothing to do with the way he was buried. His father, Abe the Just, demanded a religious funeral for his son.

"Arnold was an anomaly in the history of crime," says Sidney Zion, publisher, reporter, and expert on nogoodniks. The gangsters before and after Rothstein had all been gunmen. You couldn't earn your reputation without a kill. "Meyer [Lansky] was a major-league gunman. If you killed people, they got afraid of you. Arnold was the only guy who didn't kill people."

But how did the son of Abe the Just grow into such a dark prince? He didn't walk out of some cold water flat and sniff the air of Allen Street. He wasn't Haunch Paunch and Jowl. He was a rich kid from the Jewish West Side. Rothstein was drawn to the ghetto. He disappeared from school and hung around the Jewish faro dens. The poor little rich kid didn't have much of a future until he fell under the influence of Big Tim Sullivan, Tammany's boss on the Lower East Side. "My smart Jew boy," Sullivan called him.

A.R. was jealous of his brother Harry. Thought his parents "loved Harry more." Harry died of pneumonia at twenty, and A.R. spent his life believing he'd "wished his brother's death." Was that brooding look his way of mourning Harry? But he didn't have Wolfsheim's tiny eyes. His eyes were big and brown, his hair was dark, and he had "white, womanish hands." He was five feet seven and looked more like J. D. Salinger than Meyer Wolfsheim. But he wasn't quite so fragile as Salinger's Seymour Glass. A.R. had a "pantherish quickness," or he never would have survived as long as he did.

Through Big Tim Sullivan he made "gonnegtions" with judges, lawyers, and the police, who began to borrow money from Rothstein. Money was a special kind of liquid in A.R.'s hands. He didn't accumulate it, like other bandits. He spread his money around. A.R. began one of the first laundering operations. Stuffed gambling money into real estate. He was the only bandit who could borrow from the banks. He was the Wolf, the Wizard, the Brain.

His skills weren't really removed from those his father had. He organized like any cotton-goods man. He was the wholesaler of crime. A.R. financed different gangs. He was also a mediator; his word was enough to end a war. "Fitzgerald made him look like a bum," Zion says, wounded by *The Great Gatsby*, ". . . eating with his hands and all that bullshit. Arnold was a class act. He taught Luciano how to eat."

That shy little man changed the course of American crime. The gang became a business unit under A.R. The Italians probably benefited more from Rothstein than the Jews ever did—wilder, woolier men, like Waxy Gordon and Dutch Schultz. Luciano and Frank Costello were Rothstein's ablest pupils. Costello would inherit A.R.'s role as exclusive banker to the underworld. Costello danced between judges and Tammany pols, the way Rothstein had done. He dressed liked Rothstein, looked like Rothstein, but he didn't have Rothstein's quiet flair. He couldn't sit at Lindy's and nibble cheesecake with Eddie Cantor. He'd never go to a bankers' ball. He wasn't the man Runyon would have written about.

So much of A.R.'s ambiance depended on the *idea* of Broadway. Rothstein would have been an uncelebrated gambler sitting in the shadows, without Times Square. A czar had to be noticed, and Rothstein was seen every night at Lindy's or the Colony Restaurant. He had dinner with his mistress Inez a few hours before he was shot. "Arnold was very gay—his normal, natural self. . . . We spoke of many subjects, but mostly of love; and he said that he hoped soon to be free to marry me. He said everything would be mine—his property and the money—but I cared only for him." He was at Lindy's when he received the phone call that took him to the Park Central and his death.

Rothstein's own mysterious life helps clarify the significance of Times Square in the psyche of New York. Rothstein was the Wolf, that rootless, remade man who needed the lights of an anonymous lair. Runyon didn't invent the Brain. He could only embroider what he saw. Rothstein never clung to the Lower East Side. He'd been "schooled" in the ghetto, but the Wolf wandered from the faro dens to Times Square, a "free-fire zone" for horse players, hoods, vaudevillians, and whores who wanted to escape their own particular ghetto. In the 1920s Times Square began to take on something of a Jewish tone. Yiddish became the official argot, not because Times Square was flooded with greenhorns, but because to all the rootless souls, like A.R. himself, Yiddish represented the language of crime.

It wasn't poetry, of course. It was street Yiddish, that special patter of tradesmen and thieves, with its own metaphysics: a bending of the body, a wink, and a mixture of ghetto English and God knows what. Bookies and other sportsmen used it to baffle Irish cops. Comedians played with it in the variety houses and spoke it among themselves, to show the rubes that Times Square had a mother tongue.

Why shouldn't that tongue have been Yiddish? The garment center was only a few blocks away, and most of the bosses were Yids: tight, eccentric men who had their own little court at Lindy's, right next to the creatures of show business. Jolson, Cantor, Fanny Brice, and her gambler husband, Nicky Arnstein, lived at Broadway hotels. The humor, the style, the frantic energy of Broadway was Jewish. Times Square was almost like the East Side's secular shadow, a Yankee Second Avenue without melameds and Jewish mothers beckoning their sons to attend City College and their daughters to marry a doctor.

And presiding over this wolf's lair until the end of 1928 was a polite gangster, A.R., friend of Fanny Brice and "Roxy" Rothapfel, the movie palace king. He wasn't like Benya Krik, a boisterous, romantic outlaw in ghetto pants. He was the Jewish Gatsby. The irony of it all is that Fitzgerald had uncovered the wrong Arnold Rothstein. Fitzgerald was a perennial Princeton boy, and Meyer Wolfsheim was Princeton's version of the Broadway Jew, endearing and vulgar. It was Rothstein who could have "picked out the green light at the end of Daisy's dock," Rothstein who "believed in the green light, the orgiastic future that year by year recedes before us." And Fitzgerald never knew it.

[4]

I'm not Rothstein and I'm not Isaac Babel. I have no Odessa tales, no Moldavankas in Manhattan, or a bestiary of Jewish gunmen, labor racketeers. Lepke and Gurrah and all that crowd. Or, as one of Lepke's hitmen lamented to Sidney Zion: "We were bigger than the Italians. You think we took orders from the guineas? Meyer [Lansky] sold off the empire. We lost our farm teams."

That's the American way; images of baseball reaching into crime. And I'm not about to start a war between the Italians and the Jews. How can I say whose farm teams were the best? But the Italians had one distinct advantage. They didn't bother their heads with any maddening drive into the middle class.. The Jews went to City College and the Italians stayed at home.

The Italians haven't produced ghost cities, like Brownsville and the East Bronx. They didn't fabulate a Grand Concourse for themselves and then disappear to the ends of the earth, running from phantom tribes of blacks. The Italians weren't like those Yiddish Ponce de Leóns, with Miami Beach in their blood. But they have their own peculiar mindscape: they'd gone through Ellis

Island like goat boys, clinging to the Sicilian rocks. Those "black" Italians concocted hilly towns in the flatlands of New York. That was their genius and mad strength. Nothing existed outside the family and the village.

It was perfectly natural that families would organize into tribal units, police themselves, and turn to crime. They were ghetto brats, after all. They exploited strangers and protected themselves. And the stronger tribes began to exploit the weakest ones. They owned entire blocks, created fiefdoms for themselves. Having been the lowest order of a feudal system, little better than donkeys, they decided to become lords. But their old-fashioned ways would have doomed them in the New World. They couldn't compete with the rough Irish gangs, who had Irish judges and Irish cops behind them. They could barely enter the Irish church. There were no Italian cardinals in New York. The Irish had completely shut them out.

And so the Italians turned to their fellow greenhorns, the Yids, who were also goat boys and dreamers, with their shtetls on both sides of Grand Street, and their medieval-eyed look that was as familiar as the water of Naples. They fought the Irish hoods, became gunmen in the same gangs. And the best of them worked for Arnold Rothstein, the Wolf of Broadway.

But the young Italian lords were left without a financial wizard after A.R. was shot in the groin, and they began to organize along his lines. They weren't only hitmen. A.R. had taught them the business of crime. They had lawyers and accountants, just like A.R., and made peace with the judges and the cops. They discovered the persuasion of money outside their own little shtetls. They could buy a judge or finance Tammany Hall. Tammany might never have survived the lean years of La Guardia without Italian (and Jewish) gang money. Lepke *and* Costello contributed to the Wigwam. But Costello was the better accountant. Lepke was linked to Murder, Inc., and died in the electric chair after surrendering to Walter Winchell. And Bill O'Dwyer, who, as Brooklyn's district

attorney, helped bring Lepke down, visited with Frank
Costello, the don of Tammany Hall, before becoming
mayor of New York.

The Italian bandits persevered because they held to
their home base. The Jews couldn't sit still. They found
their own suburbs. They went to Havana and opened Las
Vegas until the dons took their little empires away. Meyer
Lansky was furious at the portrait of himself in "*Godfather
II*," where Al Pacino, playing Michael Corleone, has him
killed. Sidney Zion, who met Lansky in Israel, says,
"Meyer went crazy . . . he couldn't stand the humiliation
of a Jew being shot by a dago. It really, really pissed him
off."

But the dons still won. Lansky is dead, and five families
rule New York: Gambino, Colombo, Genovese, Luchese,
and Bonnano. Like sweet noises out of an opera book.
Their main kingdom isn't Mulberry Street anymore. The
dons crossed the bridge years ago, before the Dodgers
drifted to L.A. They have their own Little Italy at Bath
Beach, which is isolated from tribes of tourists and is run
like a Sicilian town of the New World, with capos, soldiers,
and geeps, who are at the bottom of the Mob's pole. The
geeps are not "made-men," official soldiers of the five
families. The dons import them from Sicily.

The geeps are the newest generation of goat boys, with
all the wildness of the Sicilian rocks. They act as "mules"
(dope smugglers) and hitmen. They're impossible to trace
because they have no criminal records. They're zips.
They marry here, in the Brooklyn veld, but the dons
don't like them to live in Bath Beach (too many goat boys
can spoil a neighborhood). The geeps have to find their
culture among the Latinos of north Brooklyn. Their
home is on Knickerbocker Avenue, a tiny Italian enclave
near the Queens border. But as the geeps become simple
soldiers in a crime family, their status improves. And the
dons allow them to move closer and closer to Bath Beach,
until they're on Cropsey Avenue and they've lost that
greenhorn look.

But sometimes this feudal hierarchy of dons surrounded by soldiers and geeps falls down. Tommy Eboli,

the former head of the Genovese family, was murdered by his own troops because Tommy didn't pay enough attention to their needs. Zips had been brought down from Canada to do the job. They shot him in the face as he was leaving his girlfriend's house. The family named a new acting head, Frank Tieri, known as "Funzi," or the Frenchman, because he had a thick, froggy voice. Funzi took better care of his troops and he died a natural death.

That much I knew, but it was still hard for a kid from the Bronx to travel around Bath Beach with a notebook in his hand. The Gambinos, with their two thousand soldiers, wouldn't have liked a novelist in their midst. And so I asked my brother to take me on a tour of Bath Beach. He'd worked the old precinct at the corner of Bath Avenue and Bay 22nd, which looked like a nineteenth-century bank with a castled roof. It was a good place to start a pilgrimage. I saw the limousine services, the auto repair shops, around which a Caddy parked in the street wouldn't last twenty minutes. I saw the young geeps standing outside the Caffe Paradiso, dressed in silk shirts, their eyes like dark white teeth. They might live on Knickerbocker Avenue, but the Paradiso was theirs that night.

I had dinner with my brother Harvey at the Villa Borghese on Bath Avenue, the heart of Italian country. The geeps at the other tables looked at us. Their silk shirts seemed to bloom in the dark of the Borghese. They clicked their teeth and talked in a lower voice. It was Harvey they were worried about. I was much too skinny to have the proper stink of a detective. They must have thought I was Harvey's buff, a mook in Trotsky glasses.

The owner arrived at our table, asked how Harvey was, and returned to the kitchen. "I just gave him a heart attack," Harvey said. But there wasn't much of a crisis at the Villa Borghese. The geeps drank their minestrone, and Harvey and I tore at Italian bread. There was so much eyeballing between the tables, it began to feel like a company of friends.

I talked to Harvey about our dad. But he wouldn't remember the crazy fights at home, the broom my father had thrown at him in a rage, and Harvey's swollen eye.

"Ah, I don't dwell on it," he said.

He told me about Vinnie the Mook, the ancient retarded boy of Bath Beach, who wore a phony police badge and could go into any restaurant and eat for free. Who cares how the economy went? It was a village. Even the Mob had an obligation to a mook.

But I didn't meet Vinnie, and I don't think the geeps would have sat for an interview. Yes, I'd become a scholar of the Maf. I knew which tribes carted garbage and which tribes wouldn't. But I kept searching for some clue into the private machinery of the dons. I didn't want books and magazine articles, confessions of a Mafia princess. I wanted the real thing, a disgraced button man who would talk to me. And then I found my man. That is, my brother found him for me. A former rat in the Federal Witness Protection Plan. He was living out on Long Island under an assumed name. He wasn't interested in money. He was a police buff. He liked to brag about his exploits, my brother said. But Harvey had never met the guy. We had to use a go-between. The stoolie was playing hide-and-seek. But he had stories about the Maf. Guaranteed. All we had to do was open him up, encourage the stoolie, get him to sing.

The stoolie was as temperamental as any diva. Three months went by and he still wasn't singing. He'd say yes, no, and yes again. Then my brother called me. "Kid, the meet is on." Took the subway out to Coney Island and got into my brother's car. We didn't have to hurry. The go-between was late. We went in *his* car to another village, where we finally met our man, the federal informant. He had a tattoo on his arm, and I wondered if he was like the Yakusa, those Jap button men who colored their bodies according to the horrors of their particular clan.

I'll call him Moey because I'd rather not get him killed. He lived in a ranch house with a woman who could have been his wife. She offered me Pepsi-Cola. And I began to think less and less of this Yakusa and his tattoo. What the hell were colored pinpricks on an arm? The guy had never been a button man. He didn't have the right kind of fatness. There was something Talmudic about him. He was soft in the middle, like a scholar. He had horn-rimmed glasses and an owl's eye. He'd never worked for the dons a day in his life. Wasn't even Italian.

Thought I could smell the Bronx on him. I wasn't so wrong. He was a Jew from Bensonhurst, not the kind of Jew Irving Howe would write about. Moey was a confidence man, a carryover from an earlier, rougher time. And then I understood why he seemed so familiar. It had nothing to do with memories of Brooklyn or the Bronx. This was my old friend Meyer Hirsch, Haunch Paunch and Jowl, hurled into another time and place. He wasn't a judge eating potted breast on Allrightniks Row. He was an anonymous man with a new identity card, some federal prosecutor's sweet little boy, a former pet of the United States.

But Meyer-Moe didn't behave like a pet. He was indignant about the government's protection plan, which was supposed to shield an informant after he testified, give him money, and a "new fucking life." Never worked out that way for Moe, who was one of the first witnesses in the plan. "They said, 'We'll give you twenty-nine hundred a month.' They gave me balls . . . screwed up on my Social Security. I could have gotten better papers on my own."

He bitched and bitched, but my brother had been right about him. Moe was a buff. He'd come out of the cradle with his own grift. "The witness program sucks." But he loved being a confidence man for the FBI. "The prosecutors told me they didn't care what I do as long as I don't rob banks or kill people. I was a one-man strike force."

And how did it all begin for Moe? He'd gone into the automobile business with some mook. "I was in business with the guy for thirty days . . . borrowed money from my mother, and thirty days later I was busted in five different counties, like Al Capone." It wasn't Moey's fault that the cars he was trading were hot. His partner had set him up. "I knew the guy. He just burned me. Not a dime in the bank and I got busted. He nailed my ass to the wall."

And that's when the federal prosecutors took to Moe and turned him around. He ran with the FBI, the Secret

Service, and the special task force on narcotics. Moe was involved in every sort of sting operation. "I passed off a million dollars in counterfeit money. I pulled down a hundred-million-dollar jewel case." It was hit and run for Meyer-Moe. "I went from agency to agency. . . . I did a lot of things on my own. I gave D. [one of the prosecutors] a shit hemorrhage."

Moe moved about America, working his stings. Melville would have adored such a confidence man. Drugs were Moe's specialty. "I did so much in drugs, never less than five kilos. When people begged me for a kilo, I said you can get that from the niggers on the street."

Moe crisscrossed the country like some terrible, teasing Lolita with a butterfly net. He has an active memory about all the specimens he trapped: 448 convictions, 640 arrests. "I buy weight," he said to a dealer in Miami known as the Black Jew. He'd set himself up in Miami Beach as a merchant prince, with his own prostitutes and federal agents performing as his bodyguards. Moe even had a swimming pool. It was like a story out of the *Arabian Nights,* with Moe as Scheherazade *and* the fat king who wasn't allowed to doze. And we were Scheherazade's witnesses. The Black Jew offered to sell three kilos. Moey wouldn't bite. "I need more volume," he said, offering the dealer a prostitute at the pool. The dealer took the prostitute, but he had to beg for time. They would finish the "buy" on the phone.

"Don't talk dope on the telephone, talk about shoes, black shoes," Moey said. The dealer called. He had six black shoes to sell. But he had to leave Miami to get them.

The dealer returned, got off the plane with "a gorgeous babe and six black shoes," and Moey's bodyguards arrested him on the spot. That was the end of the Black Jew of Miami.

"Did you get any of the action?" the go-between asked.

"Balls," Moe said. "I was supposed to get fifteen thousand dollars in that hundred-million jewel sting. I got five. And the U.S. marshals are still holding the jewels."

But Moe's story wasn't about money or the excitement of a sting. Moe didn't see himself as a stoolie. "I wasn't a rat. A rat spills on his friends." He was a government whirlwind, Moe the attack ship, Batman let out of his cave and lent to the FBI. But it was more than that. He'd lived a kind of schizoid life, doing scams in the morning and attending his son's bar mitzvah in the afternoon. He was like a Hollywood producer orchestrating his own skits on the government's Monopoly board. Moe had all that money to play with and agents to move around. "I did it as a challenge," he said. But there was a madness to Moe. His stings had little to do with the ordered world of the FBI. He was Haunch Paunch and Jowl, the con man who'd finally conned himself. He'd become a fantasist, a make-believe Moe, undercover cop without a badge, the ultimate grifter.

But he grew tired of the fantasy and the federal marshals who were supposed to protect his life. This was the very same marshal service that had policed the West. According to Moe, the marshals "got a few people killed because of their ignorance." Marshals shouldn't have been allowed to handle a prize witness like Moe. "They were giving me six hundred dollars a month . . . and no job."

Moe gave up the glory. "I don't want to work with marshals," he told the feds. "Give me some money, let me get away, and I'll take care of myself."

He went back to selling cars, and I wasn't any closer to the dons of Bath Beach. But the go-between saw my distress and began pumping Moe. "Did you work any stings against the Mob?"

"No," he said. "But Funzi saved my ass."

Ah, the Frenchman. We were back in Genovese country.

"Funzi buys a car from me," Moe said, talking about one of his incarnations as an auto dealer. "I ask him, how do you want it registered? Funzi sees an exit sign and says, 'Register it as Joe Exit.'"

But Moe was chased out of that dealership and bought a bar on Nostrand Avenue. A pair of geeps tried to shake him down. They were minor soldiers of a minor don, but they wanted a little piece of the bar for themselves.

"You can't have it," Moe said. "I'm a connected man."

"Who's your rabbi?"

"I'm not allowed to tell."

The geeps sneered at Moe, examined his stock of whiskey, and warned him they'd be back that night at nine. Moe got Funzi on the phone.

"Don't worry," the Frenchman said. "I'll call at nine-fifteen."

The geeps returned and Moe waltzed with them until the phone rang.

"That's my rabbi," Moe said, and the geeps picked up the phone, listened for half a minute, "had a shit hemorrhage, and walked out the door."

Moe wanted his life turned into a television series and he needed a novelist. But I wasn't the right person to chronicle his tales with the FBI. I couldn't make him glamorous enough. He was Haunch Paunch and Jowl, corpulent con man. More Zero Mostel than Robert Redford, and Zero wasn't even alive.

We left the stoolie in his ranch house.

"He's had a charmed life," I said.

The go-between agreed. "Moe couldn't have survived today with all those Colombian madmen. He's a fucking dinosaur. And he was careful. He never messed with the Chin," meaning Genovese chieftain Chin Gigante. "The Chin would have eaten him alive."

We drove back to my brother's car, and I took the local to New York. I thought of the television series I'd never write about Moe. Tales of a federal informant. With Scott Joplin in the background, a bit of sting music. And some blue-eyed discovery to play Moe as a much sleeker man. Who cares? I'd still call it *Haunch Paunch and Jowl.*

four

THE MAN WHO SAVED NEW YORK

[1]

The City weaves its legends like some collective ghost. Heroes (and villains) burst upon our consciousness, wake us from our brooding sleep, and control our lives . . . until the next crop of heroes emerges in our minds. Fifty years ago New York was in the grip of Roxy fever. Babies and bowling alleys, theaters, sweatshops, clubs and cabarets, delicatessens, dry cleaners, dogs, cats, roosters, dance steps, chorus lines (the Roxyettes), cigars, popcorn, animal crackers, and everything else was named after Roxy, motion-picture impresario and the greatest self-publicist of his time. There are still seventeen Roxys in the Manhattan phone book: Roxy Roller Rink, Roxy Wines, Roxy Window Cleaning. . . . How many of those establishments and their clients could possibly remember the original Roxy? Generations cover generations with a

frightening rust, until New York is like one enormous
archeological dig and we have to search through our
layered city for whatever past is left.

"Forget the epic, the masterwork," Nathanael West
once scribbled in a small magazine. "In America fortunes
do not accumulate, the soil does not grow, families have
no history. Leave slow growth to the book reviewers, you
only have time to explode." West was offering his advice
to young novelists, but he could have been describing
New York, where he lived at the time as manager of the
Sutton Hotel. This is not a city for slow growth. Things
and people are wont to disappear. Roxy. The old,
glorious Penn Station with its exposed ribs and "acres of
glass." Bonwit's, now entombed in Trump Tower.

And then entire villages explode into our vision. Blue
pyramids rise up near Battery Park. A broken, little seaport becomes a monster attraction and a lunching ground
for half of Wall Street. A few restaurants and boutiques
cluster near the loins of Lincoln Center and the ramblas
of Columbus Avenue is born.

Careers also begin to explode. An obscure congressman from Greenwich Village, Edward I. Koch, becomes mayor of New York and his antics are celebrated
around the world. An unknown investment banker, Felix
Rohatyn, solves the puzzle of New York's financial picture
and is declared the Wizard of Oz. The baby-faced son of
an outer-borough builder creates a hotel between Grand
Central and the Chrysler Building and is turned into
Donald Trump. A tough little lady starving in the East
Village uncovers her belly button and grows into
Madonna, the Material Girl. A wispy, eccentric ex–boy
genius lost in the Bartleby-like atmosphere of the City
Council is named parks commissioner, and suddenly we
have a genius again, Henry Stern, wearing an orange rain
slicker as he visits every park in every borough and turns
them all green. A dark, delicate beauty from the Rhode
Island School of Design comes to Manhattan and trans-
forms herself into the Egyptian goddess Mary Boone. A
burly cook in a downtown restaurant, a child of Brooklyn
and Texas, joins Mary Boone and we have Julian

Schnabel, the wild boy of American painting. An old man about to retire after a long career of building spectacular signs on Broadway constructs a gel for the Empire State Building, and Douglas Leigh becomes the greatest "illuminating engineer" on the planet Earth, just before he's seventy.

All these histories have one thing in common: they were born out of disaster, the City's near-fall in 1975. New York was "the regional basket case," remembers Peter C. Goldmark of the Port Authority. The City was in the toilet, a vassal of the state, and the stepchild of President Ford. The bankers met to decide the fate of New York and wouldn't even invite the mayor. There was talk of bumping Beame, of having his whole administration disappear—a band of Irishers, Italians, and Jews, all the old ethnic types who'd come out of the cradle of Ellis Island or even an earlier cradle than that. Those ethnics were eating up City paper, hawking bonds to finance the welfare village that New York had become in their hands.

"The City became a social democracy," says Lou Winnick, deputy vice president of the Ford Foundation. "It was taxing the rich to help the poor. It began to act like a country, like Denmark."

And the bankers didn't want Denmark on the Hudson. They demanded that City services be cut. Something had to be done about the "basket case." It seemed as if the worst fantasies of New York had arrived. The City was going dark. The country itself lay in a deep recession. New York had become so "bond-crazy," it was carrying a "third of the nation's portion of debt." And "people worried that the dollar wasn't worth a yen."

New York was moving into the Middle Ages. Hospitals closed. High-priced cooperatives on Park Avenue went down and down. No one could find Abe Beame. Riding in a helicopter, Beame fell into the sea and had to be plucked out. "Abe, please be careful," said Paul O'Dwyer, president of the City Council. "I don't want that job."

The very notion of a New York mayor had become something to scoff at: the pariah of the Western world. It was a thankless, awful occupation. The hatchet man of the banking establishment. And Beame couldn't even carry his own hatchet. He was ridiculed along with his deputy mayors. He danced inside a shadow box.

New York's great bit of luck was the coming of 1976, America's Bicentennial. The Democrats chose New York as their convention town. They must have liked the idea of a dark city: New York would be as cheap as Calcutta by June or July. And the builders and bankers, all the civic-minded men, asked Douglas Leigh not to retire. He was put in charge of "City Decor." Leigh was the magician who had built a waterfall on Times Square for Pepsi-Cola, a winking penguin for Kools, and sixteen consecutive years of smoke rings for Camel cigarettes. Times Square had lost its waterfall, but New York's civic leaders were counting on the old "Lamplighter of Broadway" to produce other miracles for 1976. Leigh began to light up various fountains, like a wicked Alice on the loose. But this Alice didn't have much of a wonderland to play with. New York was still a dark shell. Convention delegates might bump into their own shadows on Fifth, Sixth, or Seventh.

And so Douglas Leigh began to light up Seventh Avenue and line Fifth with flags. And he had the fountains spill water that was a patriotic red, white, and blue. But it was still paltry magic from the man who had a penguin wink a hundred thousand times a day and could reproduce Fred Astaire across an electric field. It wasn't fountains or flags that could charm a delegate. It was the skyline, and that skyline was as dark as the rest of New York. A tower glowed here and there (the Empire State had its old-fashioned fluorescent lamps and Wall Street had a couple of lit crowns), but a few crabby lights were nothing a delegate could dream about.

Yet Leigh himself had dreamt of skyscrapers long before '76. In the mid-1930s he had a scheme to use the outer walls of the Chrysler Building as a billboard to advertise Chrysler cars. And he wanted four powerful searchlights attached to the building so that beams could "be cast across the night sky in geometrical patterns by mechanically controlled gears."

It was Leigh's idea of a light show without Roman candles. No bursting candle could have given him the absolute geometry that he sought in the sky. Once people got tired of all the geometry, he'd get rid of the gears and hire "four men to operate the searchlights by hand, focusing them on four Goodyear blimps." The blimps would cruise over the metropolis with advertising scratched on their bellies in neon light. But Walter Chrysler rejected Leigh's plan and decided to mount an exhibit instead in Flushing Meadow at the 1939 World's Fair.

That wasn't Leigh's last flirtation with tall buildings. He had his eye on the Empire State's long needle, which had been built as a mooring mast for airships. The Lamplighter wanted to turn that needle into a gigantic Lucky Strike cigarette. The owners weren't interested. But they couldn't discourage Douglas Leigh. He had other plans. He'd select a different skyscraper and light it up as a perfume bottle. But he was years ahead of his time.

He had to wait for Henry Hudson.

In 1959 New York celebrated the three hundred and fiftieth year of Hudson's third voyage, which took him and the *Half Moon* into the mouth of New York Bay and established the idea of New Amsterdam, since he was sailing for the Dutch. Little else is known about Henry Hudson. He discovered the river that bears his name and endured a mutiny. Set adrift with his son and seven men, he was lost at sea sometime in 1611. This mysterious explorer was the City's favorite son. A Britisher employed by the Dutch, he encompasses many of New York's contradictions. He was the first greenhorn in the New World, although he never started a colony. His bones are lying somewhere in our waters.

And Douglas Leigh was allowed to reconnoiter near the roofs as lighting marshal of the Hudson celebration committee. But he couldn't bring waterfalls and winking penguins or Lucky Strike cigarettes to the Chrysler Building or Empire State. All he could do was ask the owners of the tallest buildings to keep their windows lit during the nights of the celebration and convince Con Ed to come up with the electricity he needed. The City bloomed with light.

But Douglas Leigh's own Times Square "spectaculars" grew obscure. Billboards began to rot. Pepsi-Cola and Camels had turned to television. People were too involved with *I Love Lucy* to consider an old Camels sign. Leigh had to take his light shows to the Ginza, Tokyo's Times Square. He'd become a traveling magician—but he still had that craze to light the City of New York. He couldn't forget those enormous searchlights he'd conceived for the Chrysler Building. He was a man who wanted his own patterned sky. Other men looked for faces in the street. Douglas Leigh counted bulbs and kilowatt hours. He was the master of colored gels and Lexan sheets in a city that was growing dark.

And then there was 1976. Douglas Leigh got his chance to play Yankee Doodle in the sky. He took the City's quintessential tower, the Empire State, former home of King Kong and the most recognizable building in the world, symbol of the metropolis *and* the twentieth century, and gave it a magical red, white, and blue. It was the first time any tower had been lit in such fashion. No one had ever thought of theatrical gel for the sides of a building until Douglas Leigh. His engineers removed the old fluorescent lamps and replaced them with metal halide housed in Lexan sheets (the strongest possible plastic). The effect Leigh could create was four times as bright and there was no leap in electrical power.

The metropolis bathed in Bicentennial colors. Leigh calls it "color with meaning," an adman's cliché. It wasn't the theme that mattered. The City hadn't fallen in love with Leigh's patriotic touch of red, white, and blue. The old Lamplighter had designed a mystery for Manhattan. Waterfalls were fine. But the lighting of King Kong's turf in 1976 was Leigh's greatest spectacular.

The City's recovery almost seemed to come out of that. Leigh had found the means to "push" Manhattan. The basket case was becoming the Big Apple. A cheap dollar brought foreigners to New York. Hotels began to fill. Slowly, the metropolis moved out of its slump.

And Douglas Leigh had his wish. "I was pushing seventy and I needed a new career." But that career fit an old fancy. "I had a zeal to light up the classic tops of skyscrapers." It wasn't until 1977 that Leigh began in earnest. With the Empire State. His various gels were slid into "the middle of a Lexan sandwich" and the metropolis burst with curious, different lights. The Empire State Building was now the psychic barometer of New York. When the Bronx Bombers won the World Series in 1977, Leigh lit the Empire State in the Yankee colors of white and blue. After Camp David, "we put up the colors of Egypt and Israel." And then there were all the holidays and mythic people and events. The Empire State went green for St. Patrick. It was amber and red on Thanksgiving; red and green for Santa. Only Kong didn't have his colors. Kong and Mayor Koch.

Leigh's work spread with its own wicked fire. He designed the lights for tower after tower, until New York began to look like Leigh's sky. It was almost as if he were taking vengeance on the City's impersonal grid. If the metropolis had moved uptown parcel by parcel, block by block, with an inevitable lack of grace, Leigh was going to light the City with a kind of lyricism that challenged the grid. Leigh's lit roofs were much more powerful than the relentless line of an avenue. He not only enhanced the architecture of a building, as *Times* critic Paul Goldberger has said; he created a new architecture, the body and bones of light.

[2]

Douglas Leigh has a gravelly voice and a hawk's blue-gray eyes. He looks like a boy in his tan suit and bow tie. The boy is seventy-eight. "I'm working like a dog," he says, a dog who's been summoned downtown to "bark" at the World Trade Center and light those twin towers. "If I live and nothing happens, as they say down South."

Leigh was born in Anniston, Alabama, on May 24,

1907. As a ten-year-old, he would watch with a child's religious ache as the town's iron-smelting plant poured off its hot slag every evening. The sky would burst into a crazy orange glow for a couple of minutes. And young Leigh was drawn to that dancing color. It was like the northern lights to him.

He went off to the University of Florida in 1927 and never opened a book. He left after two years, fumbled around, and landed in New York with eight dollars and twenty-five cents. He worked for a billboard company, but his bosses advised Douglas Leigh that only a man with some social position in New York could sell advertising on Broadway. He quit and started Douglas Leigh, Inc., a company without a dollar or a home. Leigh's offices were inside his skull. He leased a billboard in the Bronx on credit and sold the space to the St. Moritz, which advertised its four-dollars-a-night rooms on the billboard's "semi-spectacular" blinking lights and offered Leigh a meal plan at Rumpelmayer's, its own restaurant, and lent him a room, which also served as the new office of Douglas Leigh, Inc. But he didn't have to work at such bargain rates for long.

"I began lighting Times Square in 1933, the day Roosevelt went into office." There had been spectaculars before Douglas Leigh. "The first was a blinking billboard on Broadway that read 'Manhattan Beaches Swept By Ocean Breezes'—with flashing lights that had to be switched on and off by hand."

But they all died during the Depression. Broadway was like a blackened jungle. There was Lindy's and a couple of lights. But it was Leigh who began to resurrect Times Square.

His first spectacular was a twenty-five-foot coffee cup for A & P, with a continual feather of steam. There were problems at the coffee cup's inauguration. The feather was fine until "a few hundred cubic feet of steam condensed" and landed on some of Leigh's friends.

By the mid-thirties Leigh had his own northern lights on Broadway. He was the master switchman of Times

Square. His Wilson whiskey sign, with cartoons and silhouettes and rooftop water fountain, ate enough electricity to light up Hackensack.

At the start of World War II, the Lamplighter was prepared for all emergencies. In the event of an air raid over New York, Leigh could produce "an instantaneous blackout" on Broadway with a single switch inside the Wilson whiskey sign. And with the prospect of a blackout facing him, Leigh built his masterpiece: the Camels sign. It was a mixture of business and patriotic smoke rings. The mouth on the billboard was an eight-foot cone. Behind the mouth was a motor that thrust out steam. It was the "concussion that caused the rings." The first Camels' mouth belonged to a soldier. Every three months that mouth would change. The Camels sign had a soldier, a sailor, a marine, and an airman for the duration of the war. Then the Camels man crept into civilian clothes.

Leigh took to the sky after the war, leasing as many surplus blimps as he could find until he had his own airborne lighting circus. His blimps went around the country advertising American products. His most spectacular circus animal was Pegasus, Mobil's winged horse, which always seemed to fly right off the bottom of the blimp. Pegasus had various sets of wings; the master lit those different wings with a kind of staggered effect, creating the illusion of flight.

It wasn't fair. I saw that stinking horse as a child from the roofs of the Bronx. Mobil Oil meant nothing to me, but Pegasus could scare the hell out of a Bronx boy. As the blimp's propeller ground over my head, I was certain Pegasus would drop from the sky and I'd have a bloody horse on my hands. I knew his wings couldn't survive the fall. I'd have to nurse Pegasus on a tarry roof, pull his wings together somehow. The horse never fell. But I had nightmares of Pegasus shattering in my lap. Because I was clever enough to know his wings were made of glass. But that didn't make him any less of a horse. The dreams continued long after the blimps disappeared. Broken wings. A spill of glass. Thanks to Douglas Leigh.

Leigh himself became as much of a phantom as his ghostly horse. Blimps with complicated neon bellies and waterfalls on a roof couldn't compete with America's little magic box. The tube swallowed the notion of *live* entertainment. Burlesque was banished to New Jersey. Broadway comics retreated to the Catskills. Nothing but an institution like Grossinger's could save their skin. The movie palaces went dark. Only Radio City Music Hall, Roxy Rothapfel's last extravaganza, with its chorus line of human dolls in absolute sync, could survive the onslaught of television.

The Camels sign was torn down in 1967. Broadway was becoming a boneyard. Douglas Leigh lit a couple of fountains, but he had to build his spectaculars abroad. No one seemed to remember the Pepsi waterfall. And who would have cared about some neon horse that had once scared the pants off a generation of kids? Leigh himself was only another lost soul.

And then, like the metropolis, which seemed about to disappear along with its diminutive mayor, Leigh was resurrected in 1976, in the midst of the town's own worst debacle. Leigh had helped rediscover one of New York's natural wonders: the skyscraper. And by doing so, he revealed to the City that it was unique. Banks could treat it like a stepson. They could oblige Beame to fire teachers and cops. They could humiliate the very idea of city government and believe that the pols were a raving band of socialists, giving out lollipops to the poor, while Houston and Dallas and Denver thrived under the "new" capitalism. But Houston, Dallas, and Denver didn't have a downtown that filled with people day *and* night. They were automobile cities, and New York was a town of foot soldiers. Not even the grid could kill that incredible motor of the streets.

"We're now on a nostalgic kick," Leigh says. As he lights up New York, people suddenly remember his phantasmagoric signs. Because Leigh himself has passed into myth. That quiet little man is a walking explosion. He may have come from Alabama, but his history has mingled with New York's. He isn't only his Lexan sandwiches and the silver sheath of Citicorp. Leigh *is* light. And like most authentic geniuses, he's least authentic when he talks. He has a mundane sense of that fabric he's put into the sky. "I want some buildings visible for drivers approaching Manhattan from the east and west as well as those jets that are coming into the airports."

That sounds like an advertisement for Camelot. But Leigh's artistry has always been much more elusive. He's managed to couple commerce and nightmare. Unlike the priests of pop art, Leigh is deadly serious. There was no kitsch to the Camels sign. He was selling products with a tight, surrealistic dream. He's closer to Walt Disney than to the realtors and admen and architects he admires. Disney took Dumbo and Pinocchio and turned them into delicious, but scary, dreams. He dealt with archetypes that haunted us at some deep, disturbing level. Dumbo and Pinocchio are innocents abroad, inventive children in a much darker world. When we watch them on the screen, it's as if each of us were trapped inside the belly of a whale.

Douglas Leigh himself is part Dumbo, with Disney's genius. He's made us believe that an elephant can fly. The smoke rings and the waterfall and the gold-leaf light on the Helmsley Building were created to sell products. Camels. Pepsi-Cola. And Helmsley himself. Or, as Leigh says: ". . . we started out to glorify a building for its owner. Now, it is seen as a civic thing."

But all of Leigh's spectaculars—the two-story snowflake over Fifth Avenue, amber and green on the Empire State—are much closer to magic than an owner's glory and civic pride. Leigh has reinvented New York. He's taken our own shadows and thrust them into light. He's that old, quiet devil in a bow tie.

And then there's Roxy, who's like a curious, hidden double to Douglas Leigh. Leigh advertised other people's wares, and Roxy promoted movie palaces and himself, but there was a kinship between the two men. They arrived out of nowhere to become creatures of their own invention. Like Douglas Leigh, Roxy was a small-town boy. He was born Samuel Lionel Rothapfel in Stillwater, Minnesota, on July 9, 1882, the son of a German shoemaker.

The family moved into "the roiling, rootless slums" of the Lower East Side in 1895. Roxy had no schooling in the ghetto and he couldn't hold down a job. His father threw him out of the house when he was fourteen. Roxy worked in music halls and was a marine for seven years, ending up "as a drill sergeant in the Dry Tortugas."

Next he mined coal and played baseball in Pennsylvania. It was baseball that got him his "magic nickname," according to Roxy. He couldn't expect people to yell "Rothapfel" as he rounded third. So Samuel Lionel Rothapfel was transformed into Roxy on a baseball diamond in the Northeast Pennsylvania League. Somehow I don't believe it. I suspect that little Sam was Roxy as a child in Stillwater and Roxy as an old man. And I wonder if he was ever a drill sergeant in the Dry Tortugas. Samuel Lionel Rothapfel was a "chunky, Napoleonic little man" with a need to aggrandize all his moves. In his later years he looked a lot like Mussolini. He was always the very best fabulist about his own career.

But he did start a movie theater in Forest City, Pennsylvania, on New Year's Day, 1908. It was a big closet in back of Julius Freedman's saloon. Roxy had a real advantage. He married Julius's daughter as part of the deal.

He borrowed a bed sheet from Julius and the bed sheet became his screen. Roxy ran his little theater like a single-minded impresario. He had more energy than the town itself and some of Douglas Leigh's brilliance with lights. He invented "technicolor" with bulbs hidden behind the screen, created his own wonderland, the first "Roxy."

Rothapfel's Family Theater caught on with a fury in that Pennsylvania mining town, and vaudeville distributors began to hire Roxy to "glamorize the movie portion" of their variety bills. Soon young Rothapfel was traveling all around the country, saving vaudeville acts with his motion pictures. He was a wandering whirlwind.

And it was no accident that the whirlwind should land in New York. "I'm going to be the manager of a theater," he told his wife. "I don't know what the name of it is—but it's going to be famous, and so am I."

It was the autumn of 1913, and there'd never been a movie palace in Manhattan—until Roxy arrived. And the first palace wasn't even near Broadway. Roxy took the Regent, an ailing theater at the corner of 116th and Seventh, in German-Jewish Harlem, closed it down, ripped the theater apart, put in a private elevator for himself, installed an electric fountain on stage and colored windows on both sides of the screen, "dressed the projectionists like brain surgeons," and had rose-tinted lights in his new auditorium.

Roxy didn't stay uptown for long. A pair of entrepreneurs from Buffalo, the Mark brothers, Mitchell and Moe, demolished an old carriage factory at Broadway and Forty-seventh, in that dying district of carriage-repair shops, and couldn't seem to come up with the right solution for their hole in the ground until they began to consider the movies. It wasn't much of a brainstorm for Mitchell and Moe. New York had 986 movie houses in 1913. It was the one form of entertainment that the greenhorns preferred. And the Mark brothers meant to lure the greenhorns into their house. They needed a mass audience or else they couldn't survive.

Photoplays (films with complete stories) captivated immigrant New York. Even legitimate theaters began showing films between their other engagements. The Criterion turned itself into a movie house and had the whole of New York harbor pictured on its front wall, with the Statue of Liberty *and* Ellis Island. It was a marvelous piece of salesmanship: immigrants could watch silver ghosts on a screen and also relive their own ghostly entrance into the New World.

The Mark brothers hired Roxy away from Harlem and brought him to their movie house, the Strand. And Roxy exercised all his ideas of what a Broadway palace should be. He brought a cannon into the house on opening night. And the cannon boomed three times before the lights went out. Then the Strand's dark cave began to glow from the fountains that lit up like Roxy's original rainbow. He'd dazzled the audience, delivered it from light to dark, dark to light; and then he threw visions on a wall, with tinted light behind the screen, so that all the characters seemed to dance with a new persuasion, as if they were in a land of fire. But it wasn't the film that people remembered, or the fountains. It was Roxy himself.

He installed a lounging room for the ladies, a cosmetics suite "of satin and rosewood, with gold leaf on hand-carved decorations . . . Louis XVI furniture and tapestries." Soon every other palace on Broadway couldn't exist without its own cosmetics suite. And Roxy wasn't finished. He opened the Rialto in 1916 with an electric signboard that had a pinwheel of sparks and light, a "flying" eagle, and two unfurling flags. Roxy's sign was as complicated as Coney Island. But it wasn't a decorative lure. He involved you with his eagle and his flags. It was almost unpatriotic not to enter the Rialto. He'd become a showman without shame.

The Rivoli opened under Roxy in 1917. His salary was seven hundred a week. He was now a major in the Marine Corps reserves, and he'd prance around the theater in his uniform and a special cape, like Batman under a luminescent dome. Marine and baseball player, he'd become his own hero in his own time. But he was a little too lavish at the Rivoli. And when the owner balked about the money Roxy was spending on himself (phone calls to the racetrack, etc.), Roxy grabbed his cape and resigned. He floundered for a year, chasing after projects, until he took over the Capitol in 1920.

Roxy began broadcasting live radio shows from the

Capitol's floor. *Roxy's Gang* was the first variety show radio ever had. Roxy didn't have to invent fables about himself. And he could afford to stutter on the radio. He was the "Foxy Grandpa," a national hit: that's when all the Roxy cleaners and Roxy bowling alleys began. Everything was Roxy. He played handball with Benny Leonard, lightweight champ of the world, sat with Arnold Rothstein, danced with senators' wives.

And then, in 1926, he had his own theater at Seventh Avenue and Fiftieth Street, the Roxy, built at a cost of fifteen million dollars. It was his Cathedral of the Motion Picture, as Roxy liked to call it, the greatest extravaganza Broadway had ever known. He earned more than Babe Ruth, a hundred and fifty thousand a year. "I'm happy," he said at the opening of his theater. "It's Roxy and I'm Roxy. I'd rather be Roxy than John D. Rockefeller or Henry Ford."

He'd become spirit and flesh, the marine who was also the incarnation of his own house. But Roxy was wrong about one thing. He hadn't built a cathedral. It was the common man's ocean liner, the ship that never moved. It had deck after deck, his own captain's office, tunnels, a grand foyer, a cyclorama of silver cloth that suggested infinity itself, a fire pump room, a giant switchboard, public and private shower baths, a stenographer's station, a water-cooling tower, a bowel full of refrigerating pumps that resembled the deepest, darkest engine room, an organ pit with millions of wires, a music library, even a hospital, and an indicator board in the lobby with a little lamp for every seat on Roxy's ocean liner; the lamps would light up soon as a seat was vacant.

Roxy offered the illusion of unlimited luxury for less than a dollar. The "new" man and woman of the metropolis, dreamers, typists, hatcheck girls, as anonymous as the twentieth century itself, couldn't afford a trip around the world. But they could voyage through the Roxy, guided by a little lamp that took them to their own special chair. The dimmed lights offered the lull of an endless sea. And Roxy's fabulous organ could imitate the worst ocean storm.

It's Roxy and I'm Roxy. That theater should have carried Roxy to the end of his life. But he was restless, and John D. Rockefeller lured him away. Old John D. wanted the pioneer of movie palaces to install a "Showplace of the Nation," grander than the Roxy itself, at Rockefeller Center, the urban Shangri-la that was going to occupy the very heart of midtown Manhattan and become the new metropolis: Radio City, an homage to the fabulous science of American business.

And so Roxy shuffled from Broadway to Sixth Avenue. He was given two theaters as his own toys, a smaller Roxy and Radio City Music Hall. He worked at them for almost two years. The old master seemed to have tired of movies. He'd come full circle, back to the vaudeville days of his youth. The Music Hall would be a "live" house. It would stage the most spectacular variety shows in the world . . . without a single movie. Roxy demanded a different kind of theater, not a dream palace in the dark, but a recreation hall that could simulate sunrise and sunset, bring the great outdoors right into the house.

Roxy no longer needed movies; the theater itself substituted for film. His Music Hall was one enormous movie without the bother of a screen. The Foxy Grandpa had gone a little mad. He wanted to drop hallucinogens into the air-conditioning ducts. His lawyers said no. And the Music Hall opened without laughing gas. It was a disastrous first night.

The program began at eight-thirty and didn't end until after two in the morning, with all of Roxy's stars "rising out of the pit, rising out of the stage, revolving, singing, dancing, waving, bowing as the golden contour curtain lowered in swooping scallops to the stage. . . . Next day Roxy collapsed and was sent to the hospital."

He just couldn't turn a theater into film. His Music Hall was much too big to be a vaudeville house. Roxy had built the ultimate movie palace without ever knowing it. And after the first night, while he lay in his hospital room, the owners of Radio City Music Hall abandoned vaudeville, a creature out of Roxy's own past, and learned to depend on films for their main source of revenue. But the old master did have one legacy: his chorus of precision dancers, the Roxyettes (known as the Rockettes after Roxy's departure). The Roxyettes were perfect for such an enormous hall—"a scriptless chorus line without any action to sustain."

Roxy had re-created the New World for his clientele, a kind of relentless, costumed machine: industrial power with sexual parts. All the Roxyettes were standardized equipment, between five-four and five-seven, replaceable souls, like a parody of the immigrant dream of perfection. Their high kick was exhilarating and deadly at the same time. It mimicked the desire of the immigrant to shed his greenhorn status *and* his personality, to leap into the New World and become a mechanical, faultless doll, without pain, without that terrible sense of loss. Roxy had crystallized the immigrant imagination and never once received credit for it.

He wasn't really welcomed back. The owners ignored him. Roxy left without a word. He had one or two other ventures but he couldn't quite recover from his fall at Radio City. He'd argued with earlier bosses, he'd quit and resigned, but there were no other palaces left for Roxy. Without a genuine focus, a theater he could manage, he grew obscure. "I would rather die with my boots on," Roxy said. But he died in his sleep, a lonely, isolated man, about to make a comeback on the radio. He'd received seven million fan letters during his thirteen years of broadcasting. And now people hardly remember who he was.

But I mourn Roxy, father of the Rockettes, who came dancing out of Minnesota to perfect the movie palace for twentieth-century man. He didn't make movies, but he *revealed* them to a culture of greenhorns. How many immigrants learned to read at the movies, learned to dress, and also escaped the bitterness of their own lives in one or another of Roxy's palaces?

It wasn't only an audience of immigrants that invaded the movie houses. Most of America fell in love with silver faces on the screen. But movies had a particular relevance and charm for every "newcomer," from the nickelodeon of 1900 to the labyrinthian, multiscreen, impersonal complexes of right now . . . with Roxy in the middle.

He didn't create Broadway. But he modernized it, turned it into a democracy of people's movie palaces. And there was only a short leap from Roxy to Douglas Leigh. Leigh arrived when Roxy's career was almost done. But his spectaculars continued a process that Roxy began, the process of seduction. Their personal styles were different; Roxy pranced in his cape and stuttered on the radio, and Douglas Leigh winks from behind a bow tie. But they're both magicians who've disturbed our consciousness with patterns of dark and light.

Douglas Leigh rewired the psyche of New York with figures in a skyline. The figures increase. Who knows what will light up next while the magician breathes? He's much too modest a man to contemplate his own immortality. He has Lexan sandwiches to consider. But Roxy wasn't so modest. He worried about immortality all his life. He hoped his "cathedrals" would last. But all of them have disappeared except the Music Hall, which bumps along without the least reminder of Roxy. That old dead marine endured the ultimate irony. He mythologized the movie house, but there were no movies to mythologize him. We remember Flo Ziegfeld because of Walter Pidgeon and William Powell. George M. Cohan remains our Yankee Doodle on account of Cagney. They've become fictional, creatures of the mind. They might have been smarter and more creative than Roxy Rothapfel in real life. But they weren't as fabulous, or as perverse. And they didn't lunge into our century the way Roxy did. They were rather conservative souls.

Roxy dreamed harder and didn't live nearly so long as Ziegfeld or Cohan. "Death is just a big show . . . ," Roxy told the world a year before he died. But if Orson Welles or Akim Tamiroff had ever played him, we might have been able to latch on to Roxy, hold him in our heads. The man who was a Foxy Grandpa for an entire generation, whose name took on a persona all its own, is now lost in the sediment of New York, with a few Roxys left.

And what will it take to revive Roxy the man? A special

Easter pageant with the Rockettes? A Broadway musical starring Dustin Hoffman as young Roxy? A Roxy celebration at City Hall? Nothing could seize the personality of Major Rothapfel. It's Madonna's time now. The palaces were a naïve celebration of a new art. That art isn't so new anymore. It has to compete with disco and *Dynasty*. Movies were everything when I was a boy. Each neighborhood had its own little palace, sometimes two, with loges and balconies, carved angels in the walls. Who would ever notice an angel in 1986? Roxy lived in the details of his movie houses. The details are gone.

five

MATERIAL GIRL

[1]

I dream of Henry Hudson anchoring his little boat, the *Half Moon*, at the foot of Forty-second Street on September 12, 1609, a couple of blocks from Times Square and the old McGraw-Hill Building. Hudson was on his way to China. He continued up the river and, after a consultation with local Indians, he concluded that China couldn't be found along this particular channel. He sailed for Holland, a disappointed man, but was stopped in Dartmouth, England, and told by His Majesty's government that he couldn't serve the Dutch anymore. He was a captive of his own country. Started looking for China in England's name and was never heard from again.

But he belongs to New York, not to the English and the Dutch. He's our secular saint, and we celebrate him every three hundred years or so. First in 1909, and then fifty years later, when Douglas Leigh produced his own half moon at midnight, as every single skyscraper lit up in Hudson's behalf. The Henry Hudson affair was a bit ludicrous, like that old sailor himself, caught between two countries while he drifted in his little boat and "discovered" a city he couldn't have dreamed about, a city rich as China itself, the China that haunted Henry, the China he couldn't find.

In 1959 no one could find *Half Moon II*, Holland's gift to us for the earlier celebration. And the committee chairmen wondered if Holland would provide another boat. The Dutch were adamant. Didn't have the inclination to build *Half Moon III*. They would send us a modern *Half Moon*, the *Rotterdam*, for her maiden voyage. Meanwhile, the *Half Moon II* was found on Van Schaick Island, Cohoes, New York, one of the first Dutch settlement sites. It had landed there in 1924, a rotting tub, and was now a local monument. The monument wasn't moved for the celebration.

A show on Staten Island exhibiting products for the American home became part of the Henry Hudson fever. A twenty-nine-foot model of the *Half Moon* traveled to the show on the Staten Island Ferry. There was also a Meeting of the Rivers festival to mark the importance of Hudson's voyage. He was the world's own explorer. All voyages and waterways were one. The festival was held aboard the Circle Line, on a trip that followed Hudson's original course. It was absurd and poignant at the same time, this meeting of waters.

England's contribution to the festival was an Elizabethan flask with water from the River Thames. France had a wine bottle filled with the Seine. Hendriena van Hoboken of Holland arrived with a plastic bottle of water from the Maas River in a Royal Dutch Airlines overnight bag. The representative from Saudi Arabia never appeared. Were the Saudis angry at Henry Hudson, who neglected to visit their riverless country? No matter. The bottles and flasks were spilled into the Hudson. Hendriena went home.

It was a festival our Dutch forefathers might have enjoyed. They would have loved the hokum. The men of New Amsterdam were never morose about the making of money. If New York is a commercial town, it's because of the Dutch, who were a jolly bunch of traders.

We haven't given up that habit of rubbing shoulders in the marketplace, buying and selling, selling and buying. We're the bartering kind. We were born with the gift. We have it in our bones. The City itself is one huge marketplace. You can't walk ten feet without touching a bit of commerce. It's in the smoke and soot we breathe. We're all nascent entrepreneurs, seeking out some bargain in the land of buy and sell.

It's curious. The more the City recovers from its economic chill—as jobs return to Manhattan and guppies move in—the more peddlers there seem to be. Because the economics of New York has its own mad motor. It eats up the small. Manhattan is becoming an enormous franchise of David's Cookies and different chains of ice cream. Frusen Glädjé. Steve's. In ten years you won't be able to find a shoemaker. The local hardware store will become extinct. All your favorite beaneries will grow into boutiques. It's no miracle that the smaller businessman has taken to the street. It's the final frontier, the peddler's last stand.

Manhattan is becoming a movable feast. Peddlers come at you from every corner. They hawk dope or tube socks in six-pack cellophane bags. Or they set their stuff on the sidewalk until the cops break up that little corporation and they have to shift to some other turf.

There's one exception to the rule: the book peddler. Peddling books is legal in New York and doesn't require a license. It's part of any citizen's freedom of speech; the right to barter printed material comes with all the guarantees of the First Amendment. And so, as secondhand bookshops have disappeared, an army of book peddlers is emerging on the City streets, like an active beehive. And that beehive suggests a new kind of merchandising; the peddlers haven't taken to the streets out of fancy or whim. In a boomtown economy, there are fewer and fewer jobs for quirky people, misfits without office skills.

It's the age of the entrepreneur, as Ronald Reagan says. And Madonna is only a material girl in a material world, marketing her belly button and looking like a streamlined Mae West. New York has always been a material town. But there's almost an underlying rip to Madonna's song, a self-mocking sadness that hints at the bookseller's paradise that Manhattan has become. There are too many lost souls around who just can't compete for the Material Girl.

[2]

Perhaps the greatest single outdoor peddling act in North American history is the Washington Square semi-annual art show. It's been around since 1931. The show has distinguished roots. It began in the worst part of the Depression, when painters, like everybody else, had begun to starve. It was an attempt to provide an open-air gallery to poorer artists, bring their work to the public, and give them a few sales at a time when traditional galleries wouldn't touch their work. The original Artists' Aid Committee was sponsored by critics and curators such as Alfred H. Barr, director of the Museum of Modern Art.

The first few shows were primitive affairs, without judges, juries, or entrance fees, and without assigned slots; artists had to scramble for space on the sidewalks surrounding Washington Square. If they left their space, it was immediately grabbed by another artist. Fights would break out. Painters learned how to squat. Outdoor art wasn't as codified as it is now, even after judges and juries arrived on Washington Square. Painters were much less civil to one another; they couldn't afford civility when a given spot might determine the bread they took in on a particular afternoon. Franz Kline exhibited in these outdoor shows and won a fourth prize in 1939. He was as hungry as any other painter.

The show had a hard time after the war. By 1947 it had fallen into disfavor. It was resurrected by a number of concerned citizens, including Judge Thomas C. Chimera, but that spirit of the "hunger artist" was already gone. The outdoor show couldn't produce another Franz Kline. It grew like a very polite octopus until it captured Greenwich Village and occupied Washington Square. Its sponsors included the Salmagundi Club, the Lions Club, and the American Legion, and it fell farther and farther away from the disorder, the abstraction, and the risk of anything modern. It had become a safe society, a pastoral, a home for Sunday painters. And that's why I'd shunned the show.

Call it snobbery. I'd grown up on Matisse at the High School of Music and Art. I had warm memories of Van Gogh in his insane asylum. Modigliani's death. Velásquez's royal dwarfs. I wasn't going to visit any pastoral around Washington Square. Sometimes I'd sneak a look on the bias. It was as if all the fabric of twentieth-century art lived in another dimension—the pain, the lyricism, the mad distortions hadn't come to Washington Square. And I'd returned to an advanced kindergarten class, with painters sitting on sidewalk chairs, Visa Card medallions over their heads. I was back in the land of buy and sell. But I didn't feel like a Dutch trader. I'd watch a couple of watercolors—wild horses and winter light—and swerve from the art show.

But I was a chronicler now, custodian of City art, keeper of the ridiculous, the banal, and the raw. And I journeyed to the 107th show. It was May 26, 1985. I saw other wild horses on University Place, more winter light, but I was wrong about one thing. These weren't Sunday painters. They were their own kind of hunger artists. The pain was there amid the menorah art and pastel summer flowers. It was just harder to find. You had to drift around in some timeless zone of perfect apples, among the tents and little booths, until you discovered a bit of bedlam, like Phil Welscher's world of cats. Cats on the ceiling, cats in a crib. It was a ménage of animals with tranquil faces, but the artist had some private sense of doom. Transferred his cats to the scene of a woman putting on nail polish, with steam pipes behind her. And suddenly the cats were like a menacing club.

I pushed on to Harry Pincus. He had a full briefcase of etchings, some of which he displayed. He'd riffle through his briefcase for a customer while he delivered a sermon about patrons, moon, sun, and stars. "Neil Simon bought three etchings," Harry said, with the smile of a tranquil cat. He'd done a series of etchings of a girl on the roof, a childlike girl with large breasts. There was something devotional about the girl, and something quite mad. Like a catalogue of breasts. His mother stood watch, a fierce little woman guarding Harry's work, and when he talked too much she'd say, "Harry, stop it now. They'll think you're high."

And he'd continue that cat's smile. "I'm always high. My mother drives me crazy."

It was like meeting Philip Roth's characters on the street. Pincus was Portnoy, Portnoy as a portrait of the artist and his mother at the Washington Square semi-annual.

I bought a postcard from the Harry Pincus collection; it was of that same childlike girl on the roof, looking out at the World Trade Center. But you couldn't see her breasts. She had one hand in her hair. And she was slim as a boy from the back: a girl on a roof, done in gray, with a gray skyline that was about to absorb her. It was "The Big Picture"—Goldilocks in gray.

I passed other booths and tents, saw an artist sit behind a screen of small paintings like a puppeteer, saw air-brushed Indians, pewter clowns, a gorgeous photo of a black man with the City reflected in his sunglasses, two lovers with frozen faces by Peter Giaccio, whose airbrush lent the lovers a funny archaic quality, as if they'd come out of an icebox.

The more I looked, the more I found a madness of detail, a controlled universe of the talented, the non-talented, and the near-talented, who'd created their own galleries out on the street with some help from a semi-annual arts-and-crafts committee. It was moribund, perverse, and crawling with its own picturesque life: Montmartre without a hill. In the very declaration of its sanity, it was insane.

We're all artists under the skin. That was the message of Washington Square. And why couldn't any artist have his own tent in the art capital of the world? But I had to get out from under those sprawling tents; each one with a signature, a motif, a design. *Come look at me. I'm alive.*

I went down to Madonna country, where the East Village meets the Lower East Side. She'd been reborn there, the "Boy Toy" who understood that ego is an art in itself. She was unknown in 1982, a starving disco queen living in a wrecked apartment, a good Catholic girl out of Michigan, Madonna Louise Veronica Ciccone, with black hair and a crucifix in her pocket. She turned blond and tough, practiced a coy charm, until she was "a great white shark in goldfish clothing." Madonna had packaged herself. Even while she could hardly afford lunch, she'd become the Material Girl. Critics argue over Madonna's voice, call her Minnie Mouse. But her whispers exude more sex than the most accomplished diva. And her body coils and uncoils like Eve making love to a snake. The Lower East Side was Madonna's Ellis Island. She danced and sang among the rats and the rubble. Rats couldn't harm her.

Madonna looked into the mirror of Manhattan and saw her own mirage. She's as inauthentic as the City itself, and almost as tough. New York is a great Sahara of a town, a desert in the middle of the water. It doesn't have boundaries, like other places. It grows by swallowing its tail. Nothing lasts. Its land is too valuable for monuments and shrines. Trump Tower will disappear when its profit margin goes down. Realtors already have their eye on Central Park. One day we'll discover stone castles near the little canals, and we'll never even ask why. As Martin Gottlieb has said in the *Times:* "Rather than confining itself to Newton's laws of gravity, Manhattan dances to a variation of Einstein laws in which time, matter and energy interrelate with money." Henry Hudson may lose his river. It's beginning to look like "13th Avenue." And Gracie Mansion could become a houseboat while Koch is still alive.

Madonna has transformed herself in a transcendental town. It's the very same town those greenhorns met in 1900, a mindscape with no discernible depth. It's always

been like that. "A great city by the sea is humanity's powder keg, and it operates on a very short fuse," according
to art critic John Russell. The Dutch discovered that keg,
and Madonna is sitting on top of it right now.

She's like Douglas Leigh's Lexan sandwiches; the girl
gives an incredible glow. And whatever is behind that
shimmer—the beating eyes of Minnie Mouse?—she's become a glorious icon, a determined package of raw and
funny sex. It's the rawness and the fun of New York. You
can practice hard and bundle up, load yourself with energy, but like any mirage, Madonna can always disappear.

And it's exactly this *suicidal* feel, Madonna's desperate
sense of play, that's missing from all the tents of Washington Square. These tents suggest a permanent climate.
The Salmagundi Club. Pen and Brush Club. Pastel Society of America. Very serious corpses. The explosions of
our century have passed them by. And for all its snaking
movement, its slithering through the streets, the Washington Square semi-annual finally has no tail.

[3]

I stop at the Chubby Diver, my new haunt on East Seventh Street. It's difficult to find a hangout in New York, a
personal dive. But about nine months earlier I had noticed some weird construction on East Seventh during
one of my walks through the Lower East Side. Call me
Ishmael. Or Krazy Kat. *Whenever I feel a dark November in
my lungs* . . . I walk the Lower East Side. That burnt country represents all the roots I'll ever have. It's my rocking
boat, my voyage into the heartland. I long for those wild
beards who once inhabited Henry Street.

A few doors up from the Hebrew Actors Union (where
the hell can you find a Hebrew actor?), in that Ukrainian
stronghold on East Seventh between Second and Third,
there seemed to be a lot of activity going on inside a
particular storefront. The words *Chubby Diver* appeared
on the window in white paint. But when I looked through

the window I couldn't see a table, a chair, or a bench. I
didn't have a clue about this Chubby Diver.

And then, on my next walk, a restaurant materialized, with tables and all, and graffiti on the air-conditioning vent. I resisted the joint and the presumption of its name. But I couldn't escape the Chubby Diver. I had a soybean burger one afternoon, and a pot of peppermint tea, and discovered a painting on the wall of the Chubby Diver herself, a burly woman in a red bathing suit about to dive into a field of white paint, with no discernible diving board. I was hooked on the Chubby Diver.

The owner was a woman in her thirties who spoke French and would breast-feed her baby behind the counter and prepare my peppermint tea. We had one thing in common: Mayor Koch. She'd been Koch's third chef at Gracie Mansion. She'd lasted much longer than the other two. Koch hadn't fired her. She quit. Her name was Lauren Kaye. Her dad was a pol in the Liberal party. He'd been "mayor for one night under Lindsay." But Lauren wasn't into politics. She was involved with her little girl and brooded over the fate of running a restaurant all on her own. She'd begun the Diver with four partners, but most of the burden fell on her. "You have to be on when everybody is off . . . when the cook is sick, who cooks? I do."

And Lauren was a mean chef. She could make a "cubist" chocolate pie and apple cobbler that was like digging into a deep, delicious well. "You know," she said. "I was natural and fresh looking before I had my baby and the restaurant." But she was a brown-haired beauty as far as I could tell (we should all look so bad after our first baby).

Lauren went to Paris with the idea of becoming "a buyer for Bloomingdale's." But Bloomie's lost her to La Varenne, a cooking school in Paris where Lauren must have learned to bake cubist pies. "She's an intellectual cook," according to the school's president, Ann Willen.

Lauren took her cubist recipes back to New York. She got lucky and started cooking for Koch, who might have four hundred people for breakfast. She was up at six in the morning and often worked until midnight. Koch's bodyguard would knock on her door well after dark and she'd have to do his dinner. "The mayor wanted what he wanted when he wanted it."

Koch loved London broil and burnt-almond ice cream. But his first two chefs, Rozanne Gold and Shaun Philips, had been let go for telling reporters too much about the mayor's meals. Lauren lived in a basement room at the mansion and earned two hundred dollars a week. She'd prepare breakfast each morning for Koch at six—coffee and grapefruit juice. "The City ran on acid." She'd help the mayor put his collar pin on each morning. "That's as close as I ever got to him . . . I could feel his breath on my hand."

Koch was friendly, she said, but all business. "He'd come through the kitchen and ask for something to eat." Lauren, in her own time, was Koch's "longest-reigning chef." But the job drove her crazy. "Breakfast for three hundred . . . that's a lot of eggs." Ronald Reagan arrived for breakfast during his first campaign. The Secret Service was around weeks before that breakfast, and Lauren had to wear a special pin to enter or leave the mayor's house.

The job wore her out, and after Lauren left the mansion, she went "from limelight to moonlight" at the Chubby Diver. She had her baby and a restaurant that was beginning to overwhelm her with work. But I wasn't the only one who considered the Diver his haunt. Wallace Shawn, playwright and actor who's had a career of doing golems and geeks, would spend his afternoons scribbling at the Diver. And Frederic Tuten, novelist and art critic, my old rival from the Bronx—we were both in love with voluptuous Fay Levine—would come to the Diver to eat and play with Lauren's kid.

But a few devotees weren't enough. The restaurant was in trouble. It couldn't build much of a patronage on a side street. I had my usual soybean burger. Lauren talked about the cost of food. She had to keep her prices down in a "funky, wild neighborhood." A woman came in with blue hair and blue lipstick and asked for a cappuccino and some pumpernickel bread. I looked at the nearest wall. It was decorated with a playful Aztec design. Ken Hiratsuka, a local graffiti artist, had come in one day for a cup of coffee and then did the walls. That was the Chubby Diver. Business on the run.

[4]

I went east, into that heart of darkness, Alphabetland. Four years ago it was a free-fire zone that could have been invented for *Apocalypse Now*. I'd been researching a novel about those scary blocks between B and D (Avenue A, with its restaurants and bicycle shops, was still part of our own mild alphabet), and my brother Harvey and other people had warned me to keep out of there. It had its own Irish Republican Army, the FLN, which wanted to create an independent Puerto Rico in the wilderness of "Loisaida," the Latino Lower East Side. It had drug haciendas, where merchants could start "candy stores" in bombed-out buildings. The clientele arrived from Pennsylvania, New Jersey, and Connecticut for cocaine. Twelve-year-old bandits guarded the coke, stood under umbrellas in the sunshine, and also acted as steerers. Sometimes the "shit" was sold out of baby carriages. Cops didn't venture into Alphabetland alone. It had the highest mortality rate for policemen in the metropolis.

But I did go through that invisible band of Avenue B in the summer of '81. Couldn't write about those streets without a proper visit. I didn't catch any murderers or see much cocaine, even though East Third was like an open-air art show with peddlers who serviced the passing cars. I wore kinky glasses and a torn army coat, trying to look as burnt-out as I could. I saw tropical groceries that were caves with hardly a banana in stock. I saw vegetable gardens that could have doubled as burial grounds. But I was a foreigner in that place, and I didn't realize that it had its own pioneers, its clubs, its energetic life.

Should have known I was on an archeological dig. I

hadn't gone deep enough into the civilization of Loisaida. There was an art colony growing in the rubble. Young painters, writers, and musicians had moved there long before my visit. Catherine Texier had come to Loisaida like Henry Hudson, looking for the new China. She was born in Brittany and raised in the suburbs of Paris, the dreaded *banlieue*, with its soda-pop culture and gray life. "I grew up in the never-ending fifties," she recalls. America was always on her mind. But her America was the myth of New York, discovered through magazines, books, comics, and the movies. First, she had the image of "Americans saving France," Yanks at the end of a war. Then came sex and rock 'n' roll in the sixties, and New York seized Catherine, possessed her like a kind of dybbuk. Catherine dreamwalked her way across the ocean, arrived in 1969, fell in love with the City and its wild streets, the disorder of downtown, the skyscrapers, the limousines: she'd landed inside her own myth. It was the metropolis she'd been carrying around in her head. Catherine became a "poor jet-setter," who felt comfortable in Europe and the America of New York.

She settled in Loisaida in 1980, got married, and had a child. Lived on East Seventh between C and D, in the middle of Cocaine City. But Catherine wasn't the only pioneer. Other artists, like herself, had settled in Manhattan's last affordable territory south of 125th Street.

She began to write fiction in English and French, and started a quarterly magazine with her husband. The magazine's title was her own address. *Between C And D*. It was like a defiant war cry and also a song of celebration. Loisaida had burgeoned for a whole generation of younger artists, artists unknown beyond their little outpost. They read their poetry and stories and displayed their art in local clubs, like Darinka and 8 BC, and published their work in Catherine's quarterly. Her husband had inherited two computers, and that's how *C And D* got born, with the computers as a printing press. Each issue of *C And D* is a computer printout wrapped in cellophane, with a cover designed by East Side artists such as Rick Prol and David Wojnarowicz. At first, the cover of each copy was individually designed. Rick Prol did "a hundred and fifty different ones" and had to stop before he went a little berserk. The magazine includes stories and artifacts: postcards, a photo romance, and a wall-sized poster. It concerns itself with typical Loisaida nightmare themes: "Love, Lust, Murder, Molestation, Mayhem" or "Death, Disease, Heartache, Subway Crime."

The cover of the fourth issue features a David Wojnarowicz "dollar bill," with a devil's head imprisoned in barbed wire, that's like a motto of the magazine itself—its declaration against the twists of commerce. Catherine doesn't want to increase the magazine's circulation of five hundred copies. "We could sell more than that. But we can't handle it . . . it takes half an hour to print one copy on one computer."

Catherine feels part of a culture with specific boundaries. She's a nonmaterial girl, living in an artists' cocoon. Most of the writers in the cocoon have had to "develop a parallel career." They're computer programmers, typesetters; one man and woman have their own housecleaning company. They all "decided coldly that they were not going to make a living from their writing." Some of them "won't write a novel . . . they won't touch that form. They've chosen forms that are absolutely noncommercial."

Ah, I wanted to tell her; it's the usual carapace of a scribbler. Kafka had good reason to write about a man turning into a bedbug: bedbugs have the very best body armor.

Catherine doesn't think she could ever settle permanently in Paris. "I go down the street [in Loisaida] . . . half the population is black and Hispanic and not everyone is turned into a businessman," and Catherine understands where her home is. She senses the excitement of the new art culture: ". . . the way galleries have opened. This would take fifty years to happen in Paris . . . I'm not naïve. I know there's money and a market. The reasons are not always charming." But Catherine doesn't care. "My life next week is not going to be what it was last week. It's absolutely not boring . . . but it's hard to survive."

She's one more immigrant in Loisaida, a land of immigrants. The Lower East Side never had the chance to become a fashionable district. It turned into a slum right after the War of 1812, when there was a terrible housing shortage. And as the first real "tenements" were built in the 1830s, the Irish moved in along with some blacks, and it's been a home base for immigrants ever since, a landing point in the New World.

Catherine "never hangs out with French people. . . . I'm more and more involved with life here." She's a New Yorker now, "but not an American. I fight American influences in my daughter, fight American junk food, fight American TV. If I go to Florida [where her husband's parents now live], I'm going to America . . . but of course America is here. America is the devil, the god and the devil, and I want to see the devil up close."

[5]

Catherine isn't the only one who's involved with the devil. David Wojnarowicz, who designed a cover for Catherine and whose fiction has appeared in *Between C And D*, has been chasing the devil's tail since the time he was ten and started to become a street rat in Manhattan. Wojnarowicz has a street rat's sensibility, a kind of war-weary libido. He couples murder, mutilation, and homosexual gang bangs with a cartoonlike exuberance. Wojnarowicz himself is a warrior of the gutters, a mean cavalier. "When I walk down the street, I come away with violence," Wojnarowicz says. He was born in Red Bank, New Jersey (Edmund Wilson's home town), in 1954. And we can only wonder what Edmund Wilson would have made of Wojnarowicz. Wilson helped bring Proust, Joyce, and Flaubert to an American audience, but Wojnarowicz attended a much rougher school of combat than Flaubert. He's close to Céline, Genet, and Jack Abbott in the germs of his art.

"Self Portrait in Twenty-Three Rounds," his kinetic monologue that appears in *Between C And D*, gives us a

rough picture of a street cavalier. The author has just left
a drag queen's house "after three days of no sleep and
maybe a couple of stolen donuts." He starts to hallucinate,
sees "large rats the size of shoeboxes." David and his
buddy walk around with meat cleavers, "lookin for someone to mug. . . ."

Both of them wander the streets in a killing mood.
"Some nights we'd walk seven or eight hundred blocks
practically the whole island of Manhattan criss crossing
east and west north and south . . . on nights that called
for it every pane of glass in every phone booth from here
to southstreet would dissolve in a shower of light. We
slept good after a night of this in some abandoned car
boiler room rooftop or lonely drag queens palace."

They sit in the automat next to "a table full of deaf
mutes and they're the loudest people in the joint." One of
them, a seventy-year-old man, "takes me to a nearby hotel
once a month when his disability check comes in." And
David remembers the time a fetishist picked him up and
dressed him in "this sergeant outfit with a pair of rubber
sneakers." After the fetishist masturbates inside his own
rubber sneaker, "he says he loves the way my skeleton
moves underneath my skin when I bend over to retrieve
one of my socks."

There's a lyricism to the writing, a dizziness of the
streets, but I doubt whether Wojnarowicz could continue
it much longer. The adventures would begin to melt and
sink into one another and produce a stylized sense of
shock.

But the same rough lyricism is found in his drawings,
stencils, and signs. Wojnarowicz mixes media like an alley
cat—because he is an alley cat. He began his active life as
a painter by marking up the walls of West Side piers. He
was an artist who rose right out of the debris. Lean, with a
horsey face, Wojnarowicz looks like he belongs in
Endgame, hiding in one of Samuel Beckett's garbage cans.
He's an urban guerrilla who's stenciled his scary stuff on
walls, ceilings, posters, everything in sight.

He helped organize a guerrilla art show on the piers
that was shut down by the police before it had a chance

to properly open. And he disrupted a 1982 exhibition at P.S. 1 in Queens by placing "cockabunnies" on the floor—roaches with rabbit ears. But the cockabunnies went away and Wojnarowicz has moved his images of urban battlefields from West Side docks to Civilian Warfare and Gracie Mansion, two of the East Village's most active galleries.

Wojnarowicz, who performs with a band called "3 Teens Kill 4," is like a one-man art battalion. He waltzed right out of the streets into Civilian Warfare.

[6]

There had been noncommercial galleries in the rubble since 1974. But loose confederacies like Kenkeleba and ABC No Rio were involved with local minority artists and weren't part of this "white invasion" into Loisaida. They distanced themselves from the gallery blitz that began in the fall of '81 with the opening of Fun on East Tenth Street. Fun celebrated the archeology of the Lower East Side, lending its walls to graffitists when none of the SoHo galleries would touch graffiti art. These "cave drawings" launched the careers of artists such as Jean-Michel Basquiat, Fab Five Freddy, Keith Haring, and Kenny Scharf. The gallery had "slum festivals" that featured the South Bronx and Loisaida, with rap music, breakers, and graffiti from both sides of the cultural fence (uptown *and* downtown). Fun itself was a corroded storefront, a mad, dark cave: the perfect environment for street art. It was filthy where SoHo was neat, and concerned with play rather than self-importance—until it lost its graffiti artists, as they fell into a kind of international fame.

A second gallery, 51X, opened a few months after Fun, with its own stock of graffiti art. But the gallery went into self-exile after a year, calling itself Muzeum 51X. "We were street artists and these were street galleries," said Rich Colicchio, the owner of 51X. "Now it's all business."

He mounted a "dilapidation show" as his farewell to the business of art. "I considered breaking the toilet and installing drips from the ceiling." He hung linoleum on his walls instead.

But while 51X committed suicide, other galleries sprang up in the rubble. Nature Morte, Civilian Warfare, Gracie Mansion, Deborah Sharpe, P.P.O.W., Pat Hearn. . . . "There are a lot more young artists now than ever before," said Peter Nagy after Nature Morte's first year. "We're the post-Korean baby boom. It's now or never. Do it. Get it up. Get it talked about. That's the '80s."

Gracie Mansion, artist and gallery owner, arrived a little earlier than that baby boom. She was born Joanne Mayhew Young in Braddock, Pennsylvania, in 1946. She graduated from Montclair State College in 1979, moved to Loisaida because she couldn't afford to live anywhere else in Manhattan, and took a new name in 1981. "I wanted a name that was actually a thing, like Tommy Gun. . . . I considered Selma Alabama and Andrea Doria, but picked Gracie Mansion because it seemed so New York. When I first heard it, I knew immediately that it was the right one."

But she couldn't launch herself as an artist. She was locked out of the SoHo galleries, like her artist friends. There was no room for Gracie Mansion's special kind of flair. It was the dark days of minimalism, when fun, trouble, and the human figure had been pressed out of art. "All my friends were great artists who couldn't get into SoHo," said Gracie Mansion, who'd already found her calling as a promoter of other people's art.

Mocking what she felt to be the antiseptic world of SoHo, she started a "gallery" in her bathtub, with all the paraphernalia of a press release:

> Gracie Mansion proudly announces the opening of her new gallery, Gracie Mansion, Loo Division, at 432 East Ninth Street, Suite 5.

The Loo Division was a great success until her landlord put a stop to the shows. And Gracie Mansion had to seek

less difficult quarters. She settled into a storefront on
Tompkins Square and soon had the most famous of all
the Loisaida galleries. She wouldn't simply mount a show.
She'd create a "habitat"—redesign her gallery, put in
wallpaper and furniture to go with the decor of a particular artist.

But Gracie wasn't the only aggressive one. Loisaida
galleries held to a downtown schedule, staying open on
Sundays. And in the summer of 1983, while most other
galleries were asleep, a little explosion occurred. New
York "discovered" Loisaida, and the archeology of the
Lower East Side was reborn. People began to visit the
caves and burnt-out buildings with those cute little
galleries tucked into the corners somewhere. Alphabetland was "the art world's newest monster."

The monster took hold. East Village art began to tour
the country. A large show, "Neo York," with a complete
iconography of the landscape and the artists—like Sue
Coe, Rick Prol, Rodney Alan Greenblatt, Gracie Mansion,
and David Wojnarowicz—was mounted at Santa Barbara's University Art Museum in November of 1984. Articles began appearing in London, Paris, Rome. Suddenly
those bombed streets with their cafés and flecks of color
became an international icon. You heard less Newyorican
on the Lower East Side and more Italian and French. The
codifiers were coming, students, art dealers, journalists
from foreign towns. Buses would stop outside Gracie
Mansion with tourists from New Jersey to inspect the local caves . . . and the archeology was complete.

Now we have a new material girl, the galleries themselves. That amateur spirit is gone. There will be no more
Loo Divisions on the Lower East Side. A map of the place
that appeared in a 1984 issue of *New York* magazine already looks like an heirloom, an illustrated guide to an
earlier century. Civilian Warfare and Deborah Sharpe
have moved to Avenue B. Gracie Mansion has gone west
to Avenue A. Her old gallery is now a gift shop, which she
calls the Gracie Mansion Museum Store; but she sells a lot
of baubles in her new museum.

Ah, I don't blame Gracie. The Eiffel Tower has a lot of

baubles too. Business is business. The girl can't help it if she's become a local landmark. There're seventy galleries on the Lower East Side. Three years ago there were two. And the galleries on Avenue B are no longer caves. These storefronts have the same glassy look and sanded floors of SoHo. They're little bits of Mary Boone. Boone is the presiding witch of Loisaida, the demon lady. Her startling success had to create some kind of electrical impulse in those young gallery owners. *If Mary can do it, why not me?*

And how many painters in the ruins want to be Julian Schnabel? Schnabel must have populated half of Loisaida with young pioneers. *I remember when Julian was a cook. He sat down next to Mary Boone and said hello . . . a kid from Brooklyn and he built his own hydrogen bomb.*

But there is a difference between Mary Boone and Avenue B. SoHo may have been dilapidated in the sixties, but it was never a ruin. It didn't have a hundred and fifty years of immigrant tales in its streets. David Wojnarowicz's devil masks had to be nursed in the rubble. And Deborah Sharpe has an awful lot of glass in her windows, but she can't keep the graffiti off her metal shutters, no matter how many times they're washed with white paint. The buildings near her gallery may become co-ops in a couple of years. As Tom Pollak, a young "speculator" from Aspen, Colorado, has said: rent-controlled tenants will "all be forced out. They'll be pushed east to the river and given life preservers. It's so clear."

But meanwhile, the buildings sit in ruins. And my own favorite piece of art in Loisaida never sat inside a gallery. It's David Life's "Worms," his own resurrected storefront of an abandoned building on Avenue B. "Worms Have 5 Hearts" is written on the door. The windows have been punched out, and only the slats are left. Life has painted worms on the slats and an entire allegory on the wooden boards behind the windows. Worms fighting for their lives. "There's Buzzards in the Bushes," David Life says over the left window. And we see those buzzards swallowing worms. But they can't devour all five hearts. Worms will always win.

six

KING KONG

[1]

I'd lapsed into illiteracy after the High School of Music
and Art. I could spell, yes . . . and think a little. I hadn't
forgotten Modigliani. I'd pick up girls at the Metropolitan
Museum of Art. I'd wander down to the Frick Collection,
stand in front of Rembrandt's *Polish Rider,* wait for that
light, lovely sound of the Frick waterfall. I'd been a cartoonist once. I could draw every hair on King Kong's
head and paint the blue of his nostrils. But I wanted to be
Modigliani and elongate everything until hands, feet, and
faces were stretched out like a choo-choo train. I was a
counterfeiter. Modigliani manqué.

Might have grown rich if I'd remained a cartoonist.
Could have joined the Batman club. But I had the smell
of art in my own blue nostrils. And I failed. All the sim-

pletons in my class could draw better cubist apples and pies. I fell away from art.

Ah, I was loyal to a couple of ghosts, particularly when the ghosts were sad. Arshile Gorky leaving nooses in his orchard before he hanged himself. Jackson Pollock ending in a dumb stupor, where he couldn't paint (the last photographs were of a chubby, walleyed man). Mark Rothko sitting under a million dollars and freezing in his loft because he couldn't afford to buy an overcoat. But my ghosts were gone and I was beginning to lose track. Art itself had become a ghost to me in the seventies. SoHo. Holly Solomon. And the old don himself, Leo Castelli, the prince of modern art.

Of course I'd heard of Schnabel. He'd entered the eighties like a burning house. His show with Castelli and Mary Boone in 1981 had created a bonfire over Manhattan. It burned for half a year. People couldn't stop talking of Schnabel. The jackals waited for him to sink. But Julian burned some more. He left Mary Boone and Leo Castelli and began to show on Fifty-seventh Street. No one had ever left the don in such a cavalier way. Schnabel was the first young painter Leo had bothered with in ten years. And now Schnabel turned his back on Leo and went to the Pace Gallery. The don was very bitter. "I don't want to see him again. . . . He had it very good here with Mary and me. But he wanted to be King Kong."

Suddenly I was interested in art again. I imagined Schnabel with wide blue nostrils and a hairy back. I appealed to my friend Arthur Cohen, who is an art collector and a connoisseur. I couldn't write a book about New York City, art capital of the world, until I mastered Schnabel, Mary Boone, Castelli, minimalism, Gracie Mansion, post-graffiti, and the new figure painting. We were at an Indian restaurant in Little Bangladesh on East Sixth, a few blocks from Civilian Warfare and Gracie Mansion. I nearly spilled mulligatawny soup onto Arthur's knees in my panic. I felt like an invalid. I had all those years to cover between Pollock's death and Julian Schnabel. And what about the latest tidal spills of the art market? Somehow we got onto a different topic.

Arthur and I had one or two things in common. We
were novelists who'd never earned a dime and both our
dads were a little crazy. It didn't matter that Arthur's dad
was rich and mine was poor. We were like helpless children in front of our tyrannical fathers. Arthur's had
never been through Ellis Island. He was born on the
Lower East Side in 1897, Isidore Meyer Cohen. The family had started "in the area of Minsk," but Arthur couldn't
say who the original Cohens were. "The family came
from nothing. The Cohens were dirt poor. I don't remember anything about them. There was no style of
memory . . . no magical rabbi or revolutionary. I have no
idea what the original name was . . . it could have been
Katz, Cahan."

Arthur's dad was the oldest of six children, "all under
five foot three." He wore Adler elevated shoes. The Cohens were in the textile business. They manufactured
"suits made to sell in the Negro market." These suits had
"outrageous linings," Liberty Bells and silk American
flags. It was "jazz clothing" for the new black bourgeoisie.
That bourgeoisie disappeared with the Depression, and
so did the Liberty Bell suits. But Arthur's dad was a mercantile genius. He started a new line, Arthur Allen
Clothes, named after his son. Arthur was the "good-luck
mascot of the company." Isidore made a deal with a
number of textile mills in New England and was the only
man in America who could sell a two-pants suit for nine
dollars and ninety-five cents. "He lost a dollar on every
suit he sold, but he was the most famous manufacturer in
the U.S. . . . everyone was indebted to his company."

Ah, if only my dad had found his mark in America. It
was all a question of merchandising. Liberty Bells. Two-
pants suits.

Isidore's mother "was also a midget, but a tough Jewish
matriarch." She kept live fish in the bathtub. Arthur remembers seeing those carp swim. She was the family general. "Passover was conducted like a review of troops on
Sutton Place." She also had the habit of giving old discarded shoes to beggars. And once, when Isidore was a
little boy, she absentmindedly gave a beggar the wrong

shoe—all the family wealth was stuffed inside. She made her son get up at four in the morning "for the next five months" to find that beggar. He never found the beggar or the family jewels. But "the necessity of making money was crystallized in that episode." Money became a kind of "obsessional commemoration of these trinkets."

Isidore married a woman who was much taller than himself. She was "the public protection of his avaricious libido." He had a preposterous image of success. He once boasted to Arthur that he could buy five thousand Cadillacs if he ever wanted to. But he was quite ambivalent about having a son. "My sheer existence was threatening to him." Isidore beat Arthur with a strap. He bought boxing gloves and gave Arthur a bloody nose. And in 1934, when Arthur nearly died of nephrosis, a kidney ailment that had him peeing blood for months, his father completely abandoned him.

When he was twelve, Arthur got sick again and had to lie in bed for eight months. During that time he wrote a play about the Spanish Civil War. Isidore took the play, rewrote it, and put his own name on the cover.

Couldn't tell Arthur I was envious after a story like that. I'd have considered it a sign of caring if my father had ever "borrowed" a play of mine. But Isidore was a mad genius, harmful to his son. I thought about those Liberty Bell linings and wished I had my own jazz coat. America was merchandise. And New York was the merchandise mart of the universe. Why should art be that different? Once it left the workshop, it was as much a product as a two-pants suit. Pollock had never earned more than nine thousand bucks from a painting. Now Castelli asks half a million for a Jasper Johns. The myth of the starving artist has fled from the marketplace. They're all heavy hitters now. King Kong.

"Until the beginning of pop art, there was virtually no money in American painting," Arthur said. "You were successful if you could pay the rent." There was a minimum of abstract expressionists, "twenty artists monopolizing the scene." And you could count the number of collectors on the back of your hand, according to Arthur.

And then, as pop art emerged in the sixties, middle-class America began investing in the stock market, and there was "brand-new money, surplus capital," and you had an art movement "that began overnight." By the end of the sixties there were a lot more galleries than baseball clubs, and a full league of artists. The art market went out of its mind. "The number of painters working in New York now equals all the painters who worked in Europe from the Renaissance to our time. There are more galleries, more alternate spaces, more museums than ever before in the history of painting."

Art had become "clear investment." The notion of patronage was gone. The artist has to produce thirty-five to forty paintings a year—"one finished painting every nine days"—or dealers can't market his work, and the artist is dropped. Basquiat has already confirmed this. With a show scheduled at Emilio Mazzoli's gallery in Modena, Italy, Basquiat was put in a big warehouse and told to paint. "They set it up for me so I'd have to make eight paintings in a week. . . . It was like a factory, a sick factory. . . . I hated it."

And Mark Kostabi, who shows his paintings wherever he can, believes that an artist has to stimulate an appetite for his work. Kostabi markets himself. "It's a myth that artists have to make art 24 hours a day. . . . The belief that the artist should be a lone visionary, laboring for that one spectacular show a year, without a Rolodex, who are you kidding? Picasso had a telephone."

[2]

Arthur Cohen led me to Robert Hughes, *Time* magazine's art critic. Hughes had written a disturbing article for *The New York Review of Books*. Called "On Art and Money," it revealed the monstrous embroilment of art *as* big business. "More Americans go to museums than go to football games." Art has really arrived in the major leagues. But Hughes isn't trying to perpetrate the saga of the bush-league artist who struggles in obscurity and is rewarded after death. "The idea that one benefits from cold water, crusts, and debt collectors is now almost extinct, like belief in the reformatory power of flogging."

Yet art has become canonized in a way that Hughes deplores; it's grown into mock-religious spectacle, with museums replacing the church "as the emblematic focus of the American city." And like most spectacles, there's enormous interest and enormous pomp. Art is over-adored. That adoration generates money and the worship of artifacts, not as cultural pieces that tell us things about ourselves, that limn our psyches and unmask us in a profound way, but as pseudo-magical events, totems that are mingled with dollar signs. "Art prices are determined by the meeting of real or induced scarcity with pure, irrational desire, and nothing is more manipulable than desire."

The old Dutch traders of New Amsterdam would have loved Robert Hughes for that word, because *desire* is the real ticket of any sale. You can't have a commodity without some irrational, burning need. *I want it, I want it, I want it.* That's the purest creation of price.

Most museums may not buy Schnabel. Critics may not adore him. But after Castelli and Mary Boone, he's become that obscure object of desire: primitive and hot, like a hulking genital. King Kong. With the whole planet as his Empire State Building, Kong has different promoters—Castelli, Boone, and Fifty-seventh Street—but one Fay Wray: his own blond public, hysterical and half-undressed.

But if museums aren't buying Schnabel, one day they will. And it has little to do with Schnabel. He won't have to lobby for himself. With the deification of the museum in our society, all art becomes instant artifact, ready for resurrection. "There is no oblivion. Today, virtually everything that was made in the past is equally revived . . . the universal resurrection of the formerly dead is pretty well an accomplished fact."

Who can predict what will happen? As the gentrifiers move into Loisaida and all the older, meaner storefront galleries are destroyed, we might find the entire East Village art scene, with its caves and clubs, in some new wing at the Met. The truth is that *all* resurrections are thrilling. We love miraculous rebirths; restored emblems of our past comfort us in a town that eats up its own tail every five or ten years. It's a touch of immortality. And isn't that what we older and younger artists seek? A chrysalis of future-present-past, a timeless bubble that's outside sickness and bad reviews? Because the great American secret of the twentieth century is that every man and woman is an artist under the skin. It's no accident that Wall Street and the cave art around Tompkins Square are in the same village. In a culture devoted to the accumulation of wealth, art becomes the softer side of money—the conscience behind the stick. And so the example of Isidore Meyer Cohen as a "playwright" isn't as extreme as it sounds. In our own schizophrenic time, the drive for money *is* the drive for art.

And look how we're driven. There might be as many as a hundred thousand artists living in the metropolis at this moment. Who can keep count? The Census Bureau doesn't have a listing for artists. But we do know that thirty-five thousand "painters, sculptors, potters" and potential gallery owners graduate each year from American art schools. "Behind them are millions of people interested in art . . . and hundreds of thousands who collect it."

And Hughes has woeful words about these collectors. An exploding art market requires a body of people "whose apartments are shifting anthologies of the briefly new"—people dazzled by young artists "who can be obsequious one moment and mysterious the next." It's like Disney World to them, "full of rides and haunted houses and historical fictions; and they are tourists in it." They're identical with all their wealth, "moving in great schools, like bluefish."

It's no surprise that he has little love for Mary Boone, Schnabel, Basquiat, or David Wojnarowicz. In "Careerism and Hype Amidst the Image Haze," an article written for *Time* magazine, he compared Schnabel to a meatball hero, called Basquiat an "art-world Eddie Murphy," found Wojnarowicz's work repulsive, and said the East Village was replacing SoHo as the "Montmartre of the Neo." And he wasn't too fond of the postwar baby boom, which stampeded through American art schools "like an antelope through a python," before settling in Loisaida. He couldn't feel much "neo-expressionism" in the new art. "In this republic," he said (Hughes himself is from Australia), "the 'expressive' comes down to another form of pop art, retooled for an audience strung out on fictions of personal authenticity."

Hughes's *Time* article reads like a bitter sock in the face, as if there were nothing good at all about the young. There isn't much hope for a generation that acts like an antelope rumbling inside a python. He has no sympathy for street art. Caves mean nothing to him. Hughes sounds like a strategist summoned from Capitol Hill to stick needles into all those annoying kids, like Wojnarowicz, who are disturbed about this same republic and are looking for icons to describe it.

But that still doesn't invalidate his earlier article. Hughes has touched upon the central crisis in our art and our lives: the escape into money. Creativity can only be defined by big bucks. There is a python lurking around, and it's called "Manhattanism." Some of us are being swallowed up by that snake. The old Dutch island is becoming one more Xanadu, a pleasure dome with caves of ice riding down to a sunless sea.

[3]

I was still an archeologist on the outside of things. I could visit a few caves in the East Village, but I didn't know Schnabel, I didn't know Castelli, I didn't know Mary Boone. I couldn't rub up against the new Babylon of art. So Arthur Cohen scribbled a letter for me to Mary Boone. I waited a week and called her on the phone. I didn't get Mary. I got a gallery aide. The high priestess was busy at

the moment. I thought she'd bury my call, but Mary
Boone got back to me in five minutes. She wasn't harsh.
And there was no sense of sale in her voice. "I remember
. . . you're Arthur's friend."

And I made an appointment with Mary. But I couldn't
arrive cold, without some sort of fact sheet on Mary
Boone. Details. Details. I began to dig. I unearthed as
much as I could about "the Boonette" (as Robert Hughes
called her). Born in Erie, Pennsylvania, in 1951 (the same
year as Schnabel). Moved to California when she was six
months old. Her father died when she was three. Both
her parents had Egyptian blood. Her mother married
again. Mary studied at Michigan State and then moved on
to the Rhode Island School of Design . . . and Hunter
College. She worked at a minimalist gallery, met Schnabel
in '76 (the year Douglas Leigh lit the Empire State Building). Had her own gallery before she was twenty-seven.
Schnabel was one of the first painters she took on. Mary
had a tiny space at 420 West Broadway, the mecca of
modern art. 420 was Castelli's address. The don wouldn't
condescend to notice Mary Boone in her little closet on
the ground floor.

Schnabel began to show with her in 1979. He did
strange, nightmarish figures in a sea of mud. There
wasn't much of a thunderclap for Schnabel. Mary met the
don in 1980. Schnabel showed with her again, introduced
bits of crockery into his paintings. He was being noticed,
but there still weren't many ripples. Schnabel had to do
most of the singing for himself.

And then, in 1981, there was that "double-barreled"
show at Castelli and Mary Boone. It was the don's im-
primatur, his "interest" in Julian, plus Mary's spiderlike
involvement with Schnabel, that guaranteed Schnabel's
fate. The don had discovered Rauschenberg and Jasper
Johns, and Mary had a feel for the eighties; she was a
"killer" in the coolest of clothes. The don was like Diaghilev, a temperamental master. He gave his artists sti-
pends, carried them when they were broke. He would
weep in public, and if he had breakfast with David Rockefeller, it was the don who paid the bill. Mary was much

more cool-blooded. And in April 1981, Mary, the don, and Schnabel made a murderous combine. King Kong was born. Who cared if the critics weren't magnanimous? It was *news*. And Schnabel was blunt about the whole thing. "I think Mary is famous because I'm famous and I'm famous because Leo is famous. But what artist is really famous, say, compared to Burt Reynolds?"

Schnabel was wrong. Burt Reynolds had never shown with Castelli-Boone. Schnabel's name was boomeranging off every wall where a gallery could be found. His paintings were huge, and so was his appetite. He'd arrived almost without a past. Schnabel had conceived himself in Castelli's courtyard. With his barrel chest, he was like the bully of the Western world. And the bully could promote himself. He'd created his own season: 1981 was the year of Julian Schnabel.

And you were finding Mary Boone on a lot of different magazine covers by the middle of 1982. She looked like a dark, slender witch. Mary painted her toenails for *Life* and people began to notice that she loved to drink champagne, that she had four rings and over a hundred pairs of shoes. A syntax was built around her, a special vocabulary. Everyone had to know who designed her suits. Women began dressing like Mary Boone in sleek gray outfits—there were Boonettes all over the place. But at least Mary could joke about herself. "People feel sorry for short people—that's how I became an art dealer."

And in 1985, when I met Mary Boone, she was long gone from her little closet. She had a big glass wall on West Broadway. Nothing was revealed in that glass. Nothing was advertised. It could have been a token window, with some cluttered paradise inside, a warehouse for marketing umbrellas, gowns, and shoes.

I entered that opaque world. It was the coolest sell I'd ever seen. You had to look hard to grasp the paintings on the walls. They were like bits of decor planted there. I didn't have to sing much about myself to Mary's sentinel at the door. He buzzed the back room; a girl arrived and brought me around the bend to Mary Boone. She was my first witch: a short, styled woman with olive skin. We sat on leather chairs in Mary's conference room. I couldn't find champagne on the premises. The witch wore three rings today and a handsome scarf. She was a curious contradiction: frail *and* tough, like some Third World marine. The lady had high cheekbones and a strictly tailored suit. I tried to talk about the mythology that had been built around her, Mary as the forceful art machine, emerging with her own tight politics of style.

"I'm not a myth," she said. "I don't know how to sell a painting. I love every artist I show. My enthusiasm and belief in an artist are contagious."

Ah, but I wondered how that contagion spread; there had to be a clockwork somewhere, the inner design of Mary Boone.

"I'm not so great. I was lucky. . . . I'm successful because I work harder than anybody else. I never go on vacation. I don't go to lunch. Anybody can be successful if they work hard."

I didn't believe the witch. There was more than modesty to that song of self-denial. She wouldn't explore the topic of Mary Boone. She was playing businesswoman's poker, hiding red queens under her scarf.

"Christ," I said. "Look at the East Village. Avenue B is like your own little corner . . . Boonetown."

But she wouldn't linger on Mary Boone east of West Broadway or take credit for the arrival of other galleries. "There were many galleries opening at the same time. That accumulation of energy tends to propel as well as distill a group of artists." She had her own group of artists. That's all she'd say.

But she would talk about Mary Boone the art dealer. "I made art dealing a young person's profession. Historically, art dealers were wealthy . . . independent figures of the leisure class. There were leisure-class men and wealthy wives up to ten years ago. Men would buy galleries to keep their wives happy."

And Mary wasn't a rich man's wife. She'd come out of nowhere, a girl from northern Pennsylvania. We talked of Schnabel. His paintings were primitive and funny, like a child's obsession with play.

"Yes," she said. "They were humorous, but also really sad."

They weren't sad or funny to Robert Hughes, for whom Schnabel was only a meatball artist. We talked of Hughes and his sense of reality about recent art.

Mary laughed and touched her scarf. "Does Robert Hughes have a sense of reality?"

We talked of Castelli. "He tried to keep me from moving into 420 [Boone's first address on West Broadway]. He wasn't crazy about the idea of working with me."

And finally we talked about Mary Boone. Boone's "Egyptian blood" was no publicity scheme. Her mother and father and both sets of grandparents were all Egyptian. They were the Toneys, not the Boones. And when her mother remarried, Mary Toney became Mary Boone. Her stepfather was "a five-generation New Englander." Her real father, who'd been an engineer, "was tall, dark, and handsome" in Mary's mind. Her lunacy about art comes from her mother, "a strong woman . . . totally a dreamer, powerful and nonrational. My mother always loved art."

And Mary Boone? "I'm like a great Horatio Alger story," she insists, with a wicked beat of her dark eyes. "Everybody tries to turn things into bigger than life. I'm a human being."

And now I have to believe her. But that leather we've been sitting on speaks of something more than luck. Mary markets her painters, rather than their art. She's no Diaghilev. She's the ice mama who manages a "stable" of men. (Basquiat has recently become part of that stable.) Artist and critic Thomas Lawson claims that Mary "has moved beyond hyping her artists, beyond hyping herself, to hyping the idea of hype. . . . Her immaculately manicured gallery is itself a diagram of this strategy, with its sophisticated play of seduction and refusal."

Isn't that what the eighties is all about? The invention of inventories for success. Boone is as much a material girl as Madonna herself. And even a better strategist. The critics don't count. Robert Hughes can scream his head off and the meatball hero will continue to thrive: sixty years ago Edward Bernays, the granddaddy of public relations (and a nephew of Sigmund Freud), realized that anybody could sell anything if he could sense the outline of the period he was in. *Image was all.* Soap manufacturers complained that children didn't like to wash. Bernays simply shrugged and started an Ivory soap sculpture contest that was soon a craze among twenty-two million kids. And when Lucky Strikes lamented that their green cigarette packs were out of fashion among women, Bernays turned green into a fashionable color.

Mary Boone might never have heard of Edward Bernays, but she's been his secret disciple. She applied Bernays to the marketing of Julian Schnabel. Mary presented Schnabel as her version of "super soap" (with the Castelli seal). And no matter what the critics said, a whole population of artists, dealers, and collectors immersed themselves in the dream of Julian Schnabel.

[4]

You can find him between the covers of *Vanity Fair,* the meatball hero hugging his wife, as he broods in a Marlon Brando undershirt. Unlike the Humpty Dumpty he painted in 1984, a mock image of himself, Julian isn't about to fall.

A lot of people figured he couldn't survive his apotheosis, that he'd begin to fade after the year of his big show. But Humpty is still here. If his work was left out of the 1985 Whitney Biennial (the most important year-by-year survey of recent American art), it only focused more attention on Schnabel. *Where's Julian? Where's Julian?* It was as if all the artists in the exhibition had to define themselves against Humpty Dumpty's ghost. If Schnabel hadn't left Mary Boone, the entire art colony of Manhattan might have sworn that the biennial was another one of Mary's spectaculars, that she and Castelli had staged the whole thing. Deprive them of your presence, and they'll only love you more. . . .

The brutal fact is that the biennial needed Schnabel. People were just too curious about his art. You can't depict a sensibility, rotten or good, without its centerpiece. It seemed like the six curators who planned the show were trying to punish Julian for becoming the bad boy of art. But it wasn't only these six curators. Schnabel's always been considered a brute. Even before the big bang at Castelli-Boone, artist Sherrie Levine, who was sitting on a panel with Schnabel, pronounced: "I take umbrage with the institutions that have made art what it is—the expression of brutish but brilliant shepherd boys discovered and patronized by sensitive landholders." The shepherd boy's art was "transparent as a masquerade of alienation. . . . Alienation becomes a heroic disease," the disease of Julian Schnabel.

Schnabel couldn't break away from Marlon Brando's undershirt. He'd committed the sin of talking about "feeling" and "psychological resonance" in his work. He believed in epiphanies before his own paintings—as if he could talk to God. That was hardly post-modernism. It was theater spectacle for Sherrie Levine.

"I think people still have religious experiences in front of paintings," Schnabel insists. But that "religious experience" is close to kitsch. It creates an overload of hysteria in his work. His paintings are often like cartoon explosions, with a madcap, delirious energy, as if Schnabel himself were God, reinventing the entire world with pony hair, antlers, bits of crockery, velvet, linoleum, and paste. Schnabel produces objects with a "Frankenstein presence," Rene Ricard declared in *Artforum*. And according to Jeff Perrone: "The best of Schnabel's paintings appear like memories from silent horror movies . . . they manipulate our most basic, primal, childhood fears involving sex, authority, religion, and violence. They're the first kitsch nightmare paintings."

For Schnabel, there's little distinction between high and low; he's incorporated all images into his art, appropriated *everything*, seized art history for himself, turned it into a monstrous joke. It's almost as if Joyce were writing

Ulysses in comic-book form and declaring that the comic book was his Song of Songs.

Robert Hughes says Schnabel can't paint. But Humpty Dumpty prefers to hide behind his own technique. He's been painting and scribbling since he was four years old. He could scribble any of Hughes's chosen masters into the ground. Hughes admires Eric Fischl, Brice Marden, John Alexander. Schnabel is a better painter than them all. Even his *worst* paintings have an exuberance, a boyish need to startle and dismay, that's much more exciting than Hughes's "younger" artists. Schnabel may stare "at his brushes like a gorilla looking at a knife and fork," but I'd rather have that gorilla, with his Brando undershirt and his kitsch, than all the painterly painters Hughes can summon up.

Schnabel was born in Brooklyn and moved to Brownsville, Texas, when he was fourteen. He earned a BFA at the University of Houston and also studied at the Whitney for a while. He drove a cab in 1973, returned to Texas, and had his first one-man show in 1976 at the Contemporary Arts Museum in Houston.

"The show was tremendously unpopular," said James Harithas, who was the museum's director at the time. "I liked it. He [Julian] liked it. His father liked it." But the museum's trustees hated the show. And Harithas found it extraordinary that Schnabel "had so much self-confidence when he had no audience."

But that's the nature of Julian Schnabel, a boy from Brooklyn who lived on the Rio Grande. Perhaps it's this odd wedding of cultures that formed Schnabel—bravura in the throat of extreme isolation. He was no ordinary kid from down the block. Humpty in his undershirt, perched precariously on a wall. He goes to Europe. Visits Barcelona and wanders through Guëll Park, Antonio Gaudí's wonderland, with its long serpentine bench of many colors, paved with bits of ceramic tile. That "crockery" helped inspire Schnabel's plate paintings, though he likes to deny it now. But Gaudí's vision of "enchanted" architecture isn't so removed from Schnabel's energetic kitsch.

Both have a child's sense of the modern: a witch's plunder of mad designs. Schnabel goes to Madrid for five days and sees *Last Tango in Paris* every single night. It's like Brando chasing his own undershirt.

Then came Mary Boone. Schnabel was still a chef in Greenwich Village. He urged Mary to increase the price of his paintings. Humpty had to live. "And I was tired of cooking." Then came Castelli . . . and Schnabel grew rich. He gave interviews, stopped, and started again. "Painting makes me feel I don't have to kill myself," he told Gerald Marzorati for a cover story in *ARTnews.* He was playing Dostoyevsky and Artaud. He talked about God to other interviewers and prepared some kind of "credo poem" for *Artforum,* calling it "The Patients and the Doctors" (the title of his first plate painting). The credo is pretentious, poignant, silly, and wise, like a lot of Julian Schnabel:

> Agony has many faces. One need not talk of agony but it is the reason why I began to work. . . .
>
> Modernity has nothing to do with linear progression from figure to the absence of figure, from the distillation of the outside edge of the painting to the painted rectangle. It has to do with the accuracy of the artist in making a usable X ray of biological fear. . . .

Ah, I liked that—"a usable X ray of biological fear."

> I have two little girls and a beautiful and intelligent wife,
>
> people are buying my paintings,
>
> people are writing about me; people will write about any-thing—
>
> people are writing about people buying my paintings.
>
> I can go where I want,
>
> eat whatever I like, make a pig of myself—and will con-tinue to do so as long as I've got money.
>
> As you all must know by now
>
> I am a "success" (conditionally).

If you think that I am satiated, not hungry anymore,

that's what *your* morality is.

A chemical need, like displaced love,

is not a profession. Not a career. Not a choice.

I don't matter. What I have to show you does.

[*5*]

I met Schnabel through my friend Frederic Tuten. Tuten
was another wild child of the Bronx. He had a Sicilian
mother and an aristocratic father from the South, a father who abandoned him. Tuten decided quite early that
he wanted to be another Gauguin, but he soon discovered
that everything he drew looked like a coffeepot. He abandoned art and had to settle on becoming a tinker of
words. (The two of us were "post-modernists," that is,
failed painters who'd never quite recovered from our
"coffeepot" period.)

Schnabel greeted us in blue pajamas. His Belgian wife,
Jacqueline, was indeed beautiful, as Schnabel had said.
And his daughters, Lola, three, and Stella, two, were the
loveliest litle girls I'd ever seen. Their beauty was beyond
simple flirtation. Lola never even looked at me. But if I
could have become a Venetian prince from five hundred
years ago, I would have requisitioned Lola, signed a marriage contract on the spot, and waited for her until she
was fourteen or so.

Tuten had said that whatever I thought of Schnabel's
work, Julian was a "great father." He didn't talk to Lola
and Stella like some daddy in a playtime world. He was
interested in their particular needs. Jacqueline disappeared for the afternoon, but not until Julian kissed her
and smiled: "Promise me you'll be back."

I gave him a signed copy of my last book. He glanced at

the inscription and said, "You definitely have a psychotic handwriting." How could I dislike Humpty Dumpty after that?

There were barbells on the floor and a bicycle machine.

Schnabel paused next to one of his paintings, *Leaves of Grass,* and laughed. "I gave it to Jacqueline . . . a couple of times." He took us into the children's room. He'd designed the beds for his two little daughters. The room had a Venetian chandelier. The walls were a replica of Pompeii. He'd built a tiny fortress for Lola and Stella on East Twentieth Street. "They don't know how horrible it is outside."

Then he showed us the bed he'd designed for Jacqueline and himself, made of rolled steel. "It's the iron age. . . . I like the patina of it. I like the weight of it." The bed had a bit of Schnabel's own *substance.* You could feel his specific gravity under those blue pajamas. He looked from the window to the wall and turned claustrophobic in his duplex. "I have to get out of here." (He was going to India to join his friend Francesco Clemente, one of the few painters of his generation he admires.) He stood near the window and pointed at the "dots" of people downstairs. "They feel like worms crawling in the street."

He sounded just like Harry Lime in *The Third Man.* He's a fanatic about movies. "I watched *Viva Zapata* and *Heaven's Gate* yesterday and couldn't work."

And of course I asked him about that human wreckage Brando played in *Last Tango,* an ex-prizefighter who ends up managing a miserable hotel in Paris, shows his buttocks to a band of ladies at a local tango contest, and is killed by his former "mistress," a girl whose name he doesn't even know. It was the performance of Brando's life because the ex-prizefighter was hardly a persona at all, just an excuse for Brando to play Brando without the clutter of an organized existence. He was mad, vulnerable, masochistic. "His death was in that somehow," Julian muttered. Brando's performance *was* like a vision of his own death mask. Julian could quote Brando, line by line. "'If we live a hundred years, a man will never know what's going on in his wife's head.'" Was he thinking of Jacqueline, or the general condition of husbands and wives? I didn't ask Humpty Dumpty.

He took us downstairs to his studio, removed his pajama tops, and I swear to God, he looked like a younger, thicker Brando in his torn undershirt. His favorite film as a kid had been *The Fugitive Kind*. We were all Brando freaks, Tuten, Schnabel, and I.

He climbed a ladder and worked on a new painting, *The Idiot*, while he mixed some wax emulsion. "It's harmful or fatal if swallowed," he said out of the side of his mouth.

He hopped around the studio, attended to three other paintings. One of them, still untitled, was inspired by the war machine in *Spartacus*, the contraption that Kirk Douglas and the other gladiators had to duck around or lose their brains. Schnabel himself was built like a gladiator. He might have withstood that war machine with his own barrel chest.

He'd painted Rimbaud (*Portrait of the Artist Near the Congo*) and Artaud (at the edge of a house painter's drop cloth). I referred to them as his heroes. Julian said no. "They're casualties of their own insistence." But that sense of casualty was important to Schnabel. He'd read about some destroyed creature in William Burroughs, and "the description was so crystalline, it scares the shit out of you." Schnabel likes casualty lists. "It's important for things to overstep the boundaries," he said.

I told him that his titles were often funny to me. I liked *Nicknames of Maitre d's* and *Resurrection: Albert Finney Meets Malcolm Lowry*. Schnabel didn't laugh. "Albert Finney said something stupid." Schnabel had been watching him on the tube one night. *An actor deals with feelings,* Finney said. *An artist deals with color and form.* And Julian thought of Finney: "You don't know anything about painting, do you?"

I touched on the subject of Gaudí and Guëll Park. "Gaudí's idea was to make a mosaic," Julian said. But the bits of broken crockery Julian worked into his own paintings were "less decorative and more psychological." Ah, he still couldn't escape the ghost of Guëll Park.

He began to hurl blobs of paste on the wall with his hand. He called them "blood clots." But these clots were very white. "I don't want to end up like Robert Motherwell. I don't want to be decorative."

He looked at the clots, squinted hard, and threw some more paste, like a burly acrobatic dancer. Tuten teased him a bit. Told Julian I was a phenomenal Ping-Pong player.

"I can play a little Ping-Pong," Julian said.

"That sounds ominous." (I hadn't held a paddle in my hand in six or seven years.)

He sprayed gold on his blood clots with a can. And I tried to tear some history out of Julian, who was reluctant to talk about his past, as if he'd been some bloody child born out of the Medusa's stone scalp. But I did get him to mention his dad. His father had come to this country from Czechoslovakia in 1924, when he was thirteen. "My father did everything . . . he was in lots of different businesses. He was supposed to be in the fur-collar business." That's what he told Julian's mother before he married her. "My mother's people investigated that business. They found an empty warehouse. 'Hey,' they said, 'that guy doesn't have anything in his warehouse.'" But Julian's mother married him anyhow.

"I was always a painter," Julian said. "That's what I used to do . . . fiddle around. I read the *Iliad* when I was very young. Those were heroes. Achilles and Ajax . . . I didn't have too many friends."

Julian hurled some more paste and then looked down. "I can't believe what I've done to my silk pajamas. I guess I knew it was inevitable. They're my favorite ones." Then he reminded himself that the paste would peel off.

I made another appointment with Julian, and I took off with Tuten. Schnabel had staged a séance for us, a private ritual of Julian at work. But the painting he did was no less authentic for all his artifice. He was playing Picasso, a bull in silk pajamas. Hadn't Picasso done the same thing—performed for whole companies while he painted? That old master wasn't any less "political" than Julian Schnabel. He'd milked all of Paris with his art. He wrote plays, nattered with Diaghilev, while Matisse was nearly forgotten.

I couldn't forget those silk pajamas, Schnabel on his ladder, hurling paste across a velvet field on the wall. He was like some impresario in motion. It had nothing to do with critics or collectors. "He ordained power on himself," Tuten said. It was as simple as that. Why couldn't Schnabel paint God along with Maria Callas? He'd pulled the world inside his undershirt.

"He has an instinct for killing." Nothing was going to get in King Kong's way. I returned to his studio in a week. Julian was preoccupied. Those "blood clots" had been transformed into monsters on a wall, scary monsters. I was still the fox, trying to get Julian to talk about his childhood.

"Most kids mess with paint," he said.

He was the youngest child in the house. His brother and sister were much older than Julian. He sat Lola on his lap, with the barbells at his feet. He had a brooding look, like he'd just finished his own Last Tango. "I've been working out. I feel like I'm going to throw up."

I left Humpty Dumpty with Lola on his lap.

seven

THE PHARAOH
AND THE UNICORN

[1]

The Arsenal is a nineteenth-century fort in Central Park
that Robert Moses had seized during his long rule of the
City's parks, playgrounds, and beaches. Moses had been a
hurly-burly man. The Parks Department was only a tiny
portion of his empire. He'd ruled bridges, tunnels, highways, dams, and state parks. New York, city *and* state, had
had fifty years of Robert Moses, and for a while it seemed
like he was the most powerful son of a bitch on earth. He
feuded with Franklin Roosevelt and won. He hood-
winked La Guardia half a dozen times. He established his
own mayoralty under the Triborough Bridge. He destroyed the Bronx with one of his expressways. And he
would have destroyed Greenwich Village too, declared it
a slum and barreled a highway under Washington Square
Park, if Jane Jacobs and thousands of other people hadn't

screamed their heads off. He'd become an ogre, an impe-
rial wizard who couldn't be reached. But there wouldn't
have been much of a Parks Department without Robert
Moses. He was an authentic New York creature, the worst
and best of men. But powerful as he was, the City has
buried him under layers of dust and sand. He's become
another ancient baron, half remembered.

A new commissioner presides over the Arsenal, a slight
man with a beard, Henry Stern, who's as different from
Robert Moses as any commissioner could ever be. Moses
was an arrogant, humorless bully who growled, threatened, and glared. Stern is shy, funny, introspective, a
former whiz kid who was a shrimp until he was nineteen
or twenty and never left home until he attended Harvard
Law School. Henry Stern's idea of a shout is a hoarse
whisper.

I loved him right away. He was like some lost Russian
brother of mine. Our families must have crossed somewhere in the middle of the Black Sea (unfortunately, his
father's tribe was from Frankfurt). He scolded me on my
book proposal as we sat in his office. "It's infantile," he
said. "A leftist analysis." (I didn't want old buildings torn
down. I was demanding a moratorium on wrecking
crews.) "Houses are like people," he said. "They're not
built for eternity."

I was an "ultra" in Henry's eyes (an ultra-liberal, the
worst possible sin in Ed Koch's administration). I'd scribbled in my proposal: *artists move into unfashionable neighborhoods to save on rent and then their exodus becomes a fashion
in itself.* "They're also scavengers . . . they colonize a
neighborhood for themselves."

He'd taken my proposal and marked it all up. I'd talked
of vitality. He talked of decline—"lawlessness, the blight
of New York." When he'd been seven years old, living in
Inwood, he'd stand in the front car of a subway train,
stare into those spooky tunnels, and ride to the end of the
line. But he couldn't recommend that for his own son. It
was a "terrible loss. There's an enormous concentration
of people. You don't dare go out among them, unless
along prescribed routes."

Henry wasn't wearing any shoes. He'd greeted me in green socks. He was fifty years old, but he could have been thirty-five in his Parks Department T-shirt. He scrutinized me. "I look like you. It's odd we haven't met before."

He remembered my name from the *New York Times Book Review*. "Both of us," he said with a boyish smile, "suffer from the torment of being slightly known."

Henry is a genius on that subject: *the torment of being slightly known.* I stood under the cupola in his office and knew I'd have a Black Sea brother for life.

[2]

Commissioner Stern offered his new brother a glimpse of his territories. I was to accompany Henry on a tour of Brooklyn. We'd made our own "devil's pact." He wouldn't doll up any of his parks. He'd show me what there was to see, the whole bloody heart with all its pimples and without any promotional blitz. The ride to Brooklyn was a journey across another border because Brooklyn is like a country unto itself. It has no relation to Manhattan at all. Its politics are different. Its buildings are much, much older. And its people are wilder because Brooklyn was a city much denser than Houston or Dallas before it ever became a borough. It has the biggest Democratic machine in the United States. And whatever Republicans there were have become extinct. It has the largest black population in New York, the largest Italian population, and the largest Jewish population. It's the home of Hassidic tribes who fight among themselves over the significance of an individual rabbi, the home of Mafia dons and geeps, the home of Syrians, Albanians, and the Russian refuseniks of Brighton Beach. It has more crime, more devastation, and a lot more pluck. Brownsville is a greater ruin than most of the South Bronx. And Prospect Park is a wonderland of lakes, trees, and bridle paths. It's more like an

English garden than a city park—sculpted *and* wild, with
fabulous old entrance gates.

Wasn't only Brooklyn that intrigued me. The commissioner was a perfect traveling companion. He got behind
the wheel and had his driver sit in the back while Henry
sought out crippled playgrounds and rotting trees: the
metropolis had six hundred thousand street trees and
every single one of them was Henry's business. How
could he observe the City from the back seat of a car?

He drove like a Bronx bandit. Henry never turned corners unless he had to. So I experienced Brooklyn like a
terrifically long and bumpy line. Wasn't a street or a stop
on the subway and the el that Henry didn't know. He
rattled off stations as we drove under the elevated tracks.
He'd sucked all of Brooklyn between his eyeballs. The
only time he'd turn corners was to look for a hidden
bakery. The commissioner had a passion for the sweetest
rolls. We ran on Henry's "desire path, the path people
make to get where they want to go." And his desire path
had bakeries all along its route. But the sweet rolls didn't
hamper his conversation or that map of the metropolis he
held in his skull. He was worried about a tree some architect wanted to move from the front of a building near the
Arsenal. "Trees aren't sofas," he said. "They can't be
bought and discarded. . . . young architects love to move
trees."

He'd bite into a napoleon he found at a pasticceria on
Neptune Avenue, lick his fingers, and search his domain
like a bloody hawk. There was always a new park to discover, some triangle of concrete or grass with a bench or
two, tucked inside a roadway. It was Moses's doing. Moses
would constantly put up nameless little parks, bits and
pieces left over from some acquisition. The great land
grabber left little pockets of green near hundreds of road
sites. And no commissioner had been able to follow his
trail. That was the legacy of Robert Moses: a mystery
route of triangles, wedges, and comfort stations.

And if Henry found a disturbing landmark, a flagpole
with swastikas scratched on it, destroyed benches in a
public square, he'd climb on his short-wave radio. "Car

One to Manhattan Central, K . . ." And he'd read off the logistics and the damage done.

Henry had arrived in a boom year, 1983. For once the City had a surplus of cash. The parks had been left to rot since '75. And now they were being rebuilt under Henry Stern. He'd roam the boroughs in his orange rain slicker. The slicker had become his identifying mark. I saw him wear it on TV. That slicker was Henry's second skin. "It's like Batman in costume," he said.

Batman had been a precocious little boy and paid a price for it. "I was two or three years younger than all the other kids in my class. I went from kindergarten to the third grade. I could read and write . . . could have made me a unicorn." Because Henry had skipped two grades, he was "deemed too fragile" for regular classes and was put in an Open Air class, for "kids with asthma, kids who stuttered." There were cots in the room, and Henry could take a nap. "I was a perfectly healthy forty-pound shrimp."

He graduated from his cot to WQXR. He was on the radio every Saturday morning when he was nine as a member of the WQXR Youth Forum. "At that time I believed in the United Nations," Henry said with a wistful shrug of his orange slicker. He traveled on subways a lot.

The shrimp attended Bronx Science, where he was "too small to carry the flagpole. . . . I assumed I'd always be small. The world was made up of taller people." He entered City College at fifteen and didn't start to grow until around graduation time. "I didn't think I was ever going to form."

He was admitted to Harvard Law School in 1954. "It was like going away to college." The dormitory cafeteria, Harkness Commons, could have been "a Catskills hotel." Henry was made president of the *Harvard Law Record* during his second year in the "Catskills." His managing editor was Ralph Nader. "It was the young boy network," he recalls. Henry turned nineteen and was still growing. "My Harris Tweed jacket grew short in the arms."

A Jewish shrimp couldn't land a job with a Wall Street firm, so Henry became a junior clerk to a state supreme court justice and began his career in City government as secretary to Manhattan Borough President Edward R. Dudley. He became, known as "Ubiquitous," because he would go around to all twelve community planning boards. "I was single and I thought the meetings were fascinating . . . like a student council for grown-ups." He met Ed Koch and hundreds of other people, and as Dudley's man in charge of education, he visited every schoolyard and playground in the borough. One night he brought Ed Koch along. Koch remembers that tour. "He took me through a Harlem playground, and I thought, what the fuck am I doing here at midnight?" A caped murderer had been running around the City, stabbing kids in Harlem playgrounds with an umbrella sword.

Henry didn't have his Batman costume in those days. He smiles at the image of Koch and himself, Big and Little, in East Harlem. "I was counting on him to protect me. And Koch realized no one was there to protect him."

Henry would soon become "Ubiquitous" in City government itself, shuffling from job to job, as one commissioner would lend him out to another. He was the best pinch hitter around, a one-man team—Henry the dragon slayer, buried somewhere in the government's bowels. It was almost as if he'd come to an Open Air class for bureaucrats, but this time he didn't have his own cot. He was like some modern Bartleby who was delirious about the idea of work. During the Lindsay administration, Deputy Mayor Tim Costello offered him to Bess Myerson, commissioner of consumer affairs. "Her assistant called to say that she [Myerson] would call me in an hour. I'd never been called by anyone to announce I would be called. . . ."

He settled in with Bess, became her first deputy commissioner, until he ran for the City Council in 1973 on the Liberal line and won. It was his first victory in politics. He represented all of Manhattan as councilman at large and was something of a ferocious fly on the council, taking on quixotic causes, running, groping, fighting, as if the City Council were the center of the earth.

In the worst years of the fiscal crisis, Henry and Robert

Wagner, Jr., conceived the idea of selling neckties to fatten the City treasure chest. Beame wasn't crazy about the plan. But that couldn't stop Henry's necktie madness. He and Bobby Wagner designed a blue tie with the City's gold seal and the label "Stern & Wagner" on the inside.

Ubiquitous was an incredible tie salesman. With Wagner's help, he pulled in seven thousand dollars for the City in his first year. Henry's warehouse was the trunk of his car. He'd been schooled in the "science" of running a small business (his father was a tentmaker). And he continued selling ties in the Koch administration. He was a frequent visitor at the mayor's house. Lauren Kaye of the Chubby Diver recalls Ubiquitous's immediate presence during her time as Koch's cook. "The second morning I was there he showed up, slipped in quietly, and asked me for a piece of toast."

Did he sell a City tie to Lauren Kaye? That's never been documented. His business boomed, but he wasn't so lucky in politics. He was mired in the City Council, a Liberal-Republican in a Democratic town. And he couldn't even hold on to his council chair, in spite of all the elections he won. His job of councilman at large was abolished by a court decision. But Parks Commissioner Gordon Davis resigned on April 1, 1983, and Henry was appointed on April 2. He's worked for the metropolis all his adult life. Henry has been hired, fired, elected, appointed, and lent out so often, he's become the City's "unicorn."

But his eccentric style seems perfect for the parks. He's flourished like no other commissioner surrounding Koch. His quiet daffiness disarms potential opponents. And like any whiz kid, he's terribly efficient. "Minor obsessions can be indulged," he says. "Major obsessions get you in trouble."

[3]

It was Opening Day at Yankee Stadium and I was Henry's "date." He had an extra ticket to the Yankees' ceremonial lunch and invited me along. I wasn't dressed for the occasion. Henry hadn't warned me where we were going. I looked like a scarecrow in a tattered fisherman's vest with enough pockets to bear the weight of pencils, pens, ink bottles, and most of my research. But the Mad Hatter of Central Park took me right to the Yankees' entrance. After all, Henry was the "landlord" of this goddamn place. The City owns Yankee Stadium. Steinbrenner has to pay his rent or forfeit that piece of real estate.

Got into an elevator with Henry Stern. But we landed above the luncheon party and wandered into the owner's box. There were guards around, but no one stopped the "landlord" and his guest. We'd arrived in the middle of a buffet. Ubiquitous wasn't worried. He knew everybody in George Steinbrenner's personal foyer and introduced me to the president of the Mets. But I was interested in another man. He slumped in the corner, out of sight. He had a bald spot and graying sideburns and could have been some simple executive in a blue sports coat. That's how he blended in. But it was Mickey Mantle. And it was his first public appearance since Bowie Kuhn had banished him from baseball for his involvement in gambling casinos. The Mick had been playing golf with the wrong people. He was a paid companion to "significant gamblers." But the new baseball commissioner, Peter Ueberroth, had pardoned Mantle and Willie Mays, who'd also been a "shill" at the same casinos.

Mantle should have been another Babe Ruth. He had the Babe's raw power and his own mythic charm. He was the constant country boy, a sleepy-eyed rube in the Big Town. "I wasn't known for my brains." But he didn't need brains on the field. He was swift, and he had a compactness, like an antelope with a little bulk. Willie Mays was almost lithe compared to him. The Mick had Popeye's magic forearms. But his knees were brittle, and he hobbled around for eighteen years. What did it matter? He still was Mickey Mantle. "You don't want to get thrown out of your favorite bar," he'd said after Ueberroth had rescued him from baseball oblivion.

I watched the Mick, who was supposed to be six feet tall. But he was the shortest six-footer I'd ever seen. He must have dropped an inch or two at the casinos. His face was lined. "He's sixty," Henry said. But Ubiquitous was wrong. Mantle wasn't even fifty-five on Opening Day. He'd come out of his corner to sign a couple of autographs.

Ah, I had a notebook in my fisherman's vest. Could have sneaked an interview with Mickey Mantle. But I was slumming here. Henry and I had strayed into the wrong box. And I'd have felt like a churl begging questions off Mickey Mantle. *Mick, how does it feel . . . to be Mickey Mantle?*

We went down into the ballpark. Koch had arrived with his own war party. People shouted, "Eddie, Eddie." He walked with a slight tilt of anger, like he was daring the crowd. It was an old tradition to boo a mayor in a ballpark. But people were drawn to the fury around Ed Koch, that pull of excitement in the mayor's party, and I couldn't hear much booing. He'd come in his shirtsleeves, the king of New York.

Henry and I sat behind the Yankee dugout. Koch walked onto the field and said, "There must be a subway series." And then the Mick emerged from the dugout in his old Yankee uniform, tossed the Opening Day ball, and there was bedlam in the house. Most of the kids there hadn't even been born when Mantle retired. But the name held. It was folklore passed down from their dads, who'd grown into manhood with the Mick. It was the remembrance of a kinder past, before Vietnam, before Khomeini. For a moment, Mantle was the only hero who'd ever been, isolated from everything else, a timeless quotient with graying hair. Who would ever notice how he'd aged? He was a permanent boy in his baseball pajamas.

[4]

Could have been on a hunt, some safari into the boroughs. Our trips didn't have a prescribed route. Henry composed a trail while he sat behind the wheel. "I'm like

Ferdinand the Bull. I get sidetracked . . . once you start looking for flowers, you don't want to fight." We'd often drop in on a park site, but Henry wasn't attempting to surprise his workers. He was Ubiquitous, that's all.

The Brownsville Recreation Center had closed an hour early, and we had to find a night porter to let us in. Henry didn't scream. But I could feel the twitch of disappointment in his gray beard. He hadn't come as a hanging judge. He wanted to see the kids play basketball in one of his centers. He didn't call Manhattan Central to bring the culprits back. But I knew Brownsville wouldn't be closing early again. He has a much more quiet fury than our golem mayor, who would have gone down into Gehenna to get back that missing hour.

That wasn't the unicorn's way.

He'd rather journey than take revenge. We discovered abandoned houses with decals in the windows. The decals pictured venetian blinds and flowerpots. They'd been put up by the Department of Housing Preservation and Development along certain bombed-out routes as a kind of trompe l'oeil. The decals had been "invented" for the dead houses near the Cross Bronx Expressway to offer motorists the illusion of city life. They were ingenious in one sense. The decals did have a futuristic feel, like a dreamland in the middle of decay. I found them on the Grand Concourse, in Morrisania, Brownsville, Bed-Stuy. I hated them and was fascinated by their design: they could transform a building, give it a surreal, almost bucolic, existence. But it was like being in East Berlin, where entire streets on the far side of Checkpoint Charlie were an empty village, a fabricated no-man's-land.

We could decal half of Brownsville and declare an end to urban blight. It was the old fairy tale of Manhattanism: a center city of culture and wealth (with ice-cream parlors to replace the Chinese laundries) and decals everywhere else.

But that wasn't happening with the parks. Henry didn't believe in trompe l'oeil. He wasn't concerned about motorists' imaginations. He didn't have a love affair with highways, as Robert Moses did. He was trying to "reclaim land from the automobile and turn it green." And when he saw a tired, old playground, it angered him. "Even the trees are leaning down." He wasn't Bartleby on the road. He was Ahab in the midst of a maddening quest. We went through broken factories, through freight yards and dark, smelly lanes, looking for the least bit of green on the map.

He was also putting personnel back into the parks. He had a corps of urban rangers and special park police, PEP (Park Enforcement Patrol), officers who carried handcuffs and walkie-talkies, could issue summonses and make arrests. The rangers had become the most visible feature of Henry's parks. They wore Smoky the Bear hats and behaved like the City's ambassadors. They could turn mean, miserable parks into zones where children wanted to play. The clearest example was Crotona Park.

It was a jungle before the rangers arrived, a nightmare forest without magic children, without children at all. It was dangerous to enter Crotona Park. "Muggers would rob you for your clothes. People were murdered here."

As the Bronx began to burn, Crotona Park became a "shelter" for junkies, rats, and wild dogs. Crossing that park half a dozen years ago, on some sentimental journey, seeking out my Bronx "ancestors" before the borough disappeared, I saw those wild dogs on the rocks above Indian Lake. They moved in a narrowing circle, like neurotic wolves closing in upon themselves until they started to bump and attack each other for a bit of space, when they had all of Crotona Park.

I was on a fool's errand. I wanted to see that lake out of my childhood where I'd rowed with my brother, the oars deep in algae. There was nothing to row in now. The lake had become a huge garbage dump. And the handball courts on the hill, where I'd played blackball with a little dark glove, lay in ruins. The string of lamps that had lit the courts past dinnertime looked as if they'd fallen into bomb craters. We'd had endless tournaments of blackball at midnight under those lamps (it wasn't really midnight; more like 9 p.m.). But the handball courts had become a playground for rats . . . until the rangers arrived at the end of '83. A new Crotona Park was built out of the rubble. The wild dogs were gone. Paths have been repaved. Cooking grills can be found. The old boathouse has become a ranger station. The park has a lake again, and the water is "postcard blue." There are only eleven rangers assigned to the park, but they've brought back a whole population.

"You get a lot of bank for the buck from these guys," says Adrian Benepe, director of public information for the Parks Department. *A lot of bank for the buck.* It's almost as if a new kind of economic babble has emerged after the fiscal crisis. The City couldn't take a chance with state exchequers sitting on its shoulder. Sixty rangers was all it would allow, sixty rangers for five boroughs, and eleven of them were in Crotona Park.

And the Mad Hatter, Henry Stern, that quixotic councilman, suddenly had to deal with the power of the buck, sell the "idea" of parks to the City of New York, when he'd been dealing with lost causes most of his life. But he's grown much more pragmatic, and his nine years on the City Council haven't hurt his persuasiveness as parks commissioner. "Henry understands how the purse is opened and closed," says Adrian Benepe. "He knows who butters the bread, who has to be courted." And he butters, courts, begs for money.

I stood with Henry Stern on the bow of the Crotona Park pool, built by the great pharaoh himself, Robert Moses, when he had eighty thousand federal workers on loan to him in the middle of the Depression. The pool was "larger than a football field," but it had fallen into disrepair while the Bronx became a ghost town. Children were frightened to enter its cavernous locker rooms. Finally, the pool was shut down, and it was as if all the pharaoh's monuments had crumbled around him. But Robert Moses is enjoying a renaissance in his old bailiwick, the Parks Department.

The Bronx's Riviera, Orchard Beach, was created by Robert Moses in 1936. He borrowed some sand from the Rockaways, packed it between Hunter's Island and Rod-

man's Neck, and produced a crescent-shaped beach that
was the playpen of an entire borough. I grew up at Orchard Beach. It was like having cousins in the sand, feuding cousins. But nothing was left to chance. Each
eccentric group had its own section under the sun: communists, socialists, vegetarians, furriers, hermits, bodybuilders, bums. Of course, these cousins began to vary
with the years. The bodybuilders went out to California.
The vegetarians died. The communists disappeared. Latinos and blacks established their own sections. The old
Jewish couples continued to pluck their mandolins. The
"Hollywood" section was for kids on their first dates. And
the handball courts were a home for gamblers.

But Orchard Beach went the way of the Bronx. It's as if
a fire burned through all the sections. The grounds were
ravaged. And the Bronx Riviera grew into a wasteland.
"The City lost control," says Adrian Benepe. "It was a
disaster area." A tent colony of prostitutes, Las Vegas
Valley, rose up in the middle of the beach, a mad little
town of booths and blankets and colored tents, like a
phantasmagoria out of the Arabian Nights, a den of
wicked people along a crescent that wasn't policed. Ah, it
might not have been so wicked at all. Prostitutes have to
vacation somewhere. And why shouldn't illegal vendors
have their own booths on a beach that had fallen outside
the City's pale? But the City reclaimed its right to the
beach. The tents are down. And the Bronx Riviera has
been restored . . . like the Crotona pool.

I walked with Henry among the bas-reliefs at the side
of the pool—the work of Robert Moses's craftsmen.
There was more delight in those raised emblems than you
could discover in a fleet of store windows. We found a sea
lion, Medusa, Old Man River, an amphibian (a water
monster with a human eye), a scorpion, a flying fish, a boy
riding a whale—perfect motifs for a Robert Moses pool.
They read like hieroglyphics out of the pharaoh's past.
Moses's personality was in that amphibious creature. The
old man loved the sea. He swam like a flying fish. He'd
given beaches and parks to the City before he became the

monster who destroyed an aquarium out of spite (who will remind us of that wonderful cave in Battery Park with its fish tanks reflected like a diorama on the walls?), declared neighborhoods a slum out of some deep desire to put up concrete bunkers or build one more bridge.

But there hasn't been another pharaoh in the Parks Department since Moses. Ubiquitous is no master builder. He sold ties and is obsessed about trees. And there's no army of federal workers on loan. Henry Stern has to sing before the City Council to have his sixty rangers.

[5]

We were at a marathon out in Queens, near the old summer mansion of Mayor La Guardia at Flushing Creek. Fiorello had become an authentic City ghost. He was like some incarnation of the grand old days, the Little Flower who crippled slot machines with a sledgehammer, traveled around in a fire truck, and had his own police court. He's remained in the City's consciousness as the *good mayor,* incorruptible, kind, reading comics to the kiddies on the radio. But he was also a pain in the ass who bullied his people, did a lot of bending to bankers, and allowed Moses to grab more and more power until he was beyond the reach of any mayor. It was Moses who ruled the town during the days of Impellitteri. And neither Lindsay nor Robert Wagner could control him, though Lindsay did try. Whatever Moses wanted, Moses got.

The pharaoh had funny ideas about black people. He'd lower the temperature of his pools to discourage blacks from swimming there because he "was convinced that Negroes did not like cold water." And when he began to put up his housing projects, Moses decided that the poor weren't civilized enough to need toilet-seat covers.

When I talked to Henry about the pharaoh, he shrugged like a rabbinical student and asked me what I expected from a man who couldn't admit he was Jewish. And we continued on our way, with Henry at the wheel, a guy who's "been in government service since his bar mitzvah," according to Mayor Koch.

Back in the Bronx, the unicorn discovered a misspelled street sign near Southern Boulevard. "Call someone in traffic," he said to his aide sitting with the chauffeur in back of the car. He knew about my connection to Crotona Park. "Where's your candy store?" he asked. "Do they have egg creams?"

"Henry," I said, "how can they have a candy store? My whole street is gone." The corner where I'd lived and played off-the-curb disappeared from the City map and was reborn as Charlotte Gardens, those ranch houses in the rubble.

We passed an empty schoolhouse behind Hoe Avenue. The school had blackened windows and a ratty roof. Henry watched that roofline with a dreamy eye. "Another neighborhood that ran out of kids."

We toured a playground on Fox Street. The watchman there was proud of his "vandal-resistant, stainless-steel sink." He was getting rid of graffiti as fast as he could. We waltzed around the comfort station, which had a dark chocolate color to discourage graffiti artists.

Graffiti was the parks' number-one sin. Koch had a sense of humor about everything except graffiti and the Soviet Union. He wanted to outlaw the sale of "bombing" cans to teenagers and to set up a special court in the subways for muggers and graffiti artists (or vandals, as he called them). Graffiti had become the totem word and taboo of his entire administration. The Parks Department spends over a million dollars a year to rid its sites of graffiti (the squiggles keep coming back, like haunted children), and Henry was just as religious as Ed Koch on the subject, but he still was a unicorn, and he was able to smile at the graffiti artist of Fox Street who'd written his lament on a handball court, declaring that he'd run out of paint.

We followed the graffiti trail into Brooklyn, Henry searching for bombed-out handball courts and comfort stations. Howard Golden, Brooklyn's dapper borough president and Democratic party boss, joined us on the trail. We were visiting playgrounds that were part of a restoration program in Howard Golden's turf and Henry had stopped to examine a tree. Golden stared at him.

"Henry, in Brooklyn the trees are healthy. It's the people who aren't so healthy."

He wore a dark suit, the boss of this wild borough that seemed to have no perimeters. You could get lost in Brooklyn, lost for life. Howard Golden wasn't Haunch Paunch and Jowl. He was thin, like an aging street kid. I could imagine him tossing marbles in the Brooklyn gutters fifty years ago and winning every game. He could smell that I was a scribbler.

"You're taking notes," he said. His neck tightened.

He would have been the most powerful Democrat in the universe during ordinary times, the boss of bosses, as Meade Esposito had been. But these weren't ordinary times. Koch was a party unto himself. He prospered without precinct captains, and the boss of Brooklyn was left somewhere out in the cold.

As Meade Esposito once said: "Hey, I've been dancing on a charlotte russe for 16 years and I never dented the cherry." It doesn't matter anymore how Golden dances. The charlotte russe is gone and Ed Koch owns all the cherries.

But Brooklyn still belonged to Howard Golden. And Golden was on a walk with Henry Stern, visiting playgrounds together, and declaring war on graffiti in his borough. But one member of our little army said, after looking at the graffiti on the ground, "It's like herpes, this stuff. It's forever."

And we went on to visit more graffiti. We stopped at a playground in Bath Beach, passed the old police castle in the heart of Mafia country. It was the Mad Hatter who noticed the first irregularity. "That precinct has two numbers on it." The sixty-second precinct had once been the seventieth, it seems: the words *70th precinct* were written on the castle's side wall. It felt like Alice and her looking glass, as bizarre as Brooklyn itself. Mafia, police, and a playground within a few hundred yards. I wondered if

the Bonnanos contributed any basketballs and swings.
And then I decided it wasn't Alice's fault. It was the logic
of the world: crime, cops, and recreation on the same
street.

We traveled on to Brownsville, a haunted village with
people here and there. But the playgrounds were packed.
Golden scrutinized the red and green squiggles on the
back of a comfort station. "Henry, do something, so they
won't graffiti it. The place for good art is on canvas, not
on buildings." And I thought, Howard, where the hell
have you been? A whole generation of cave artists had
sprung up around him, but Golden lived inside a clubhouse. He was like a handsome wraith who could kiss the
mamas and ask the little kids, "Children, who am I?"

"The president of Brooklyn," the kids would always
answer.

But he had no sense of those anonymous graffiti artists
and the territory they were claiming for themselves with
their personal "tags." It was like some cosmic mystery
show, seeing the care they took to decorate a wall—and
also the lack of care, the ruinous slashings, the dumb
spraying of a park bench that was like an appalling,
artless cry. *I live in a ruin. I am a ruin. I'm adding to the ruin.*

I scribbled in my notebook.

"Watch the bum," Golden said, sipping Diet Coke.
"He's taking down everything."

I liked the man, imagined him as a Jewish Mafia don.
But there were no Jewish dons. He was only the president
of Brooklyn.

I returned to the Arsenal with Henry. One of the City's
own lawyers approached Henry on his castle stairs. She
was attractive, around thirty-five. There'd been a problem in Riverside Park: a federal marshal had arrested a
boat at the Seventy-ninth Street basin. I was curious about
all the procedural stuff. How does a marshal arrest a
boat? The lawyer looked at me.

"Who are you?"

Henry didn't smile. "That's a good question. I often ask
that myself."

And I shoved out into the street, away from Henry and his fortress in the park, thinking of marshals, boats, and that invisible graffiti artist who was spraying all of us, front and back, with the design of our own lives, twisted green and red curls that we'd never come to know.

eight

A MAN CALLED ALVARADO

[1]

I'm a public-school brat. I went through the whole bloody system, starting in 1942, with a couple of hours of kindergarten. I ate wooden blocks. The fiber was delicious. An Irish spinster lady pulled my hair in the first grade because I'd picked up this lousy habit at Hebrew school of starting sentences on the right side of the page.

.BOY BADDY THE AM I

Took me a whole season to learn where the margin was. And I never quite recovered from that fall to the left side of the page. I couldn't spell, and my father, who spelled worse than I did, knocked the habit of spelling into my head. So please don't tell me how the nation has grown illiterate. I was illiterate enough for two nations. Henry Stern may have been a reading, writing unicorn in kindergarten. But even in the whitest of ghettos, it was hard to read.

The public-school system has been a problem child ever since I can remember. It functioned beautifully in "homogenized" neighborhoods like Douglaston in Queens and along the Madison Avenue belt, or in that middle-class Jewish enclave on the Upper West Side, with its famed citadel, Joan of Arc Junior High. Every other little genius from Manhattan had gone to Joan of Arc. A fabric existed between the school and its general population that was like a dancing, singing ship. It was in the pull of a neighborhood, in its streets, its homes, its stores. And the schools could neither create nor destroy a fabric that wasn't there.

Sometimes a school manufactured its own "neighborhood," if talents were specially picked, as they were at Bronx Science and Music and Art. But the competition was so fierce that gifted students often had to suck their fists and resign themselves to a second-class education in an inferior school. The system just couldn't absorb its own talent. It has always been a sluggish machine, and in the worst ghettos, black and white, the students were mostly invisible. I would have disappeared into the woodwork, crawled under some urban stone, if I hadn't gotten out of my neighborhood and gone to Music and Art.

I was a wild boy, filled with paranoia and greed. And because Music and Art was considered a sissy school, good for girls with a violin cello between their legs, it was desperate for guys, guys with a minimum of talent and reasonable grades . . . moon children from Crotona Park. I wore muscle T-shirts to Music and Art. I was blessed with Brando's profile. I mumbled like him, I twitched, but the girls with violin cellos between their legs never seemed to notice. They'd come riding out of Joan of Arc, dreaming of concert careers or a ticket to Radcliffe and Swarthmore. And I was like a cave animal to them. Stopped wearing muscle T-shirts. My palette went from maroon to charcoal gray. I discovered how to eat with a fork at the school cafeteria and was on my way to becoming a "squire," while the kids from my old neighborhood sank deeper and deeper into Crotona Park, disappearing into the air force, getting married at seventeen, or dying on some roof with a dirty needle in their veins.

My brother Harvey became a cop. It was both a disgrace—Jews didn't wear handcuffs—and a survival kit; got him out of the ghetto. And I learned the genealogy of manners at Music and Art. But I never picked up an idea that stayed with me, or a vulnerable thought. It's as if those mandarins from the Board of Ed had reached into Music and Art and mummified all my teachers. We piddled with Shakespeare (every line of smut was removed from the text). We knew about George III's nasty treatment of his American colonies, but no one bothered to tell us that he grew incontinent near the end of his reign and had to wear diapers on the throne. I wouldn't have despised an old king in his diapers. It would have been as familiar as Crotona Park.

I'd never heard of Dostoyevsky or Sophocles or Kafka and Freud. Marx and Lenin weren't players in my history book. The Russian Revolution was mentioned in some paragraph we weren't required to read. Washington was tall, brilliant, and brave. Jefferson never had a mistress in his life. The Chinese were welcomed like any other stranger. The Irish were never pissed upon in New York. The Italians and Jews sailed past the Statue of Liberty, searching for their citizenship papers. There were no blacks around except Joe Louis and Jackie Robinson (Music and Art sat in the middle of Harlem). American history was a long unfolding flower of democratic ideals from the Battle of Bunker Hill to the bringing of baseball to Occupied Japan. It was the dumbest kind of distortion, as relevant as a mouse. The public schools had prepared a curriculum for dwarfs—while the Board of Ed was manufacturing the myth of its own greatness as overseer to the largest school system in the land. Hadn't it seized a hodgepodge of immigrants for over a hundred years and turned them into a small nation of readers?

The title of Diane Ravitch's book, *The Great School Wars: New York City, 1805–1973,* cuts into that "legend of success." Long before the bitter fights that erupted in the late

1960s over the destiny of local school districts—who should control them, who should set the curricula, who should teach—the schools had become a battleground between natives and newcomers. The Irish had been the first to be hit. They weren't considered teachable at all. They arrived like stinking mules in the 1820s, lived like stinking mules. The almshouse was packed with Irish souls, the public hospitals, the jails, the "homes" for juvenile delinquents, the houses for the insane. But the Irish got their education soon as they started dancing with Tammany Hall.

That education wasn't in the first "public schools," which were part of the Free School Society, established in 1805 to enlighten and enlist every depraved and poor boy in New York. The society operated a mechanistic universe, where everything was learned by rote. It produced a series of talking dolls who could multiply and spell and weren't supposed to be "saucy to a monitor," make noise in the street, stare at persons who entered the classroom, soil their books, have dirty faces and hands, scratch their desks, or move after the bell rang. Besides its idiotic rules and its condescension to the poor, its textbooks treated Catholicism as a form of devil worship.

It's no wonder the Irish stayed away and attended parochial schools. And thus began the first great school war, between a Protestant Public School Society and the Catholic Church. Both sides lost in that donnybrook. The public schools didn't get their poor Catholic students, and the Catholic schools failed to get public funds. The society itself was soon absorbed into a new Board of Education. And that's how "modern" schools began in the City of New York.

These modern schools had between a hundred and a hundred and fifty pupils in a class, while ten to thirty thousand brats lived in cellars or the City's streets. There was a whole vagabond army of beggars, bootblacks, and thieves that makes *Oliver Twist* look like a fairy tale. The fact is that neither the Church, the Board of Education, nor Tammany Hall cared enough, or had the will, to help this beggar army. And all the Protestant reformers, the

"Goo Goos" (Good Government Boys), were so incensed about the dirty Irish in Tammany Hall, they never bothered to see the waifs.

And those democratizers, the good gentlemen from the Board of Ed? They'd never heard of kindergartens or public high schools. Some of the system's best teachers were senile, deaf, or nearly blind. "One school had the same principal for fifty-five years." Another school had a janitor who was a hundred and five. And that was the golden age. Teachers, janitors, and principals were long-lived in those wooly years before the stampede of Sicilians and Russian wild beards shook the public school rafters and roofs.

This wave of immigrants was worse than the Irish. The Irish were unclean, yes, but they had a slippery tongue. That brogue of theirs could be considered an English of sorts. The filth from Eastern Europe had no English. And the *Tribune,* in 1896, suggested as a joke "that the first exercise in each school be to give the pupils a bath."

The "natives" who taught them, mostly German and Irish spinsters, had little feeling of generosity for greenhorn kids. The dropout rate was horrendous. Soon as the kids reached fourteen and could get their working papers, half of them left school. And there were grave problems among the other half: they could neither read nor write; you had twelve-year-olds in the second grade. The myth of "instant success" never happened. Some researchers in the 1920s wondered whether "inferior genetic endowment" was keeping Italian children behind. The researchers didn't stop to think that it might be the schools that were a little stupid, not the kids. The kids didn't want to become Yankee Doodle. They preferred the Sicilian life in the streets.

And the Jews? They were the Board of Ed's biggest success story. The little wild beards helped sustain that myth. Some of them failed at school, of course. But they had a wish to get ahead, a kind of rabbinical fever that didn't come from the quality of teaching in the public schools. The Sicilian brats had had a homeland, even if it was only a bunch of medieval rocks. But the Jewish kids had nothing but an America they invented with their eyes. That Pale of settlement their parents had come from, that in-between country, was only a shadowland the czar had cut out for the zhids. With all its isolation and loneliness, America had become their last Eden on earth.

The sons and daughters of the Russian wild beards would have been successful at school even if camels and donkeys had taught them. They believed in the Constitution and all those articles about the rights of man. They brought their own wonder to twentieth-century New York and helped transform the town. They took a mercantile village with its own tight rules, an aristocracy of bankers and insurance brokers and old-line gelt, and ripped it apart with that Jeffersonian democracy they'd discovered from the Irish schoolmarms: a fantasy of the real.

They had a fine model, the German Jews. If the German Jews couldn't enter Rockefeller's bank or the large insurance companies, they could still become investment bankers, mercantile wizards, newspaper tycoons. They formed their own aristocracy, built country clubs, moved to Park Avenue, these gentile Jews.

Not all the wild beards wanted the same thing. They reinvented America with their hunger for democracy, and in the process, they fabulated the City of New York, where everything was possible along their own crazy lines. There were a million and a half of them in 1920. While the Italians built their Little Italys in all five boroughs, the Russian Jews were establishing their own civil service. "More than half the city's doctors, lawyers, dentists, and public school teachers were Jewish by the 1930s."

The metamorphosis had been so absolute, it was like a population of golems, with failure, success, despair as different colors of the very same flag. New York had become a Jewish town in twenty, thirty years. It was also a black town, but a lot of people didn't know it. Harlem had as much energy as the Lower East Side, but it was all locked in. And its contours were felt in a different way, as a terrible implosion, a wound that wouldn't bleed dry.

The National Origins Act of 1924 cut off the flow of

Italians and Jews into the United States and soon put Ellis Island to sleep. It also calmed the Board of Ed. With very few immigrants to bother about in the 1930s, the public schools began to reach the ideal of a one-hundred-percent promotion rate. But it was a lie. The Board of Ed had fallen in love with its own promise of infallibility. And the myth began of the public school as "melting pot, the great cauldron of Americanization. . . ." It was bringing up a wonder class of white and black. Bess Myerson, the first and only Jewish Miss America (and one of the first Miss Subways), graduated from Music and Art. Lewis Mumford was a Stuyvesant boy. Nathan Quinones, the current schools chancellor, went to the High School of Commerce. There were Nobel laureates, novelists, divas, Pulitzer Prize journalists, gangsters, psychopaths, corporation chiefs, real-estate czars, Mayor Koch (who began his schooling across the street from Crotona Park before his family pulled out of the Bronx), Rita Hayworth, Lauren Bacall, James Cagney, Arnold Rothstein, Dutch Schultz, Danny Kaye, Al Pacino, Hank Greenberg (who hit his first home runs in Crotona Park), Kate Simon, Lee Harvey Oswald, Norman Mailer, Son of Sam, Woody Allen, Abe Beame, Bobby Fischer, Lionel Trilling, Lou Gehrig, Grace Paley, Groucho Marx. . . .

And what about all the black laureates, like James Baldwin, who attended public schools in Harlem? Stokely Carmichael went to Bronx Science. Diahann Carroll and Billy Dee Williams, "the black Gable," went to Music and Art. Franklin Thomas, president of the Ford Foundation, went to Franklin K. Lane High School with Assemblyman Albert Vann. But I'd love to know how many foundation presidents attended high school in the Morrisania section of the Bronx.

The Board of Ed democratized itself by pretending the ghettos didn't exist. It promoted everybody, until some kids entered high school with bewilderment in their eyes: they couldn't read. And this was long before whites ran to the suburbs and the schools went Latino and black. There was a two-tiered system, Herman Badillo remembers, one for whites and one for Latinos and blacks. The Latinos weren't expected to learn. Badillo went to school in East Harlem, where students spent the morning "throwing erasers at the teachers." Badillo couldn't progress "in an atmosphere of turmoil." He was shunted off to a non-academic program at Haaren High and would have remained there, become a mechanic, a fix-it man. But he happened to drift into the offices of the school newspaper and became involved with the newspaper kids, who were all white. "I got an academic degree because I was with the whites." Otherwise, he would have been invisible to the school administrators, like the other Latinos in his class.

The son of a Puerto Rican minister, Badillo is a man with a fierce Castillian air. Former Bronx borough president and deputy mayor during Koch's first administration, he's pissed at the Board of Ed. "The City schools are a disaster for blacks and Hispanics," he says. "The system is not geared for doing any dramatic improvements." It's a cauldron with a crippled fire. The pot itself is melting away. It's still a two-tiered system, only the tiers have gotten worse. It can seize most of the top honors in the annual Westinghouse Science Talent Search while it produces an army of dropouts—illiterates who "live in an amputated present tense," as Jonathan Kozol has said. Badillo feels a hopelessness about this army; the nation itself is growing more and more ghettoized.

Midtown Manhattan has become an insulated village, "with a disaster two miles up . . . and another disaster two miles down." It's like a mirage kingdom in a dead borderland. Badillo doesn't see much hope outside this mirage. "Cities are no longer essential" because "there are so many blacks. . . . In America, cities are the places to stay away from," he says.

"The average American doesn't give a shit about blacks and Hispanics." Most people would love to see them "disappear." There's "progress for the rich and progress for the upper classes," but not for the "black, Hispanic, or elderly Jewish lower middle class . . . cities are dead in this country."

Whether Manhattan can become more than a mirage

for the rich, Herman Badillo has gone through the City schools himself and witnessed their essential flaw, the flaw of most public education—that it is a disguised form of charity work rather than a right and a privilege of the children themselves. As the trustees of the Public School Society said in 1830 of the Irish boys living in the Five Points (the worst slum New York had ever seen until the South Bronx): they are "destitute of literary and moral instruction," and not fit to associate with the "orderly children who attend the Public Schools." Therefore, the trustees were going to build a special school for dimwits in the Five Points, so that the righteous children would not be corrupted.

That attitude still prevails. The "righteous children" have fled to the suburbs or a phalanx of private schools, or are lucky enough to live within one or another white mirage.

[2]

For about nine or ten months in 1983–1984 a rattlesnake gripped the public schools and wouldn't let go. That rattlesnake was Anthony Alvarado. He'd just been named chancellor by some fluke. Ed Koch had wanted Robert Wagner, Jr., his own deputy. Wagner is a compassionate, intelligent guy who grew up in Gracie Mansion as the son of a mayor. He has a feel for the City that few other bureaucrats have. And he might have made an excellent chancellor—but he was also the mayor's man. Whatever independence he might have had inside the Hall of Education at 110 Livingston Street, he would have been a bit too close to Koch. I doubt whether he could have taken too many unpopular stands.

Alvarado, who was superintendent of District Four in East Harlem for ten years and had been only a minor rattlesnake until then, shaking up the district, closing a rotten high school, creating Las Escuelas Alternativas (alternative junior high schools with their own catalogues and themes), was supposed to become Wagner's deputy chancellor. But things didn't turn out that way. The state education commissioner vetoed Wagner. And the rattlesnake went into office.

He had little patience for bureaucrats who weren't eager to try anything new. The whole system was bounded by an infernal cautiousness, an almost pathological absence of adventure. And Alvarado was an adventurous man. He could also be reckless—he didn't always have his figures right—but he preferred action to endless sloth. He realized that if he didn't move quickly, another year would be lost. And in nine months he exhorted, harangued, danced, and shouted harder and longer than the system had ever seen in a hundred years. And the Board didn't quite know what to do. Alvarado wasn't trying to "warm up" the ghettos, feed candy to hapless kids, or juggle statistics until he could find a slight improvement here and there. He was talking of quality education in a system where the schools were haunted houses and the kids were defeated before the term began: the dropout rate for Latinos and blacks hovered between fifty and sixty percent. Alvarado was either a madman or a wizard.

He was both. He was a visionary who couldn't afford to bury himself in other people's lack of dreaming. And he wasn't a token Latino who yapped about minorities. The rattlesnake was going to educate *everybody* or no one at all. He didn't depend on statistical charts. "You walk into a school, take a sniff, and you know right away whether the school is good or bad."

He did an awful lot of sniffing in those first few months. But he wasn't a public-school brat like me. Alvarado received a Catholic education. He's seldom talked about his childhood, and when he has, he's given confusing tales, sometimes saying his father was Puerto Rican, sometimes not. His father was born in Cuba. Alvarado himself was an only son, born here on June 10, 1942. His mother had come from Puerto Rico. He grew up in the South Bronx, something of a Bartleby, a loner who read a lot of books. He was trained by the Jesuits in local schools and at Fordham University, but Alvarado says "he is not religious."

His first job was teaching English at a junior high. He was a rattlesnake even then, curling his way through the system, becoming a principal and then superintendent of District Four, in the same East Harlem where Herman Badillo went to school. Kids were still throwing board erasers and doing much worse. Alvarado had entered a bombed-out country, ninety percent Latino and black, with the lowest reading scores in the "continent" of New York.

Benjamin Franklin High School, which was in his district but under a separate authority, looked like a war zone with a lot of kids who went AWOL all the time. I'd pass Ben Franklin on the East River Drive, and it reminded me of some Cambodian nightmare that Pol Pot had produced—a ravaged monkey land without people. I wasn't so wrong. Ben Franklin was losing its population. Kids rapped in the hallways, beat up on teachers, sold drugs, and forgot to graduate. It was that familiar life of a ghetto school, with students and teachers stuck in a place where no one wanted to be and each was a prisoner of the other. Ben Franklin was like a wound that faced the sea.

Alvarado pressured the sachems at 110 Livingston Street to close it down. He converted that dropout temple into the Manhattan Center for Science and Math, a whole fort of learning, from the first grade to the twelfth. The metamorphosis was astounding. The school had a waiting list rather than a gang of absentees. And suddenly this Harlem complex was matching the attendance rolls of Bronx Science and Music and Art; Alvarado had discovered a school where students wanted to go. And he'd destroyed the fable of ghetto apathy. Kids had been dying in dead schools. The rattlesnake woke them up.

But it was in East Harlem junior high schools that Alvarado left his most controversial mark. He'd grab a floor in some old worn-out school and declare it one of his "mini-colleges," academies that he'd design with a particular teacher, emphasizing sports, art, acting, writing, music, maritime skills—twenty-two "magnet" schools that were drawing kids into East Harlem from every borough.

Alvarado had invented his own public-school system. It

was a kind of madness and also a miraculous birth. Alvarado was saying that Las Escuelas Alternativas in the middle of Harlem could compete with the offerings of any private school or college. He'd willed the schools' success with his own energetic push, a bit of finagling, and teachers who felt concerned again, alive in a public wasteland. He'd overspend, take funds from one program and stick them into another. That's how the rattlesnake worked. "Alvarado seemed to float through life on idealism; he had the ability to cast spells on his friends and associates."

But more important, Alvarado loved kids and believed in their perfectability. Perhaps he'd remained closer to the Jesuits than he was aware of. The Jesuits were an incredible teaching order: logicians, wizards, and priests. And Alvarado could bewitch people with "great swoops of words and arcs of thought, in a voice that was loud one moment and soft the next."

A perfect rattlesnake.

[3]

As chancellor he took on Ed Koch, the Board of Ed, and the whole slothful system that delivered "second-rate services." His values and his own scrambling style were "at polar odds with the nature of functioning in a bureaucracy." He had no particular discretion or desire to soften past and present failures. He hadn't come to apologize. He saw the stranglehold the system had, its ability to destroy teachers and children, and he compared it to "an octopus with grasping tentacles." The rattlesnake was going to squeeze right back.

He started all-day kindergartens. It was unheard of. Five-year-old brats were entitled to half a day. But Alvarado sprang his plan on the Board of Ed during his first week in the chancellor's chair. The sachems couldn't deny him money for all those latchkey kids. Koch himself liked the idea. And there was never a "kindergarten war" at 110 Livingston Street.

But after hearing about Alvarado's coup, I had a bit of
cockeyed paramnesia. Kindergarten remained so dim for
me because there was precious little of it. I remembered
being shuffled back and forth between the schoolyard
and my house on Longfellow Avenue. I ate wood, that's it.
But I couldn't conjure up the hint of a teacher's face.
There was nothing, nothing to recall.

The rattlesnake was going to remedy all that. Critics
attacked him for moving too fast, said he hadn't properly
"costed" his kindergartens. The Old Guard sniped behind his back. *Being around Tony*, they said, *was like living
in a whirlwind.* But Alvarado realized that if he didn't act,
there would be no all-day kindergartens for another year.
He had them in place by September, four months after
he'd arrived. A different chancellor would have planned
and planned, until the whole idea fell into the maw at 110
Livingston Street.

Some chaos surrounded his kindergartens, but the children and the teachers were there. And Alvarado's kindergartens weren't a total playland. The chancellor brought
computer terminals into the kindergarten classes. His associates figured he was insane. But they weren't ghetto
brats. They hadn't been raised in the dark slumber of the
streets. Alvarado had to get to the kids, excite them, load
them up with skills, or he'd lose them to lifelong illiteracy.

Koch visited a kindergarten on the first day of class.
"The mayor walks in, there are a hundred press people, including camera crews. It was a stampede. . . . The mayor
goes over to a kid who's practicing on the computer and he
asks the kid to show him how to do something. The kid
shows him, but the mayor gets it wrong. The kid turns to
the mayor and says coolly, 'You forgot to space.'"

You forgot to space.

That was education under Alvarado's rule. But he
wasn't simply tinkering with little kids behind ghetto
walls. He meant to start a whole new cadre of high
schools, schools that would advertise and develop particular gifts. A high school of computer technology. A
high school of international studies. A high school of finance. A high school for writing and journalism. And

he'd enlist professionals, talent outside the system, to serve as career models. Businessmen, writers, computer scientists. He wanted to release the schools from the vacuum they'd been sitting in for so long, that land of the mediocre.

Alvarado had a shrewd sense of real estate. He'd close the worst high schools, as he'd closed Ben Franklin, and "redesign" them according to individual themes, so that kids could attend the school they desired. Every single kid would have his own Bronx Science.

The rattlesnake brought a sense of revolution to the job. He was going to service all the souls he could find. Children in welfare hotels. Grown-ups who couldn't read. The handicapped. The delinquent. The disturbed. The preppies who might prefer one of his own schools.

Alvarado wasn't behaving like a ghetto brat. He had aristocratic notions. No one had dared dream of excellence when the dropout rate was so high. A madman. Tony the Terrible. A self-styled prince in a disaster area. Who can say what he wouldn't have accomplished? The perception of movement had become movement in itself. The momentum began to build.

And then, in February, the chancellor took a fall that was sadder than any school war, though it felt like war. An anonymous school official, John Chin, fired several shots into a neighbor's apartment in the early morning of February 27, 1984 . . . and Alvarado's unraveling began.

"From the moment the shots were fired," Alvarado said, "this has been a script that could've only been written by Kafka." Or Alvarado himself. Chin was arrested. The cops found guns, drugs, and certain documents in his safe. Those documents were decidedly weird. Anthony Alvarado had signed his own car away to John Chin. And Chin held two checks worth $10,450 in Alvarado's name. They seemed like some kind of markers, a system of debt.

Alvarado never quite recovered from those contents in John Chin's safe. Chin himself was a mystery man. He held some obscure title at the Board of Ed—the deputy to the deputy of an assistant deputy—and drove around in an Eldorado. Was he a hitman in deep cover at 110 Livingston Street? A dope peddler? A pimp? It didn't really matter. The scenario darkened. A vast skein began to weave itself around Anthony Alvarado, a web he couldn't get out of. He'd been borrowing money from his own employees. He'd gone into real-estate ventures that sounded a bit like a scam.

He complained to *El Diario:* Los Americanos No Comprenden. The gringos couldn't understand. He was in some cultural crossfire. But the fact was that he'd been golemized, suckered into the American dream, like a lot of other gringos. He had a house in Brooklyn. A second wife. A mortgage. Four kids from two marriages. And his finances were a mess.

He waltzed a bit, but he had to resign. The Board of Ed felt redeemed. The system just couldn't tolerate a visionary like Alvarado. It returned to its old stance of "deep quiet," promoted a virtuous, safe functionary, Nathan Quinones, who also cares about kids but is no maverick, and immediately dropped most of Alvarado's schemes into some wide "Sargasso Sea."

[4]

Alvarado produced no miracles. Teachers dropped out as fast as students did during the three hundred and twenty-seven days he served as chancellor of the schools. Six thousand eight hundred and thirty-two new teachers accepted jobs that September, and "1,393 quit within two weeks and 775 never appeared for work." In the poorest neighborhoods, children watched "teachers come and go." Alvarado might have had a chance to change things. He deplored the hiring of teachers with a lack of commitment to kids. They were recruited according to some mandarin "mirror test," he'd told the *Times.* "You put the mirror under the nostrils, if it fogs, you're a candidate." And what is most brutal to Alvarado and the kids of New York is that his ideals will be lumped with his life, and the vision he had will be dismissed as just another bad dream.

We're already witnessing the failure of the old, dead style. The very committee that investigated Alvarado declared the system so ineffective "it cannot police itself and does not even know how many teachers are teaching children at any given time. . . ." A coalition of concerned parents and civic groups, the Educational Priorities Panel, issued a scathing report, "Lost in the Labyrinth," that verified everything Alvarado felt: the fate of children is controlled by the Board of Ed in a helter-skelter fashion. No matter what special high school a kid applies to, most of the time he ends up in his own "yard," at one of the disaster schools Alvarado wanted to close down.

Alvarado knew that the guidance program was pure folly. "Lost in the Labyrinth" revealed that counselors would spend as little as eleven and a half minutes with each kid on admissions matters and were often ignorant about the programs they described. Counseling was only one more part of the educational octopus.

Through his desire to enter the great American middle class, Alvarado had practiced a form of economic banditry. He was as schizoid as the town itself, a town of Jekyll and Hydes. But his departure was the worst thing that could have happened to our children. The Board of Ed will hide behind figures, as it's always done, and nurture its own fantasy of improvement, while kids are lost in the labyrinth, without Alvarado's energy, his mad strength to rip through the maze.

"Someone like Alvarado comes along once every twenty years," Herman Badillo says. The system couldn't handle him. Alvarado was the Humpty Dumpty of 110 Livingston Street who provided his own fall. Another casualty of his own insistence (as Julian Schnabel said of Rimbaud)? Or just an unfortunate man who had a little too much of his autobiography in John Chin's safe?

Franklin Thomas despairs "at his demise . . . you felt a pulse change that was beginning to take place." But he doesn't think that Alvarado could have survived. A tough administrator needs "vision, imagination, almost recklessness to break out of the structural restraints that exist, an irreverence to challenges," which Alvarado had, "but all that has to be accompanied by a hardheaded understanding of the system." And Alvarado dreamt on his feet. There was no one to "protect the dreamer from the ravages of the system." He didn't have a "support structure" to bail him out. He was only a rattlesnake.

[5]

I was sitting in a vestibule on the "commissioners' floor" at One Police Plaza, waiting for the PC, Police Commissioner Benjamin Ward, while I considered Alvarado's fate. The PC had also had a bout with recklessness. The newspapers had gotten on his back. He'd "disappeared" for a day or two while he was driving around the country, had been out of radio contact with the Police Department, in some sort of commissioner's twilight zone. There'd been talk of a drinking problem. The PC's life had suddenly become everybody's business. He didn't like to give interviews. He was busy, tough, and shy. But I had a "rabbi" in the Police Department, my own Chinese connection, who'd appealed to the PC in my behalf, told him I was serious. The PC liked crime novels, and I'd written four of them, invented my own police commissioner, who was twice as reckless as Anthony Alvarado and had a tapeworm in his gut. My PC had murdered people.

I had forty-five minutes with Benjamin Ward. He *was* imposing and shy. He played with a penknife and a rubber band while we talked. He'd told a *Times* reporter that racism was as American as apple pie, and the *Daily News* jumped on Ben Ward, asking him what he had against apple pie. He was also the first black PC in a department that had always been run by an Irish mafia, and people kept whispering that it was "a political appointment, a political appointment," that Koch needed a black man in the commissioner's chair. There had been too much friction between blacks and the police.

Ben Ward didn't look like someone's political toy to me.

He'd been a detective out in the yards of Brooklyn. And I'd swear he'd broken a lot of bad guys' backs. Wouldn't have wanted to be a bad guy in his presence.

He was nearing sixty. "I'm old enough to have been on bread lines, old enough to have stood on coal lines and coffee lines." His mother had cut holes in his pockets so he could collect extra doughnuts at the police station, where doughnuts were given out during the Depression. "The Depression lasted longer for blacks." He was born and raised in Brooklyn, he said with a tip of pride that I understood. He'd never been yoked to Manhattan. "I have no relatives outside New York City, none outside Brooklyn." He'd lived on Hunterfly Place, the last remnant of Hunter Road, near the old village of Canarsie. "All of our heritage is traced to that area." It had been a home for Indians and blacks, who lived side by side and often intermarried. The myth he remembered was that these same Canarsie Indians had sold Manhattan Island to the Dutch and then returned to their Brooklyn hunting grounds.

But the PC wouldn't limit himself to local lore. He talked about the nineteenth century, when the Indians and the blacks were much more "integrated" than they are now. They were boatmen together, hunting whales off Long Island. "The Indians were harpooners, and the blacks did the rowing." It was like reading *Moby Dick* as I listened to Ben Ward on the subject of Canarsie whalers. I thought of Queequeg, with all his tattoos, and Ishmael, the outcast, who could have been black. What had happened to those Indian harpoon artists? And the black boatmen? Were they in Ben Ward's own blood? Or in some hidden museum of bone, brick, and dust, bequeathed to the old city of Brooklyn?

I was with the police commissioner, for God's sake. We talked about crime, cops . . . and the racism that was constant to America, constant as apple pie. "How could it not be, given the way blacks were introduced into this country . . . in chains. They might not even have come in chains. They were pieces of personal property, with no more rights than of a cow or a donkey or a horse . . . and no

ASPCA in existence," he said with the puzzling smile of a police commissioner with harpooners in his family tree.

I told him about Herman Badillo's experience of being tracked into oblivion at Haaren High until he'd joined the school paper and gone over to the whites. The PC didn't share Badillo's opinions about school. "I was a big wise-guy kid, big enough not to have trouble with anybody." Yet he did have to "pass a white junior high school" on the way to his own junior high. He was one of the smartest kids in his class, but he didn't go on to an academic high school, though that had been his mother's wish. She'd attended "an orphanage for colored children. She got paroled out of there and was raised by a German-Jewish family."

I was confused about that word *parole.* "Did they adopt her?" I asked. But it was a dumb question. Black orphan girls didn't get adopted into German-Jewish families.

"My mother wanted me to be a doctor. I talked to the guidance counselor. She told me to learn a trade." And the PC passed the entrance exam for the Brooklyn School of Automotive Trades. "I was steered to that school. The woman thought she was telling the right thing . . . it was realistic tracking. It was a wrong assessment, but she thought it was right."

The PC didn't feel bitter about her. He was the tenth of eleven children, and his parents were quite old by the time he was born. He went to Brooklyn College, where he had to take the algebra and the geometry he'd missed. He was a provisional student, even though he was on the dean's list "three or four times." He finally got his BA, but with all that algebra, he had enough credits for two degrees.

Ah, that guidance counselor might have meant well, but she'd shunted him along some invisible trolley track in her brain that said "colored boys' line." He'd overcome the damage. He was the PC. But I couldn't help thinking, *Benjamin Ward, you should have gone to Bronx Science.*

nine

HOME

[1]

I left the parental cave when I was twenty-four and moved into a closet on those Heights where George Washington had once held off the British, and was now a neighborhood of Latinos, middle-class Irish, and old German Jews. I lived like a rabbinical student on chocolate pudding and cans of tuna fish and read all the catechism books I could find because I was in love with James Joyce and knew I'd never write novels until I understood the holy rood. I turned Catholic in that nutty heart where a young writer spends his spare time and wanted to know what the hell had happened to my foreskin. Then I discovered Isaac Babel and baptized myself as a Cossack Jew. I was as nimble about identities as any ghetto wolf. I'd grown up like Peter Quinn, an assistant to Governor Cuomo, believing that America and the Bronx were "a country of Catholics and Jews." Protestants hid out in Pennsylvania somewhere. They belonged to that quota of dummies Columbia College had to let in because it was an Ivy League school and the Ivy League might get scared if Columbia didn't have enough Protestants to go around.

It couldn't bother me. I was living in a closet and learning my craft. I also had a practical bent. I'd enrolled in the Teacher Ed program at Hunter College and took the train down to 110 Livingston Street to get my substitute teacher's license. It was like the Kremlin down there. I sat with other candidates in a long room until some local commissar led me into the examiner's station. The examiner had white hair. He gave me a list of words to read like a kindergarten fool. I remember mispronouncing *horizon*.

The examiner smirked. I had visions of becoming a short-order cook. But my license arrived in the mail. And I began doing one-day tours at Music and Art. It was like the Count of Monte Cristo returning to his roost. My old teachers were a little embarrassed. They'd expected something better from one of their own. I'd entered the system, as they had done. I could just as well have been a fireman or a cop. My tours grew longer as a couple of teachers got sick. And I sensed the Gulag those other teachers were in. Five classes a day, with lesson plans, until the alphabet whistled in my ears and I'd have amnesia by 1 p.m. I'd forget Hamlet's father and Jane Eyre. It was crippling work. Three classes might have been human. But a hundred and seventy kids a day . . .

Stanford hired me after I'd grabbed a little from James Joyce and published a Catholic novel about an old Yiddish actor. When I crossed the Nevada border with my wife in our ancient Cadillac, I was an immigrant all over again. California seemed like some Aztec land of the sun, a country to worship in. I'd come out of the Bronx caves. I'd never seen an eagle before. Or people who were polite. Protestants, I presumed.

I settled in Palo Alto, the town of the tall tree. Bank clerks didn't snap at you. No one verified my signature to prove that I exist. A cat scratched my eye, and in the

emergency room at Stanford's own hospital I chatted with
an ophthalmologist who, as a boy in Oxford, Mississippi,
had fished with William Faulkner. He saved my eye.

I lived near an old folks' home, and there was none of
the sadness or that evil medicinal smell I'd remembered
from the homes I'd visited in New York—discount places
for the dying, where my grandparents had spent their last
days. New York had a private misery quotient that said
despair was built into the fabric of the streets. You endured it with one eye shut.

But I couldn't love California. I'd ride through Palo
Alto on my Japanese motorbike, like a golem searching
for his grave. What I missed was a goddamn New York
face, someone who slouched and talked to himself or
tried to sell you rubber bands and a hot radio. That level
of nervousness I needed didn't exist. But as a Californian,
I began to develop a paranoia about New York. After all,
I'd gone out there forever to the land of the Aztec sun.
Forever was three years.

I was warned, just before I returned to Manhattan in
'68, to keep my bathtub filled at all times and stock my
shelves with a month's worth of tuna fish because some
great army was going to blow the metropolis away, a
freaky liberation front, commandos of the world. The
invasion never happened. I filled my bathtub for a week
and then forgot about it. But I was a former "native" of
Palo Alto (anybody becomes a native after six months),
with a driver's license and an eye that shed its old
scratched "skin," and I'd absorbed some of the country's
ambivalence about New York, which really means Manhattan because no one is threatened by Staten Island or
the precincts of Brooklyn and the Bronx. But Manhattan
was a hairy monster, a vaudeville show that barked sex
and high culture. It was the place where you stuffed yourself with violin concertos and went to sin. Like the dark
side of Coney Island, a lunatic mirror that encouraged
your fantasies and let you choreograph your heart's desire—until it was time to get out.

But I wasn't a tourist. I hadn't returned with fantasies
in my head. I needed a bloody apartment. For a while I

lived in a room on West Eighty-fourth, the worst block in town. It was a junkie farm, a village of single-room-occupancy hotels, where crazies hurled garbage out the window, had their fix, and spoke to God in the hallways. It felt as if half of Manhattan was becoming an SRO hotel. And the other half was out searching for a lease. The SROs were from some distant lagoon where people were born into a state of instant distress. And we didn't stop to consider that they were also looking for a lease . . . and weren't able to find it.

The word *home* takes on a coloring in Manhattan, a particular shape, a philosophical density that it has nowhere else on the planet. Home is where landlords and tenants engage in guerrilla war, and the City becomes a constant referee. We don't have oil. We don't have diamonds under the street. But we do have land. And people have been known to kill for it, lie, cheat, and take their own fathers to court. "Real estate may be New York's most valuable commodity," says the *New York Times,* as if it had just discovered America. Real estate is what the hell New York has always been about. Until the nineteenth century, a man had no recognizable worth without a piece of real estate. He couldn't vote. He couldn't say boo. He was considered an orphan, some homeless thing who happened to be around. New York's three "perpetual children" were women, slaves, and landless men.

De Witt Clinton guaranteed the City's fate when his own commissioners introduced the idea of the grid; it was a gorgeous invention, to divide the future city into perfect lots, so that the metropolis could encourage, limit, and control the sale of all land. It was, according to Rem Koolhaas, author of *Delirious New York,* "the most courageous act of prediction in Western civilization: the land it divides, unoccupied; the population it describes, conjectural; the buildings it locates, phantoms; the activities it frames, non-existent."

But that was no problem for De Witt Clinton, who was the virtual dictator of New York. He resigned from the U.S. Senate after he was appointed mayor of New York in

1803. The office was a creature of the statehouse, which Clinton controlled. He served ten years; during some of that time he was also a state senator and lieutenant governor. He ran for president in 1812, while he was still our mayor, and helped conceive "Clinton's Ditch," also known as the Erie Canal. But that town he envisioned with its ghostly grid of streets may have been his one perfect achievement; it stimulated the growth of real estate like mad, although the dictator didn't invent land speculation. The Dutch had been speculators long before De Witt Clinton. But that magical city now on the map, with its contradiction of finite space and an infinite future (because of Clinton's canal), started a frenzy of buying and selling that's never stopped, and helped turn New York into a city of realtors and renters, castles and slums. The poor just couldn't compete for a parcel of land, not along a grid that was like a realtor's dream, a giant Monopoly board.

The first modern slumlords housed the Irish in hovels and made a quick buck. It was an open marketplace until World War II, when the federal government created a system of rent controls to curb wartime inflation. These controls were meant to disappear when the vacancy rate climbed above five percent. But it never happened in New York.

Forty years after the surrender of Japan, the vacancy rate in New York is a touch over two percent, and closer to one percent in Manhattan, which means landlords and renters are in a killing mood. The perception each has of the other is filled with an endless rage. Landlords see most tenants as squatters in their buildings, and for tenants most landlords are "one notch above child molesters."

New York is like a nation apart in matters of real estate. Homeowners are an invisible breed. The City has eleven percent of *all* rentals in the United States, one million nine hundred thousand units; and they're going more and more to single women and men. The notion of a "family" is disappearing from New York. "Children," says

former *Times* columnist Sidney Schanberg, "are slowly becoming an endangered species in this city. The predomi-
nant household is either single or childless."

Young children are particularly absent from our
streets. Eighty-eight percent of the City's households
don't have a child under six. New Yorkers are growing
into Bartlebys—isolated beings. The average City household contains 1.9 people. In Manhattan it's 1.5, "the
lowest figure for any county in the country except for a
county in Hawaii—Kalawao County—that serves as a
leper colony."

But lepers or not, New York isn't unique. Paris is un-
dergoing much of that same movement toward isolation.
Paris has "fewer couples, fewer families, more rich people, more old people, more people, especially women,
living alone." French statisticians talk about "the rise of
solitude" in a city where the average number of people in
a household is shrinking to New York's proportions.

A similar thing is happening in London, West Berlin,
Los Angeles—the family, as we know it, is becoming one
more fossil of big city life. And the phenomenon of Columbus Avenue suddenly grows poignant and begins to
make real sense. Yuppies? Gentrification? The young rich
arriving like barracudas, ripping a neighborhood down,
turning it into a row of restaurants and boutiques, where
the window becomes almost a mystical enterprise, a frame
for everything—the desire to be discovered, protected,
seen. That stasis of the window, the transformation of
people into mannequins along a dreamlike boulevard, is
like a ritualistic dance without steps, a courtship rite in
which people look but seldom touch. Columbus Avenue is
a perpetual mating season where people never marry. It's
a rich person's Times Square; white instead of black and
brown, but equally anonymous. A voyeur's paradise,
where a desperate need to rub is frozen into the landscape and nothing is finally risked. One more boulevard
for isolated beings.

Like any New Yorker, I've been so obsessed with a "home," and the fear of losing it, that I managed to push the homeless as far as I could from my skull. Sure, I've seen all the bag ladies, but I could accommodate them into whatever psychic safety net I considered mine. They had a sense of territory, even if it was a few bags in a shopping cart. They could locate order out of disorder, and that comforted me . . . until I began to notice bag men (most of them were black). I couldn't stay settled about these bag men. Was it a simple matter of maleness, the bag men hitting closer to my own private turf? Perhaps. But they seemed more like vagabonds than the bag ladies, reckless with their shopping carts, disordered, without territorial integrity. I didn't have to spin reasonable webs. The homeless were everywhere, and I couldn't hide from their plight.

They were on the front page of the *New York Times*. City shelters. Grand Central Station. The Hotel Carter. Koch had announced that he wanted to shelve the homeless in mothballed Liberty Ships. "We're checking to see if we can get the Federal Government to give us a Liberty Ship. . . . We would house people overnight on the Liberty." Or vacant aircraft carriers. The navy did have a fleet in mothballs. But it wasn't going to lend out that fleet to Ed Koch. None of the ships was available as a hospice or a hotel.

Koch shrugged and considered trailers, but no one seemed to want the trailers around. There was a lot of grumpy talk in the City Council over the idea. Jerome X. O'Donovan, Democrat from Staten Island, declared it was okay to put a trailer park in his precincts, providing that all the homeless were residents of Staten Island. That wouldn't work, said Edward L. Sadowsky, the council's finance chairman. Staten Island would have to secede if it wanted its own trailer park.

The situation was becoming macabre, a grim parody of the metropolis, in which people were shunted from invisible aircraft carriers to invisible trailer parks in some kind of fairy tale—except that the people in this fairy tale weren't without a prince. The homeless had a lawyer, Robert Hayes, and he took on the whole metropolis in their behalf. A narrative began to build around the man, though he never sought publicity for himself. He was counsel to the Coalition for the Homeless, a resistance fighter in the land of Ed Koch and the Human Resources Administration. He'd obliged the City to offer safe and clean shelter for every single man and woman who requested it under what was called "the Callahan decree."

Callahan became a rallying cry for the homeless. But who was Callahan? He didn't have much of a biography. World War II vet, short-order cook, alcoholic, and homeless man. Died in 1983: he was found one night on Mott Street. Callahan wasn't an aimless drifter. He had a coterie of friends. And he was the mayor of the Bowery, a homeless Ed Koch who understood his turf. He knew that the Men's Shelter at 8 East Third Street, the City's dispatch station for homeless men, was neither safe nor clean. It shipped men out to barracks and hotels that were little better than hovels. Callahan sued the City and won his case with the help of a Wall Street lawyer who was still in his twenties at the time. Robert Hayes.

"He became my guide to the Bowery," Hayes said of Callahan. "There were tricks to learn. If one sneaked into a mission at the right time, you could get a bowl of soup and avoid the sermon. He knew about the bathrooms in the courthouses. He knew which grates blew dry heat; he knew park benches that were, well, pretty safe. He had the pride and the sense, back there in 1979, to avoid the Men's Shelter except in the dead of winter."

Hayes didn't disappear after the Callahan decree. He left the firm of Sullivan & Cromwell and devoted all his time to the homeless. He became a gadfly *and* Goliath, attacking, stinging, and taking on the golem, Ed Koch. The mayor wasn't the easiest of enemies. He loved a good fight. He'd gone to the Men's Shelter and ladled beans. He was providing more beds. And he had a game room built at East Third that was like a poor man's Waldorf,

with chess pieces and Ping-Pong balls. But for Hayes
nothing would ever be enough. He embarrassed the Human Resources Administration, forcing it to allow Hayes's own people to inspect the City's nineteen shelters and all the hotels where homeless families were housed.

"If we knew the homeless as human beings, doing the bare minimum would not be enough," Hayes told the *New York Times*. And he'd touched upon a troubled nerve. In a city where "home" was a permanent obsession and a gnawing wound, it was better not to think of the homeless as very human. Because you didn't want to rub that wound. You might fall into some dumb fever if you had to imagine yourself without a home. A kind of funny curtain went up, a soft screen, and you satisfied yourself with a little song. *They're street people. They have nothing to do with the rest of us.*

I went to see Robert Hayes. He was the politest Goliath I'd ever met. Couldn't conceive of him badgering City lawyers like some Roy Cohn of the underclass. He didn't snarl. And he didn't have Roy Cohn's aggressive stance. He wore a sweater to breakfast. He looked a little ruddy under the coffee-house lights. It was half-past seven in the morning. He had an English muffin. I had toast. A typical power breakfast. But there were no contracts to sign.

The idea of a coalition began during "the purge of Madison Square Garden" in 1980. The Democrats had come to town. It was the year of the Carter debacle. The Republican candidate, Ronald Reagan, would soon visit Koch's mansion and make the Democrats scream. But the golem knew what he was doing. He liked to give Carter a bit of heartburn. And he was also intending to capture the Republican line in his November bid for reelection. Koch was everybody's mayor. And he didn't want Democrats or Republicans to think that hobos ran the Garden. There were about a hundred and fifty homeless men and women "living in the environs," and they might bother the conventioneers and embarrass Koch. So the mayor decided "to weed the Garden." But he hadn't counted on Robert Hayes, who helped establish a refuge for the homeless in the churchyard of St. Francis of Assisi. The mayor's plan misfired. He'd "put hungry people in the spotlight." There was a soup kitchen a couple of doors from Madison Square Garden, where the pols delivered speeches about poverty in the U.S.A.

Hayes wasn't really organized. He had a band of "students, saints, loners, and lots of Mother Teresas." But NBC had sent a crew from the *Today* show to talk to the homeless, and Hayes had to identify his little band. He scratched his head. "Christ, what's our name? . . . Coalition for the Homeless."

And that was the birth of a nation that's been at war with the City ever since. Hayes describes it as "a healthy tension. . . . New York does a lot for the homeless," he admits, "but more has to be done . . . there are interagency squabbles and rank incompetence . . . you have to criticize, and the criticism works against you in terms of government."

The coalition was incorporated in 1981. It has a tiny warren of offices on East Twenty-second, with a makeshift sign on the door. The sign is dotted with hearts. There's almost a savage innocence to the place. Pamphlets, old desks, wild-eyed volunteers. It wasn't like Koch arriving at City Hall, creating whirlwinds around him. Because the mayor's energy is fierce, and City Hall is a constant show, with Miss Puerto Rico one minute and ship captains from Castile the next. Hayes slipped into his office like a ghost. I still couldn't picture him in court. But he'd become a legal magician after he left Sullivan & Cromwell.

For the first time, thanks to Robert Hayes, homeless people could enter a voting booth. Federal Judge Mary Johnson Lowe had ruled in the coalition's favor. An address was an ambiguous and arbitrary thing: the homeless had a constitutional right to vote. They could declare whatever address they pleased, so long as they considered it "permanent." A park bench would do, or a lamppost, the Bronx Botanical Garden, one of the City's six hundred thousand street trees, a handball court, Herman Melville's grave, a restaurant in Bath Beach. . . . The significance was enormous. It was like the breaking down of the old property laws. The court had declared that you didn't need a "home" to exist; no man or woman was defined, or made any more human, by an address.

Callahan wasn't suffering from delusions when he called himself the mayor of the Bowery. Those streets were his. And like him or not, Koch's enormous power came from the fact that he considered the City a grocery store and would spend only what the store took in. But other people also had ideas about Koch's grocery. One homeless man, Harold, sat down on Eleventh Street, claimed the sidewalk, and said: "My home is New York City. . . . I live here like everybody else."

[3]

"There's twenty thousand people in emergency shelters, and either two or three times that much in the streets," Robert Hayes told me during breakfast. "There are more and more homeless . . . a twenty-five to thirty percent increase in the last five years, a tripling in homeless families."

He'd just had another encounter with Ed Koch. Three hundred homeless men and women were parked in Grand Central during the bitter cold of February '85, until a few of the "briefcase people" had been hurt and Koch ordered the terminal closed at night. The three hundred didn't go away. They lived in the steam tunnels under the station and near the borders of Grand Central. And the coalition rented a van to feed them every night. "But the police are touchy, because the mayor made a stink."

Hayes feels there's no mystery about the homeless. It's a matter of housing, or the lack of it. "It's an impossible housing market . . . there are more kids under sixteen living with their mothers in emergency shelters and barracks, in cots and cribs, that look like Louisiana refugee stations during hurricanes."

For Hayes it was "a chronic crisis ... you can't talk about job training when someone has nowhere to sleep and is hungry." The City schools were treating shelter kids like lost refugees. At one Brooklyn shelter "kids are kept in separate classes to avoid disruption" because they were constantly "coming in and out" of class. "Separate but equal went out some time ago," says Hayes.

"Politics is played with these folks' lives. It's not an intractable social problem. There's game playing by politicians of every party."

I wondered how long he could dance in the political haze. Didn't he ever feel like giving up?

No. "It's enraging, but you try not to burn out ... someone died of malnutrition in Grand Central."

I mentioned Koch's plan to put the homeless in mothballed ships. "It's like a crazy parable," I said. "The City's affairs are becoming a piece of absurdist fiction."

Hayes didn't agree. "As bizarre as some of these things sound, I would take them seriously because things are so desperate." He talked about abandoned luxury liners and appeals to Greek ship owners. "The City pays through the nose for these welfare hotels" (as much as three thousand a month to house a single family). "The boom times have no effect on the poor." They couldn't compete in a housing market where the middle class had no place to go and was gobbling up all the railroad flats that were left.

People lucky enough to have an address tried to dismiss the homeless as disturbed shadows, a collection of misfits and the mentally ill. It wasn't so. There was "street-induced psychosis" because the homeless "were missing sleep all the time." But our conception of the homeless was distorted by the need to shove them into a shadowland of crazies and alcoholics. "Alcoholism is a smaller and smaller piece of the puzzle ... without housing nothing makes sense. Psychiatrists paid by the state are doing counseling for the homeless on park benches." It's housing, housing, housing, Hayes says.

"The shelters stink no matter how good they are. . . . " The poor were shoved from place to place. People were "avoiding the poor, the unsightly, the unpleasant."

And part of this was the mayor's fault. "The mayor is nuts in his own way. He gets obsessed on issues, and obsession leads to paralysis." But nothing could really change the shelter system. "Half of the homeless feel the streets are safer. The shelters are dumps . . . degrading."

The homeless weren't Robert Hayes's invention. He hadn't abandoned Wall Street to worry over a fable. He'd sensed "a disaster situation, like the wartime period"; these were boat people who hadn't come out of any water, citizen refugees.

And what were the boat people at the City shelters like? Ten percent Latino. Sixty percent black. Nearly a fifth of the boat people were white. Four out of five had never married. Less than fifteen percent had a genuine drinking problem. Only ten percent had come to the shelters from an asylum, a hospital, or a jail, which destroys the myth of the shelters as a kind of foxhole for the crazy. Twenty-five percent had lost their jobs. Fourteen percent had been kicked out of their homes.

Home.

Court-ordered evictions have been climbing in the metropolis year by year. Twenty-eight thousand in 1981. Over thirty-three thousand in 1983. And these evictions have their own ghouls, the City marshals who carry out the mandate of the courts and are paid a fee for every eviction. "To make money in this business, you got to do volume," said one particular marshal. Our golem mayor tried to get rid of these ghouls. But the marshals are protected by state law. Some of them earn over a hundred thousand a year in that eviction mill they control.

But the ghouls didn't create the crisis. There's been a terrible loss of housing stock, a loss of SRO hotels, and no matter what the City does, it can't provide enough apartments to house the poor. It slips deeper and deeper into the housing hole.

"It's like the ship is sinking," said David Beseda of the coalition. "The women and children are supposed to go first, but the lifeboats are already full with women and children, and they're leaking, too."

I'd heard horrendous tales. Security guards beating up the homeless, buying sexual favors, selling drugs. A two-year-old girl kidnapped from her cot at a shelter in the Bronx, molested, and returned the next day, like some toy. The director of social services at the Hanson Place men's shelter in Brooklyn wrote to the *Times* that the City's shelters were "dangerous for the residents and staff members alike. . . . Security in the shelters is a low-priority item in a low-priority program." There were a lot of stabbings and fights. "Grand Central Terminal is safer than the shelters. . . ."

I had to see for myself. But I couldn't walk into the shelters without a monitor's badge. And a badge wasn't such an easy thing to get. The coalition had to request a badge from some goddamn agency. Took weeks for my badge to come through; and when it did, I was an official monitor of the Coalition for the Homeless, empowered to visit men's shelters in the City's domain, check pipes, linen, and toilet seats, ask if meals were coming on time. I felt like an inspector general. All I needed was a commissar's coat.

Of course the coalition wouldn't let me wander in alone. I might have disappeared in a Brooklyn armory, become another homeless man. My mentor was Mark Bullock, a young blond volunteer from Ontario, who lived with two other volunteers in a blasted neighborhood of the Bronx. Mark was the coalition's liaison man to the men's shelters. He visited each of them as often as he could. He was a strange bird to me, without anger or that Jewish angst the City had adopted, like a permanent twitch. Koch had it. So did the Mafia dons and the old men of Chinatown. But there wasn't the slightest twitch on Mark Bullock, not one Jewish vein that pulsed. He was kind and calm, the man from Ontario.

I was wrong about Mark. He did have a good deal of anger behind that soft Canadian mien. He wasn't a shouter, that's all. He lamented the horrible waste of lives in a system that finally didn't care. The City was supposed to find housing for the people it sheltered. "The housing placement is a joke. There's no place to put people." The bureaucracy says, "Go and find an address." But there is no address. People have become invisible to the various agencies. The homeless are "without history" to them.

We took the subway and a bus up to the Franklin Avenue Armory in the Bronx. It isn't an active fort like the Seventh Regiment Armory at Park and Sixty-sixth. The Seventh still has generals running around. Homeless men lived on the third and fifth floors, but sometimes they went AWOL and drifted into the Armory's restaurant, which has a reputation for its prime ribs. One of the homeless tried to hawk Duracell batteries to a general and was thrown out of the restaurant. But there were no generals on the heights of Franklin Avenue. It was an armory for homeless men in the middle of a Bronx desert, with uprooted railroad tracks, odd debris out of some current stone age, and the grim monoliths of Claremont Village, a ghost town the City had put up. Gangs of young men roamed the sandless dunes, kids from Claremont, dropouts who preyed upon the Villagers. One Villager, an ex-merchant marine, declared: "If I stay out late, come home and the elevator's gone, I catch a cab and go to a fleabag hotel or to a friend's house. Going in those stairwells, with the kids in there, it would be suicide."

That was the brotherhood surrounding the Franklin Avenue Armory. The shelter had opened in September 1984 without much fuss. No one screamed about having homeless men in the dunes.

The security guy at the front door didn't bother to look at our badges. This was home country for Mark. He was recognized right away. Mark had warned me not to scribble too hard in the presence of these Franklin Avenue men. They'd been studied as if they were a band of freaks. "The first thing they ask is, 'Are you a cop? Are you a reporter? Are you a graduate student?'"

So I tried not to be too much of a voyeur. Or a judge. I had my monitor's badge. I was inspecting the premises with Mark. It was a barracks with row after row of beds, and who the hell was I to write parables and sermons about the men in their beds? They had lockers. They had linen. It was a home. It had its own established order. A TV set, a pool table, men sleeping in that afternoon twilight of a fort. We'd come a bit too early. The house wasn't full. But I saw enough. A man sitting politely on a bed with his girlfriend (women weren't allowed inside the shelter). A transvestite roamed the barracks, following us in and out of the johns as Mark checked for hot water. The water was cold. "Hot water comes and goes."

A group of men clustered around us. They'd gone to the circus with the shelter's recreation leader and had just come back. "I felt like a kid again," one of the circus group said. He was a black man who looked about fifty. I'll call him Bob. "Recreation been goin' down all right."

Mark asked him about breakfast. Food had its own mechanical laws on Franklin Avenue. Bob couldn't grab a muffin off the stove. There wasn't a stove at the fort, which had to depend on trucks dispatched from the central station at East Third Street. Breakfast often arrived at noon. That was the way of most bureaucracies. But Bob had had his breakfast at the circus.

He caught me scribbling inside my pocket. "Hope you're not marking down no dynamite." And he went back to his own circus group, while we inspected lockers and sinks.

"There's a lot of stealing," Mark said. "The staff steals from the food supplies." There'd been complaints about a guard at the Atlantic Avenue shelter, and some dick from Human Resources raided the guard's locker and found it stuffed with food . . . and a second locker stuffed with clothes. But it wasn't a big deal. Somebody was always pulling on the poor.

Franklin Avenue had a floating population. Men might come for a day or six months. "There's no program, no plan. . . . Guys are released from Riker's Island with a token to the Men's Shelter. . . . Nothing was done to help them get out" of that hopeless shuffle from institution to institution, whether it was a jail, hotel, shelter, or juvenile facility.

But Bob had gone to the circus that day. He had a bed on Franklin Avenue. And if the guards fleeced him, he could always get another bunch of shoelaces from the Human Resources Administration. The despair of Franklin Avenue wasn't the rows of beds like tombs on a converted drill floor. It was the recognition of how difficult it was to make a home in New York City. Took all your power and all your wits to hold on to an address.

[5]

The transvestite followed us to the front door. And that woman who shouldn't have been inside the shelter got up from her boyfriend's bed and paraded in her leather pants. People hardly noticed. I was beginning to feel like a long-time resident of Franklin Avenue.

I walked Mark home. He lived on Sherman Avenue, a couple of blocks from where I'd lived—1296 Sheridan—when I was six. It was my family's one excursion into the West Bronx to find a more exclusive address.

We passed the Park Avenue railroad tracks, with Claremont Village to the right, like a permanent brick storm. We went up to Findlay Avenue and the Daughters of Jacob Geriatric Center (it used to be called a hospital and a home), where my maternal grandfather had lived and died with baked apples on his windowsill. In the photograph I have of him he wears my face. He was much more gentrified than my father's father, the apple peddler. But I never knew his name or what he did in America. He died of a cerebral hemorrhage, like FDR. He was a young man, sixty-nine. What the hell was he doing at the Daughters of Jacob? And the only history I have of him are those baked apples on a windowsill, circa 1942.

I left Mark off at Sherman Avenue, climbed 167th Street, and was amazed to see the Kent, where I'd discovered *The Mark of Zorro,* still a movie house. And I took my old walk from the Kent to 1296 Sheridan Avenue. It was a puzzle not even Proust could have answered with all his recollections of cracks and corners. Because Sheridan Avenue made no sense. There was garbage in the courtyards, broken, littered streets, but the houses themselves were in the Grand Concourse tradition: a bit of Art Deco, a stone lion here and there, a fountain that had become a junkyard. There were boarded windows for half a block, and then a house that functioned perfectly well, with lattices in the windows, plants, a roof of lovely tile embedded in the brick.

Was it really rent control that had murdered those other houses? What secret did this landlord have that the others lacked? The Bronx had a fundamental weakness, like a chronic tear along its spine. It had become a way station for one immigrant culture to the next. And it had no fabric to give, no internal rhyme. It's always been occupied by golems and ghosts that trickled in and trickled out.

I stopped at 1296 Sheridan. Ah, the building was alive. I saw a face in a window. The courtyard was like a choppy sea. A pretty girl watched me taking notes. "You can mark this down as a fire hazard," she said.

I passed my old school, P.S. 88, where that Irish teacher had pulled my hair because of my misfortune with the English language. The school had once been a firehouse. Behind the gate I could see a full valley of wasted buildings—ghost factories, hump after hump of blackened windows, like some madness of industry determined to destroy people's houses.

Houses and homes.

ten

THE WORLD ACCORDING TO KOCH

[1]

All rivers run to Ed Koch. At least in New York they do. And in half a dozen other countries, cities, and continents. Koch loves to stick his nose into everything. He's like a chess wizard who has one line of defense: attack, attack, attack. He's been fighting with the UN for years. Called it a confederacy of cowards. And he's taken on Jesse Jackson, Jimmy Carter, the FBI, the Mafia, the homeless at Grand Central, the *Village Voice*, and the sovereign state of Bulgaria. "What Bulgaria has done to the Turkish minority in Bulgaria is a sin," he said to a panel on apartheid at the UN. He's made the solar system his personal territory, along with the planet of New York.

A cautious man could hide behind his commissioners. But not Ed Koch. When he sought legislation to pull homeless people off the street during a cold wave and keep them for seventy-two hours, he was warned it was unconstitutional, and the mayor said, "If that's true, and I'm told it is, the Constitution is dumb." Ah, what other mayor in the world would have dared admit that? Every point of opposition with Koch becomes a military affair. And the mayor has his strategies, his battlefield plans.

If Jesse Jackson comes to town and declares that the homeless don't have a chance because "the inn is full," Koch dances in front of the TV cameras with fury on his face and tells the Reverend Jackson to mind his own flock in Chicago, where the inn is twice as full.

Koch thrives on controversy. He's not the forgiving kind. As Norman Mailer has said: "This is a town where people love to get your jugular. That's why Koch is still mayor. No one can get his jugular."

Koch personifies, like a monstrous pimple, the worsening relations between Jews and blacks. Rather than soothe tempers, he's gone deeper into the storm. But it's not a storm that Koch himself created. Jews and blacks are the twin American bugbears—the image of something less than human. Jews have tails, according to the old popular legend, and blacks are soulless greedy children who love to live on welfare. And both managed to perform a curious dance in this country, as bugbears often have to do. In New York City, with its populist dreams, it was almost an alliance. But within the ghettos themselves, where blacks and Jews sometimes lived as "near" neighbors, that alliance was shaky, if there was an alliance at all.

Morrisania, where Koch was born, was one of the black-white ghettos, with the blacks living on the south side of Crotona Park. There was almost no contact, no communal life . . . a bit of anger, suspicion, fear, and a lot of name calling. *Negro* was only a word you could find in a history book. And if a particular journalist is shocked when he hears Koch refer to blacks as *"schvarzes,"* then that journalist should have been to the East Bronx, where blacks were always *schvarzes*. The Italians were guineas. The Irish were micks. And the whole gentile population was that mysterious tribe—the goyim. *He eats like a goy* was the most popular Yiddishism out of my past. What the hell did it mean? Could the whole Christian world have rotten manners? That Yiddish remark was a mingling of racism, ignorance, and village lore, a reflexive desire to locate an enemy and put him down. It grew out of pogroms and God knows what. But the czar hadn't come to Crotona Park, and the devils weren't such devils anymore, at least not in the boroughs of New York.

But the Morrisania Jews weren't the only ones caught in that racism of the lower depths. We were kikes and sheenies—killers of Christ—to the parochial school kids and for the black gangs of Crotona Park South we were the Draculas of the ghetto, white Jew motherfuckers who sucked blood and exploited people . . . when we didn't have a dime. That litany of name calling, the curse of one tribe upon the next, sprang from a narrowness and pain that marked all the ghettos, a desperate need to find the right phantom to explain one's ills. Because if there weren't phantoms out there, you'd have to look for one inside yourself. And that's where pathology began, the gnawing self-doubt, the wound of ghettos with street lines—roads rather than walls.

Of course Koch shouldn't have talked about *schvarzes,* but Koch is Koch. He was angry that evening, the journalist recalls. He was having one of his periodic feuds with blacks. And he's not genteel, like John Lindsay. He's the first mayor of the lower depths we've ever had. Abe Beame was also a ghetto brat. Born in London and raised on the Lower East Side, Beame has a civility that Koch will never have. He was a teacher for sixteen years. He ran City Hall without a single shout. He turned Gracie Mansion into a docile doll's house. And when the bankers screamed at him during most of 1975, he was much too civil to scream back. He allowed the metropolis to become a ward of the state, an irresponsible child.

The City sat in its own apocalypse for a while. The middle class suffered along with the elderly poor. The Bronx lost ten square blocks a year to its own internal ravage. Brownsville grew into a jungle garden. And then the ravaging stopped. The City started to recover, almost like a magical show. But there's been permanent damage.

The terrible loss of housing created an army of homeless people. And the blacks and Latinos, who'd suffered along with everybody else, were recovering least of all. The City's "blue collar" was gone. Blacks couldn't enter a market that had disappeared. The fiscal crisis had created its own catch-22. Blacks and Latinos could no longer start their lives without an education, and the City couldn't seem to educate them at all.

That's the mantle Koch inherited from Abe Beame. And because he personalizes everything, the City's problems have become Koch's crusade. The homeless weren't Koch's invention. But he has to ladle beans as if the shelters were his own living room. And if black or white journalists and pols attack his programs, Koch sees this as an attack upon himself, and that "incredibly thin skin of politics" begins to show. He swears as if all his First Amendment rights have been denied. And he has to stand naked, naked as Ed Koch.

But even at his worst, that naked man has considerable charm. There is no one he caricatures better than himself. He's a tall Woody Allen, with a mean streak. ". . . I get the bends when I have to leave the City," he says. He's like Zelig, Woody Allen's phantasmagoria of himself—the creature with such an inner fright, he takes on the protective coloring of whatever is around him. Koch is the ultimate chameleon. Visiting Texas, he puts on a ten-gallon hat and instantly "looks like Lyndon Johnson." And he also worries that his lizard-skin cowboy boots will "make my feet pointy." He poses with a human-sized toy pelican from the New Orleans World's Fair, and suddenly the pelican looks more like Koch than Koch himself. On St. Patrick's Day he puts on a shamrock tie, calls himself O'Koch, and you'd swear he's more Irish than anyone in the parade. In Egypt he dons a desert hat, sits on a camel, and becomes Lawrence of Arabia—our own Ed Koch, the guy who couldn't bear to leave New York. He loves his job, but he also knows: "Every day is dangerous."

He was born "poor and Polish" in 1924. His mom and dad had passed through Ellis Island as teenagers around 1910. Koch lived at 1660 Crotona Park East, two blocks from where I spent most of my childhood. His dad was a furrier like mine. But he went bankrupt during the Depression, and the Koches moved to another ghetto, lived with relatives in Newark, nine people in two bedrooms. His dad operated a hatcheck concession in a Newark auditorium, and Ed Koch worked there too. It was like a tale out of Dickens. Young Koch had to beg for tips.

The family moved to Brooklyn in 1941. Koch sold shoes part-time to support himself at City College. He joined the army in 1943, crossed Holland with the Timberwolf Division, fought like any good soldier, and was discharged when he was twenty-one, "a decorated sergeant." He entered law school, lived at home, became a lawyer, struggled with his career, and moved out of his parents' apartment in 1956, like a belated bar mitzvah boy. From that moment on, politics became his entire existence. He bumbled, he fell, he intrigued, he maneuvered, without much natural charm. He yapped, he slouched, like a young balding grandpa. No one figured him for much of a career. But the baldy loved to campaign. He was the magical rabbi of Greenwich Village. A clumsy Jewish duck in the days of the Kennedys and John Vliet Lindsay.

He had no forebears to invent, no links with another country or another past. Asked to trace his lineage, he said, "Well, I think the best I could do is back to Ellis Island."

His roots were inside that brick castle, which made him as modern as the City itself. He had no hobbies. He knew nothing about sports. He's the golem of politics, single-minded, obsessed. He was a kooky congressman, an ultra-liberal in a conservative house. He got nowhere in '73, trying to run for mayor. He was a man without constituents. He didn't have the money or the machine.

It was different after the fiscal crisis. For the first time his very Jewishness had become a virtue. The City was scared. It searched about for its roots and sought an ethnic tribal leader. Koch was coached, trained to sit on a chair without his ass sliding onto the floor. He went around with Miss America, Bess Myerson. It was like a scene out of a fairy tale. The Jewish princess and the slouching congressman.

Koch won. He rode a City bus to his coronation—and was as isolated as he'd ever been. But he was the mayor of seven million souls. There wasn't a single other mayor, not even the Little Flower himself, who was so absorbed with the substance and the style of his job. Ed Koch had finally grown out of his bar mitzvah suit, but in that "graduation" he'd altered the idea of mayor from a half-potent being who was the slave of bankers, unions, and a grim bureaucracy to a guy who ran the town. It was Koch's grocery. And he was the one who decided what the store would allow and what it wouldn't. He angered blacks. He angered liberals. He angered advocates of the homeless and the poor. The golem had risen out of the Depression. He'd watched his father's business go to ruin. He'd been a hatcheck boy. And *his* store wasn't going to depend on anybody's largesse. He slept in the mansion. He snored. His life was New York . . . and New York. He didn't vacation in the Hamptons, or have a summer home, like La Guardia did. "Other people go out of town," he said. "I go to my apartment."

[3]

I got to the golem through Dan Wolf. I didn't know Dan, but my girlfriend knew Dan's wife. The four of us had dinner at the golem's favorite restaurant, the Peking Duck. Dan wasn't on Koch's payroll. He was the golem's special adviser, confidant, and sidekick. Their friendship had started when Dan was editor of the *Voice* and Koch was a bumbling commando in the Village's reform move-

ment. "Can I have lunch with the mayor?" I asked Dan.
"Why not?"

Dan understood from the beginning that I was a Bronx
Iroquois, with a bit of anarchy in my blood, and might
criticize the grocery store. But the mayor didn't mind a
little trouble. And how could Dan hope to keep apart two
kids from Crotona Park?

I waited a week and called Dan at Koch's office. I could
have lunch with the golem that afternoon, June 13, 1985.
Koch was to give a speech at a Latino trade fair inside the
Seventh Regiment Armory, the same armory where the
homeless were housed on the third and fifth floors while
generals mucked about, avoiding homeless guys who peddled Duracell batteries. That was the lunacy of New York.
Nothing was isolated, nothing stood alone. The pieces
always fit into an unpredictable puzzle.

Had a problem at the fair. I couldn't get in. No one had
issued me a pass. "Ah," I said, "I'm with the mayor."

The golem's advance man looked at me. "Do you have
proof?"

"Dan Wolf," I said. "Dan Wolf."

And I was ushered into the fair. I chatted with the boss
of Expoferia '85, who wanted to "expose" large companies to the Latino market in New York. I walked past
the feria booths: White Rose, Pepsi, Coca-Cola, Cham-
pale, AT&T. . . .

The golem arrived. There was a wind around him, like
an energy wall.

"Alcalde," people said. "Alcalde de New York."

Koch climbed onto the platform. The feria boss affixed
the longest title I'd ever heard to a man's name. It
sounded like Koch was Don Quixote, Sancho Panza, the
moon, the sun, and the mayor of all the people. Alcalde.
He pecked Miss Turismo de Puerto Rico, "opened" the
fair by cutting a ribbon, and suddenly he wasn't Ed Koch
of Ellis Island. "I couldn't be mayor of New York if King
Ferdinand and Queen Isabella had not sent Columbus. . . . I am a direct descendant." People clapped. Koch
stepped down from the platform, was serenaded by a
mariachi band, and the whirlwind went out the door.

Dan Wolf stood on the armory stairs. I got right into the golem's car with Dan. The golem couldn't decide where to eat. We passed a Broadway sign of Sylvester Stallone as Rambo. Koch intended to see the film. "I love violence," he said. So do I. But we still hadn't found a place to eat.

"Neary's Pub," the mayor said. He'd met the publican in Rome, during Cardinal O'Connor's ordination, and had promised to visit the pub. So the car took us out of Rambo country and east to Neary's Pub. Neary marveled for a moment at the waltzing figure of Ed Koch. "For a man I met in the Eternal City, he's a man of his word." He was proud to have the golem in his pub. "I said, 'If we don't get him out of Rome, he'll be the mayor of Rome.'"

And Neary was right. Mayor. Cardinal. Pope. Not even Zelig could acquire a habitat quick as Ed Koch, who'd been Queen Isabella's nephew half an hour ago.

Koch talked about his trip to Ireland with Dan. He'd stayed with Maureen O'Hara. One of my knees began to twitch. A phantom out of my childhood, Maureen. I fell in love with that Irish bitch soon as I saw *The Hunchback of Notre Dame*. She was Quasimodo's sweetheart, Esmiralda, the loveliest wench in all of Paris. Charles Laughton had died, his tongue thick in his mouth, thinking of Esmiralda. I'd have gone out to Hollywood in my teens, looked for O'Hara, but one of the film mags insisted she couldn't be with a man outside her own unhappy marriage.

"Ed, is she still beautiful?" I asked.

"In your mind," he muttered, eating his lamb chop.

He discussed the martyred life of Mayor Koch. "I really run the City. My enemies can't abide it. . . . There's one guy in charge. I have fired twenty commissioners and deputy mayors. That's never been done." But the golem didn't torture himself about it. "I sleep the sleep of the just."

Neary came around with a brace of Irish coffees on the house.

We gulped the coffee and ran. A guy at the bar waylaid Koch, grabbed the golem by the hand. "I'm a Republican and I love you."

The golem stood on his heels and turned to me with mischief. "I'm twice as tall as Abe Beame."

We were in a hurry. Ed had to deliver a speech before the Council of Senior Centers and Services. "Lights and sirens," he said, and his car began to break through traffic, crossing Central Park in one gigantic push, with the banshee whoop of the sirens and the twirling red lights that glimmered through the glass and made us look like Martians on a mission. We sat author to author, the golem and I, and he talked about the chapter he'd added to the paperback edition of his book. "I take on Arthur Schlesinger, the prick." Schlesinger had helped start a "Dump Koch" campaign in '81 and had trashed *Mayor* in *The New York Review of Books*. Koch glanced at the speech he was supposed to give. "Who can read such a dull speech?"

We passed Jimmy Breslin outside the park. The mayor's body preened like a zaddik on a magic quest. He had a glint in his eye. "Jimmy Breslin, that dog. We could have run him down." He'd been feuding with Breslin for years. The golem wouldn't have bumped Breslin. But he loved the sheer pleasure of thinking about it—another battle in his head. He glanced away from the window.

"Did the Irish coffee pick you up? I'm slurring my words."

We arrived at the Jewish Association for the Aged. The golem got out and gave a terrific speech. He bent, he shivered, and wove fable after fable on his feet. And then he started to field questions from the audience of blacks, whites, and Latinos: women and men who must have been seventy at least. An old man stood up. "I don't know if you're responsible—"

The mayor's bald head wagged above the microphone. "If it's good, yes, if it's not, no. . . ."

We got back into the car and went downtown. He

talked like Ivan the Terrible about his tactics. He believed
in the written word. He wouldn't telephone his commissioners. "I put it in writing. . . . It terrifies people. They
know the clock is ticking."

We arrived at City Hall. I was in the middle of the
whirlwind now. No one stops you when you're a member
of the mayor's party. The golem, Dan, and I whisked past
the portrait of Mayor Impellitteri outside the Blue Room.
The portrait had a green look. Koch stared at Impellitteri. "He's dead."

It was like a note of warning, that green look. Dan
advised the golem. "Ed, you ought to get your portrait
painted now."

"I'm ageless. My father died at eighty-seven. There's a
portrait of my father at Gracie Mansion . . . people think
it's Ed Koch."

He disappeared into his office. I stood around with
Dan until the mayor invited us in. Four Spanish admirals
from the *Juan Sebastian de Elcano* had come for a courtesy
call. Koch played Voltaire.

"I like the king. He's a good man."

The admirals seemed like children in Koch's presence.
They had to keep looking up. They were intimidated by
his height.

The admirals left and the golem was stuck with a chore.
He had to investigate a claim that his staff had destroyed
a precious mural at the State Supreme Court Building.
We marched over to the court. Miss America met us in the
rotunda, Bess Myerson, his commissioner of cultural affairs. A tall, ravaged beauty wearing an exquisite scarf. I
sensed no particular warmth between her and the golem.
But I wanted to say hello to Bess. Somehow, she'd crystallized the acceptance of those Yiddish wild beards in the
New World. She was a kid from the Bronx who'd gone to
Hunter College. And when she'd become Miss America in
1945, she wasn't just another gorgeous girl. She'd "played
the Grieg piano concerto and some Gershwin on the
flute" for the judges at Atlantic City. And it was as if an
entire population—every *citizen* of Ellis Island—had been
redeemed in the simple stroke of Bess's coronation. One

of their own children was Miss America, and immigrant New York had become part of the country. It was the sort of symbolic act that can't happen twice. Koch's own coronation was almost like an end point to Ellis Island. The first golem mayor and the last of his kind.

We walked upstairs to the missing mural. Koch only had to take one look at the ravaged wall. "Bring me the head of the Philistines."

[4]

Met the golem one more time. Dan and Rhoda Wolf had invited my girlfriend and me to spend the Fourth of July with Ed Koch. The golem's car came to pick us up. We were guests of the grocery store. The Fourth of July was capital to any mayor, and Koch didn't intend to sit alone inside his mansion. We were going up to Gracie for a bite and then down the river in a police launch to watch the fireworks.

We arrived at the mansion and were let through the gate. There was another mansion out on the lawn, with carpeting and a cupola. It was the residence of Archie the dog. Archie belonged to Mitchel London, the mayor's fifth chef. And he had the tallest doghouse I'd ever seen. It wasn't built out of fancy. Archie was a big dog.

The mayor had a mezuzah on his door. I couldn't tell if the mansion had been consecrated or not. But a Jewish grocer had to live in a Jewish house. He said hello and barked about the food Mitch had prepared. "Try the gazpacho. It's great."

Rhoda Wolf took us on a tour of the house. She fell in love with some antique wallpaper. "This is the wallpaper I want for my vestibule," she told Ed Koch.

"For twenty-five thousand you can get it," said the golem-grocer, who can always come up with a price.

We passed the breakfast room. Napkins and all had been placed for the golem's next breakfast: it was single setting, in a niche with a view of the lawn. We visited the

Beame bedroom, done in bright yellow. The Beame toilet was twice as big as that yellow room. There was a curious combination lock on Koch's own bedroom door, a battery of buttons. We couldn't get in, of course.

But we captured Koch's study. There were photos of Reagan on the wall, and a cartoon of Koch in a sedan chair. The caption read: "How'm I doin'? I'm the king. Hi there." Then we waltzed down to the mansion's little museum. But no one could find the light switch. The theme of the exhibit was "Merchants to Mayors," which could have been the golem's rallying cry, but we had to stare at darkened walls. The mayor smiled when he discovered our confusion. "I give them ten-minute tours . . . we're saving lights."

We went out onto the verandah and I asked Koch to tell us the definitive tale of how Archie had been kidnapped. The mayor's attention grew: he was an artful spider, Ed Koch, builder of webs. "It's clouded in mystery," he said. "The dog disappeared. We get a call from a garage . . . the dog was in Queens. The dognappers hadn't realized whose dog it was. We called Queens, didn't get a clear answer, but we heard a dog barking. The cops went out to Queens, and the man said, 'Don't hurt me.' The guy had surrendered the dog to the *Daily News*."

"Ed, that ought to be in a novel."

"I can't write novels. . . . I don't have an ear for dialogue. You can't have five people talking like Ed Koch."

I laughed, because the golem was in my territory now. "Ed, you might be an avant-garde writer without knowing it."

We got around to Koch's defeat in his bid for the governor's chair. "I'm not unhappy," he said, rocking his knees on the verandah and pointing to the strip of blue sea beyond his grass. "You think Cuomo has anything like this?"

"You should run for president."

He rolled his eyes as if he were looking at some madman out of the City's wards. "People are ambivalent about New York."

"But they love you anyway." And it was true. The City

registered Democrat, but it was becoming a Republican town. And Koch could have sat like an Iroquois (his favorite Indian) on top of both political parties. And that had been the motor behind his gubernatorial bid, I suspect. He wasn't thinking Albany. He had the White House in his head: the first Jewish president. But Albany wasn't the route. Koch had a problem. City Hall was a graveyard. No one, except De Witt Clinton, a hundred and sixty-nine years ago, had ever gone from mayor to anything else (and Clinton wasn't an elected mayor). Wagner tried. Lindsay tried. But they didn't have the raw, rabbinical power of Ed Koch.

Without that disastrous Albany battle, he might have bided his time and campaigned for president from City Hall, co-opted everybody, and grabbed the Democratic-Republican line. He has a face you couldn't forget. It's packed with mischief and grief. He's like a mourner in the New World—and a Mafia don. The Manhattan cowboy. It's hard to tell where he'll go next. The golem was a late bloomer. His career might not start until he's eighty-five.

We went down to the river in a tidy caravan: Koch, the Wolfs, Holly Wemple (the golem's photographer), Bill Rauch (his press secretary) and Bill's pregnant wife, my girlfriend, Mitchel London (with a picnic basket of wine), the golem's nephew, and another couple or two.

A little girl spoke from the grass: "Hi, Koch."

It was difficult to climb down into the launch. You had to climb backward. The mayor said to Rhoda Wolf: "Make like it's a fire escape."

The cop on the launch seemed a little embarrassed about our hard times with his boat. "The mayor can do a lot of things, but he can't get the tide up."

We struggled. We survived. All of us entered the boat—except Archie, who had the mayor's grounds all to himself.

The golem waved to people on the shore. "Bye, I'll be back." And we took off, with another police boat on our tail.

"The mayor gets a lot of protection," Dan said.

The golem was at sea. He stood on a special chair, giving his thumbs-up sign to the crowd along the river. I didn't hear a bloody boo from all the buildings that lined the water. The crowd had come for the fireworks and to cheer the mayor in his churning boat. It had nothing to do with glamour. He wasn't a decorated doll. He was a big baldy with a slouch. But there was a kind of electrical touch between him and the people on the shore. It was as if they had thrust a persona upon him, brought the golem to life. And it wasn't about a rich, white waterfront in love with a rich, white mayor. The waterfront wasn't so white or rich.

Koch wasn't seeking a constituency on his ride down the river: he was like a bald river god, come to celebrate the Fourth of July. He stood with a glass of wine. And people cheered from benches, balconies, windowsills, roofs, and the rails of a highway that had been closed for that festival of fire. The mayor loved being loved. No other mayor would have dared risk such adulation: it was absolute, reckless even, the risk of the lonely. The golem didn't have much "merchandise" outside of being mayor. The job had become the man.

We passed the Chrysler Building, with its corrugated metal hat caught in the sun, like some piece of a futuristic city out of a forgotten time zone. We passed the Empire State Building, lit with July. We passed the Water Club, people waving from that restaurant on the sea. And then there was quiet. We docked in a little cove and climbed out of the launch.

The mayor winked and smiled at me. "That was nice." He hadn't given up his wrinkles, all those laugh lines. Our caravan marched behind the mayor, who was slouching again. "Don't get lost," his advance man said to us.

The fireworks shot out of three barges in the river. The barges belonged to Macy's. Ah, the big grocer couldn't escape department stores. Macy's and Ed Koch. It was like Star Wars on the East River, an eternal Times Square. I wondered if Douglas Leigh was the wizard behind it all because this show had Leigh's clarity of light . . . and a fabric of colors that wove itself into the American flag; the flag disintegrated and spread into an orange mushroom that could have signaled the end of the world. The golem watched and politicked in that orange haze.

The mushroom disappeared, and rockets were falling down onto our necks. Suddenly it was Spinoza's sky, a patterned world of comets that revealed all sorts of truths I wasn't privy to. The golem was gone. The rockets snaked and dropped into the sea like dust. And then Spinoza's comets bumped in the sky and I could feel a shake in my heart. The hell with orange mushrooms. Macy's had fabulated the world all over again with bumping comets that provided their own glue—and miraculous, sudden daylight, worms wiggling in the sky.

One of the barges transformed itself into the Statue of Liberty, with sparks bursting out of the torch until you had the feeling that nothing couldn't be duplicated: planets, Miss Liberty, Mayor Koch. And New York was the dream that dreamt itself, a monster out of the Old World that could never rest, spitting ideals like fireworks—liberty, brotherhood, and zero-coupon bonds. Wall Street, Chase Manhattan, the Seventh Regiment Armory were only phantom stations on a grid. Events, statues, streets were nowhere as powerful as the myth of New York: smoke and fire out of a fabricated torch, a bit of neon on the river. That was the New World. Henry Hudson, sailing for Britain's enemy, the Dutch, went looking for China and landed in a river channel that was as enigmatic as himself. Ah, if he'd had a proper witch on board, she might have told him that he'd discovered a future Shanghai, a port city that sailed along its own grid and had the power to reinvent itself. The City's principal sailor was a golem called Ed. Neither Henry nor the British and the Dutch could have conceived a character like Koch, whose clay was formed on a funny little island with a brick house that processed immigrants from the Old World and turned them into something never seen before: wooly ducks with all kinds of peculiar notions. New-Yorkniks. Americans, after all, who loved the Fourth of July like any Nebraskan or native of Tennessee.

We climbed onto another launch and got to South Street. The police pilot let Rhoda Wolf fiddle with the foghorn. Koch had Holly Wemple pose him with the entire crew. He didn't walk like a whirlwind tonight.

"Ed, you're slowing down. It's the first time I've ever been able to keep up with you."

He shrugged at the sky. "I'm getting old."

We ate at Roebling's, inside the seaport's central barn. We were in the midst of a water crisis. The city's wells were dry. And the waiter asked Koch: "Do we have a special dispensation?"

"Sure," the golem said. "Everybody can have water."

The mayor started munching. Then he stared down at his plate. "It's dangerous bread."

We talked about presidents, Carter in particular. "I tortured him," Koch said. But the golem got along fine with Ronald Reagan. "I like him as a person. I didn't like Carter as a person."

"Who did?"

"Rosalynn Carter," he quipped, eating some of that dangerous bread.

The grocer saw his destiny. He'd had to administer brutal cuts to balance the budget. "I will say no to anybody." And he'd developed a grocer's ideals. "The job of government is to provide a climate for jobs and profits for the private sector." Otherwise, the grocery would starve to death. It couldn't feed the poor with empty shelves. The grocer "wasn't allowed to spend money" he "didn't have."

Ah, I could have argued with him and said the government ought to play Robin Hood a little, but my grocery would have sunk under the seaport like another Atlantis.

I asked Ed about that abysmal Times Square project, with Philip Johnson's mansard roofs.

"The project will go through . . . when I came in, there were plans to turn Times Square into Disneyland."

I'd have preferred a gigantic Ferris wheel to grim glass

roofs, but I didn't tell him that. I ate my swordfish and shut up.

He went downstairs and people mobbed him. Holly Wemple took pictures of Ed and the citizenry at the seaport. What the hell could you make of Koch? "Most mayors are police and fire commissioners," says Richard P. Nathan of Princeton University, "but in New York the mayor was the king of a great social enterprise." And Nathan laments the loss of that enterprise. Particularly in Ed Koch. "There has been a culture of doing a lot for people and caring about people. That boiled over in 1975. The symbols and rhetoric of Lindsay and Beame— there's a decided difference today." I'm not so sure.

When did this king of social enterprise come about? The first "modern" mayor was Jimmy Walker, who was a bit of a thief. Yes, there were reform mayors like Seth Low. But they're part of some prehistoric history. They didn't give a damn about the wild beards or the blacks. The reformers yelled a lot, touched a little power, and disappeared.

City government meant Tammany Hall. The mayor had always been Tammany's toy. One exception was that irascible man, William Gaynor. His years in office are mostly forgotten, but he's famous for the 1910 photograph of him with a bloody cheek and coat: a maddened City employee had shot him in the neck when Gaynor was about to leave for Europe on the *Kaiser Wilhelm der Grosse*. Gaynor served for three years with that bullet in his neck. He had to whisper instructions to his clerks. But who can recall Gaynor and his bullet?

Our memory of mayors in the metropolis starts with Jimmy Walker. He was perhaps the most popular mayor of all time. And the enterprise he presided over best was Jimmy Walker. He gambled, loved beautiful women (chorus girls in particular), borrowed money from Arnold Rothstein, and ran City Hall like a judge dancing on glass: he preferred nightclubs to any place on the planet. While scandals rocked around him, Jimmy Walker was elected again. As the bits and pieces of corruption moved closer and closer to his tail, Walker resigned and ran to

Europe. But he could have been elected mayor from the Tombs because Beau James had a style and a handsomeness of habit that the populace adored. *He looked good.* And it was Walker who began the myth of mayor as uncrowned king. The people of New York would have given him a crown to wear, but he was too busy dancing to bother with a hat.

La Guardia was his opposite: short, scruffy, and scrupulously honest. But the jazz age was gone. Fiorello couldn't afford to dance. He had to govern a town that was toppling into bankruptcy. New York owed almost as much as "the combined debt of the forty-eight states." It was like a prelude, a dancing lesson, for 1975. La Guardia lacked his own Oliver Cromwell (Felix Rohatyn), but he did have bankers sitting on his tail. "The banks had complete control over La Guardia," remembers Paul O'Dwyer, who lived through those times as a young immigrant lawyer. La Guardia "reduced the salaries of employees at the direction of the bankers." He was only rehearsing for Abe Beame.

But La Guardia wasn't a clubhouse pol. He was an independent, feisty mayor, who loved a good donnybrook. He was also incredibly naïve. He introduced the first public housing program in America, envisioned the end of all slums, the death of tenements in New York, and the beginning of model worker villages "with a window in every room and a bit of sunshine in every window." The sunshine turned to soot. And there are more slums now than La Guardia could have ever dreamed, slums within the slums of his worker villages. But at least La Guardia had a quest.

He wasn't the typical reformer, who existed in an abstract universe. He was a mayor of the streets. He helped soothe a city that had grown desperate, a city where Benjamin Ward had to stuff his pockets with doughnuts or starve. La Guardia roared like a righteous lion, beat down Tammany Hall, attacked chiselers, ate slot machines, and ran his own democratic kingdom: he was fire chief, police captain, magistrate, mayor. But he relied on Robert Moses and that was his terrible fault: Moses had become a second mayor, with an invisible jurisdiction that wasn't subject to law. Moses hadn't been elected, and he couldn't be dismissed. He gathered his own hegemony on Randall's Island, his own state within a state. He was lord of the Triborough Bridge. And he treated La Guardia like an infant. He'd tack La Guardia's name to some obscure playground, allow him to switch on the underground lights to a swimming pool so that the Little Flower looked like a magic man, and let him cut the ribbons for a new housing project. Moses destroyed neighborhoods that happened to intrude upon the bridges and tunnels he intended to build. He shuffled populations without the least thought to individual lives. And La Guardia learned not to fight with a pharaoh who could "provide him with a seemingly inexhaustible cornucopia of political benefits. If he did fight, Moses would humiliate and defeat him."

The pharaoh couldn't be voted out of office. And no mayor or governor could remove him without cause. He wasn't a crook. He just happened to crush an awful lot of people who got in his way. Administrations appeared and disappeared, but Moses was a constant commander in chief, with a flag over Randall's Island—and a seal. "Triborough had its own fleets, of yachts and motorcars and trucks . . . its own generals and admirals. . . . It had its own constitution."

He ruled thirty-four years. No one, not La Guardia, not Bill O'Dwyer, not Impellitteri, not Robert Wagner, really challenged him. Lindsay tried, and the pharaoh laughed in his face. It took *two* Rockefellers, Nelson and David, the governor of New York and the chairman of the Chase Manhattan Bank, to wrestle Robert Moses to the ground. And the old man was seventy-nine.

Herman Badillo is eloquent on the subject of Robert Moses. "Basically," Badillo says, "he was full of shit." By building Lincoln Center, Moses "destroyed an Hispanic community" and created a house of "culture for the upper classes . . . he filled in the Hudson River for the rich" and left pockets of doom for those who couldn't afford that culture.

"No mayor shaped New York," says Robert Caro; "no

mayor—not even La Guardia—left upon its roiling surface more than the faintest of lasting imprints."

But Robert Caro wrote *The Power Broker* before the arrival of Ed Koch. He couldn't have anticipated a golem. Robert Moses was an aristocrat with one pair of shoes, a pauper most of his life, living off the largesse of his mother, a guy who "would have been happy with a ham sandwich—and power." Koch would have demanded a bit of Peking duck. He didn't have Moses's cultivated sloppiness. He hadn't gone to Oxford and Yale. He was a graduate of Crotona Park. He wouldn't have tolerated a second mayor, a builder with a royal seat on Randall's Island. Koch would have seized that empire with a rash of helicopters and hurled that old man into the sea.

And it's to the shame of New York—its mayors, its builders, its bureaucrats, its journalists who puffed him out of proportion—that Moses wasn't stopped. He created ghost towns, left a deep scab along the spine of the Bronx, coveted Ebbets Field and the Polo Grounds (for housing projects), until he helped convince the Dodgers and the Giants to leave town. He would have crippled lower Manhattan, bulldozed Gramercy Park and most of Greenwich Village if he'd had the chance. And here's what Roger Starr (author of *The Rise and Fall of New York City*) has to say about Robert Moses. The man was "unbearable," Starr agrees, but he "was also courteous to a fault with the aged and charming with children. He removed his hat in elevators when any female person entered, regardless of age, race, or previous condition of servitude."

Removed his hat on elevators. That's how Moses will be remembered.

Koch doesn't wear a hat. He's not so courteous. He's crazed at times. His critics declare that he "cherishes vindictiveness—getting even—as his chief political currency." Yet what other "currency" does a politician have? Koch has to get even to stay alive.

Wagner was much more compassionate than the golem. But he hated controversy. He saw the ruin that Moses did

in East Tremont, eating up a neighborhood out of spite:
the pharaoh could have "bent" his highway to preserve
that section of the Bronx. With all his compassion,
Wagner permitted the neighborhood to die. He was, perhaps, a legitimate king of social enterprise, but he was also
a better man than mayor. Wagner wasn't courageous.

Lindsay was. A patrician knight. "We wanted and
needed a patrician, a special kind of WASP outlook," Paul
O'Dwyer says. "We hungered for it subconsciously." And
the patrician knight was going to change the social order,
educate the poor, and get rid of the slums. Wagner was
cautious enough, and clever, to know that the slums were
like a dark looking glass to miracle Manhattan—the land
of those who'd never make it. And Wagner understood
ethnicity: that lower-middle-class drive. The patrician
never did. It was evident from his first encounter with
Michael J. Quill, head of the Transport Workers Union.
The patrician was hit with a strike immediately upon entering office. Quill called him "Mr. Linsley . . . a boy in
short pants." And the patrician couldn't quite recover
from Quill.

Then came Beame, the clubhouse kid, who knocked
Badillo off in the primary. Badillo had a temper. He
wasn't sweet. "He's a most quixotic person," Koch told me
at lunch. "I like him . . . an innocent he's not. But he has
an innocent smile, a sweet smile, that belies his toughness." Toughness wasn't enough. The pols and a white
ethnic majority pulled Beame in. Ah, but what a different
scenario there might have been in '75, with Herman
Badillo as mayor. He'd have screamed back at the bankers. And the metropolis might not have become a sick,
dead dog. But Badillo wasn't there. And Beame person-
ified the bumbling mayor. Different people have different stories to tell. Felix Rohatyn says that bankruptcy
would have been like "slipping into a tepid bath and slash-
ing your wrists: You might not feel yourself dying, but
that's what would happen." And I believe him.

But Badillo insists that the bankers themselves promoted the crisis. "The bankruptcy deal was to protect the

bankers. The newspapers made it appear that it was a great victory . . . the solution of the crisis was screwing the middle class and the poor."

Wagner and Lindsay had been performing the same tricks that Beame did—shuffling short-term notes to cannibalize the grocery store. But conditions were much more volatile during the days of Beame. There'd been an oil embargo. The biggest banks were losing fortunes on their foreign loans. And Nelson Rockefeller was no longer around to placate them: he'd gone to Washington to be with Gerald Ford. A border war had developed between Jersey and New York; companies were escaping across the river, and the bankers began to feel that the City didn't care. It was too involved with administering services to a populace that had become more and more Latino and black. There was a loss of confidence in the very nature of the City itself, a monster that was eating everybody's blood. The banks began "dumping" City paper in '84, and the crisis began.

Enter Koch. The golem slouches, sings. He's not tailored to perfection, like Jimmy Walker. He doesn't have Lindsay's chiseled features. And he's not an invisible man, like Abe Beame. He's Ed Koch, an army of selves and souls. Funny, morose, he's formed from City clay. He's gruff, mysterious, obscene. A born grocer, tight with money. He conjures up indignities like a vengeful toad. "Those of us who served in World War II remember the Salvation Army provided coffee and doughnuts free, while the Red Cross charged." He can curse and also bless. He'll grunt into a TV camera about New York's rotten marriage with the UN, and on the very next day he'll smile and swear "that this match is a good one . . . this match is forever."

He becomes J. Edgar Hoover and prepares a list of the City's hundred most-wanted crooks, including a lady bandit with a star tattooed on her cheek, and announces that they're "dangerous people, the dangerous of the dangerous." And then tapes are discovered, proving that the golem can't be bought. "Billy the Butcher" Masselli, a meat packer in the South Bronx, declares with all the clarity of Spinoza's suns and moons: "This is a thing here that, I don't think this Koch you could do business with him on this level with this guy. He's not that kind of a guy, maybe the people around him I say yes, but in himself, he's a [expletive deleted]," according to the *Times*.

That missing word is "mother——," Ed Koch told the *East Village Eye*. And if the Mob considers Ed Koch a motherfucker, how bad can the metropolis be?

Yet Paul O'Dwyer understands what New York does to its mayors: "The mayor is the choice of people who want that person at that time. Each mayor has a feeling that they will survive, then time and the town destroys them and their ambitions."

It happened to Lindsay, it happened to Wagner, it happened to La Guardia even. Will it happen to Koch? The City has never had a mayor like him before—a huge protean clown with a grocer's resources and an endless appetite, a golem out of the dust, indestructible—and it will never have a mayor like him again. . . .

Suddenly it's 1986. Several days after Koch's third coronation. And something weird happens. Donald R. Manes, the portly borough president of Queens, is involved in a mystery show. The cops chase his car off Grand Central Parkway early in the morning of January 10th and find Manes with a bloody wrist and a bloody leg. Koch visits him at the hospital, pecks him on the forehead, and blames it all on Donny's liquid diet (Manes had been trying to lose weight). But no "killer diet" could cut Donny's wrist. Then Manes comes out of his dream state and declares that he'd been kidnapped. The kidnapping involved a hooker who wrestled with Donny in his car. A hooker? Who cares, says Koch. "He's still my friend."

But not for long. Manes is linked to a scandal in the Parking Violations Bureau. It's the old story of extortion and graft, with Manes in the middle. The mayor turns on Donny and calls him a crook. Donny dances a bit on a very thin wire and then steps down, admitting that he himself was the phantom hooker. The business in the car had been a suicide attempt. But the scandal widens, and Koch is caught in a black hole. The man the Mafia couldn't buy is now sitting on an administration that's been selling off pieces of the grocery store. And O'Dwyer's words seem more and more prophetic. Can *time and the town* really destroy Ed Koch?

The mayor has a conundrum on his hands. He can't distance himself from a bureaucracy that's like an enormous heart of darkness. The bureacrats work for him. He can scold and scream, wave his scimitar, but he isn't battling Bulgaria now. He has to cannibalize his own store. City government has always been a killing ground, a grim, gray machine. How can Koch wield a scimitar when half the City's sewer inspectors have been arrested for taking bribes? (And Manes? Despondent and sick, he stabbed himself in the heart on March 13 and finally managed to kill himself, as City, state, and federal prosecutors were moving closer and closer to his tail.) And one begins to understand the perils of being mayor in New York. Ed Koch is an acrobat surrounded by entropy, performing in a world of stupefying arrogance and sloth. He appeals to us because he does get involved with everything. The golem makes that grim machine a little less grim. "I'm gonna be around for at least another four years," he tells his critics. "So you have to live with me. I'm kind of like the 800-pound gorilla."

King Koch.

eleven

MADNESS, MYTH, AND MELANCHOLY

[1]

Whenever that melancholy hits, the rub of New York, the realization that we're a town of such cruelties, with the relentless rise to fortune as our biggest theme song (we're all Mafia men), the grasping, the clutching, the hundred little dances we do to keep alive, from eating Stresstabs to showering and shaving, shrugging off the ghosts of sleep, the dread of a girlfriend gone . . . I put on my shoes and walk to the Chrysler Building. The whimsy of that steel top, a witch's hood with a host of triangular eyes, is enough to shake the sadness out of me. It's a reminder that New York once had an element of pure play, the belief in its own modernity. The building is slightly mad, with hubcaps in the walls, gargoyles borrowed from old Chrysler machines, and futuristic cars trapped in a design of brick. Chrysler has an innocence, a total trust in the passion and good of industry, that's all but gone. Its entrance looms like a church celebrating the dream of the automobile, and its own breathless future, as Walter Chrysler saw it.

But I didn't put my socks on for an automobile show. The lobby of the Chrysler Building is one of the great hidden spectacles of New York. It's not a tourist attraction, a hangout, a home for shopping-bag ladies. It's a spa for melancholics like me. You enter into the softest light you could imagine, as if bulbs had suddenly become quiet worms under glass and you'd gone into a land of burnished red marble that bore no resemblance to the streets. It's like one of Roxy's movie palaces: a dreamscape with elevators, a clock, and solid chrome. The clock is set in a dark wall, and its illumination is almost the drama of time itself—as if the dials were inventing each moment, and Chrysler caught you, held you in its sway. Nothing jars. Nothing hurts your system. Elbows never bump along those walls. You've fallen into the design and you're cradled there, crazy as it seems.

There's a letterbox with an Aztec eagle, and the most beautiful elevators in the world, with laminated wood, green lights on top, and the picture of a pharaoh's plumed hat staring at you out of another age. I can imagine Nick and Nora Charles in those elevators, or Hammett himself, the original Thin Man. I wait, but Nick and Nora never come. Not even their toy dog, Asta.

Chrysler cured me, as it always does. It's my private sanitarium in a public place. I can walk downtown again, go about my business. But the idea of sanitariums sticks in my head. Where do the melancholics go when they haven't discovered the resources of the Chrysler Building? Is melancholy an inherited thing, passed from one bloodline to the next? Did my maternal grandfather have it, sitting in that "island" on Findlay Avenue known as the Daughters of Jacob? Is it the immigrants' disease? Because it seems so partial to our metropolis. It's where melancholy was born. Freud could have found his "wolf man" and "rat man" on our streets . . . or in Bellevue.

That's where the screamers go. I've always been curious

about that brick house on Thirtieth Street, where all kinds of "immigrants" were processed and kept. Bellevue has the most celebrated crazyhouse in existence, after London's Bethlem Royal Hospital, or Bedlam, and France's Charenton asylum, where the Marquis de Sade wrote his best works. The marquis was as lucid as hell at Charenton. And I've often fantasized how it would be to scribble in my own corner of Bellevue. I wouldn't have to cook or search for restaurants, have bloody fights with my girlfriend, or worry about the rent. But Bellevue isn't a permanent hospice. You can stay only a couple of weeks. And that's not long enough to write a novel.

But my curiosity wouldn't go away. Bellevue seemed like the natural climate of any New Yorker—the house across the road from whatever bit of sanity you had left. Bellevue has had a long career. The Dutch put up their own city hospital and asylum for those melancholics who'd lost the art of making money. But the first official Bellevue (without that particular name) was built under English rule in 1736, on the grounds of the old City Hall. The hospital was moved uptown to Belle Vue Place, near the East River, during the dictatorship of De Witt Clinton. It's been in that neighborhood ever since.

I was fortunate enough to meet Mary Guerriero, a lovely silver-haired woman who happened to be an administrative assistant to the chairman of psychiatry at Bellevue. I'd met her at an auspicious moment. The brick monster was closing down and Mary could take me inside for a look. I felt like a voyeur preparing to visit his own living room.

Bellevue Psychiatric Hospital had globes in front of its doors, like a police station, but these globes were white, and they were gone. There were scavengers around Bellevue, grabbing everything—the ghouls of an old, dying hospital. "I'm amazed these doors haven't disappeared," Mary said. But globes are much easier to shove inside an undershirt than heavy doors.

This Bellevue had been built in 1931, during the Walker administration. But according to popular legend, the City couldn't complete the job. It ran out of money and wanted to turn the hospital into a tubercular center, which could survive with a much smaller staff. But the chief of psychiatry moved all his "clients" in overnight, and the City had to capitulate. I believe in a legend like that. It takes one inspired general to defeat a whole stinking bureaucracy.

Once I stepped inside, I was startled by the house that Walker built. It wasn't a barn with nondescript floors, a lunatics' alley. Bellevue had all the grace of a country inn. Marble benches, marble floors. A king could have lived there . . . until it fell into decay. Bellevue was like an old haunted house, another Ellis Island, with vaulted ceilings and decorated stairs. The doorknobs were gone. The sconces were gone. Bellevue's bones had been picked. "It's a crime to see it deteriorate," Mary said.

She showed me a spot under the vaulted ceiling where you could shout or sing or cry and your voice shot right back at you. I stood on that spot, said, "Hello, hello," and heard the roar of God come down from the ceiling.

I followed Mary like a mouse.

There were murals under the walls, accomplished by the patients themselves, and art students had been hired "to chip away at the walls," but the students got lazy, and those murals were never revealed. There'd been no general to supervise them in this falling house.

We couldn't get into the auditorium, which had a magnificent ceiling, two stories high. I never saw it. Mary didn't have the right key. "Everything is locked." But those gravediggers always managed to get in. They took light fixtures, pieces of the banister rail. They'd have stolen the murals too, if the art students had ever dug them out. An iron cage had been put in the stairwell, like a prisoner's roost, because "patients jumped from the top floor." I wasn't surprised. A hollow staircase nine stories deep could beckon whatever devils were inside you and this house.

We went up to Mary's old office, paneled in the richest wood. That office opened onto the auditorium roof, which functioned as a balcony. But the balcony saw little service. Doctors couldn't picnic on the roof or wander too far: patients would throw things out the windows.

One afternoon Mary felt a wind behind her. Someone fled past her desk, through the window, and over the side of the building. "He was escaping," she said, "not trying to kill himself." Bellevue had a series of setbacks in its walls. And that escape artist hopped from balcony to balcony until he made the street . . .

Mary adored the nest of rooms where she'd worked in old Bellevue. It had an elegance of detail that couldn't be found in any modern building, even though the walls leaked, "the pipes had never been cared for," and globes were missing from the solid brass chandeliers. "They don't make them anymore. They're one-eighth of an inch off the standard, which is typical for Bellevue."

I asked her why the psychiatric hospital had become one more ruin. A patient had brought a class-action suit against the City because "there were no medical people on the premises." The courts had ruled in his favor. Most essential services relocated to modern Bellevue by the middle of '75, but the war had begun between the bankers and Abe Beame, and New York didn't have the money "to finish the four floors that were to be devoted to psychiatry."

Old Bellevue lingered under the courts' death sentence. The City had to complete its psychiatric construction by September '84. "The judge said you can't admit any more patients to the old hospital." Bellevue began to discharge patients, until the hospital shrank to less than thirty souls. Mary's office "closed forever" after 5 p.m., on Thursday, August 15, 1985, and the psychiatric center moved to modern Bellevue, occupying the nineteenth to the twenty-second floors, but the "construction was horrendous." Entire floors started to buckle. And no children could be admitted into that modern ghost town. That's the nature of New York.

We toured other parts of old Bellevue. Pigeons had flown into the upper floors. "I don't want to even contemplate what they look like." And so we held to the lower depths, the bottommost rooms and wards. Every bit of frosted glass had been covered with plastic and wood: for some reason, "frosted glass was considered a fire hazard." The medical library had to be closed down because books were stolen by students and everybody else. There was an elaborate mantelpiece in the library, with winged animals in the wood, griffins surrounding a broken clock. We stepped out of the library and entered the wards of Belle-vue. Mary had to use an enormous key to get in. The words ELOPEMENT RISK were scratched in big letters on the door. "That's a euphemism," Mary said. A lot of people had eloped from the wards.

I saw a playground for children, and it was hard for me to imagine two-year-old melancholics. But Bellevue's children "ranged from infants to teenagers." Mary mentioned "autistic babies," and my reasoning collapsed. Babies with a psychic wall around them. I had a fool's knowledge of psychiatry. I understood metaphors, myths, but walled-in babies were outside whatever artistry I had—or attitudes about New York. I couldn't invent fables any longer. I listened. I looked.

The major group of admissions, Mary said, were chronic schizophrenics. And they had no color line. White, black, Latino. Oriental too. The women's latrines had urinals, just like the men's. And all the bathrooms had an enormous tub with a wraparound curtain. I thought of Peter Weiss's *The Persecution and Assassination of Jean Paul Marat as Performed by the Inmates of the Asylum of Charenton under the Direction of the Marquis de Sade*. Charenton was right here. And I recalled that the inmates of Bedlam once challenged the entire U.S. team to a game of postal chess—and won. The mad have better concentration than we do, and more time to think out a move.

The bathrooms all had metal mirrors. Glass was too dangerous to have around. I read the scratchings on the wall. "First blood then guts and then staff infection and then death to you all, signed, Anna S——."

And I had to puzzle out a bit of Spanish. "No Es Lo Mismo Enterió Saturnilo" (It's not the same until you enter Saturn).

That was it. *Entering Saturn.* New York, Bellevue, and
Ellis Island were like wards on the same wing. Madness
and adventure. Risk. Journeys into some fanciful America. That's what New York was. Chrysler's hubcaps on a
wall. Those hubcaps wouldn't have been so out of place in
Bellevue.

Depressives, schizophrenics, attempted suicides, that
was Bellevue's population, and visionaries who talked to
themselves and might have received hydrotherapy in one
of Bellevue's big tubs. The fire alarms had to be
padlocked because children were setting off alarms "a
couple of times a day." But, said Mary, "there was very
little to burn." This hospital was all "marble and air
pockets."

There were mice all over the place, even in modern
Bellevue, but Mary had been assured that mice meant rats
weren't around. She worried about that constant route of
the patients, "the old revolving door." Patients would be
discharged, then returned to Bellevue, and discharged
again . . . on a ship to nowhere.

There'd also been celebrities around. Woody Allen had
used the front of the old building for *Zelig.* And, Mary
said, "they brought in the guy who shot John Lennon . . .
never saw such security. Policemen with shotguns looking
up at the windows."

We crossed the old complex of buildings and went to
the modern Bellevue, visited the adolescent unit, which
hadn't opened yet because of the buckling floors. It was
like walking on a sea of wood. The patients all had a river
view, while the doctors and staff were stuck in the core of
the building. Mary had a windowless closet, after working
in an office of wood with her own high balcony. "The
doctors ought to go and live with the patients," I said.

Mary received a lot of calls from actresses and actors.
*We're playing schizophrenics. Can we come in and observe the
patients?*

"This is not a theater," Mary had to tell them. She remembered the first time she saw the patients. "They're as
sick as anyone with heart disease or diabetes . . . it's very
sad. They walk around hearing voices all their life."

Ah, I wanted to tell her how a novelist feels. Had enough voices in my skull to repopulate the old Bellevue.

"They're their own worst enemy, not anyone else's," she said. In the wards one day, she felt a hand on the back of her head. A woman patient smiled at Mary. "'You have such beautiful hair.'"

We strolled along the corridors, from window to window, like a great city carnival. One window seemed to pull in the entire downtown depth, an endless jigsaw of buildings, like brick teeth, brown and red, much more convincing than skyscrapers themselves because there was an infinity in those bricks, a heartland that could never really be absorbed. Mysterious, mean, and bountiful.

[2]

Couldn't stop thinking about an article I'd read in the *Times*. It concerned black kids in Philadelphia who hardly ever saw a white person until they entered school at the age of six. That isolation, in itself, is a form of madness, a Bartleby complex, both for blacks and whites. Ben Ward swears that no child in New York could live six years without meeting a white person. "New York has lost its neighborhoods . . . the old concept of turf is gone, except in Chinatown." A black child could get lost in Philly, not New York. What about Brownsville, where even the grass is bleak? I've walked for miles in Brooklyn, passed cave after cave, and there were no whites inside or out on the street.

Claremont Village is far more frightening than those caves. It suggests the worst despair one can imagine: the closing in of walls, the sense of home as self-imprisonment, the idea of absolute exile. Why shouldn't young black women get pregnant? The single engine they can rely on is their own body. And so we have twelve-year-old mothers. Grandmas of twenty-five. Children nursing children. Pathology? It's more like a terrible desire to claim *something* in a world that seems invisible. *I'm a mama,* says the twelve-year-old child. *The little white girl, she play with her dolls. But I can get a real live baby.* It's a dreamlike, delirious act, full of courage and craziness, stupidity, love, hate, a child's desperate need to find her own endearment . . . and adulthood. It's better than going to school, which is so removed from her needs and her vocabulary that it makes her feel even more of a child.

And now we have an epidemic of infant mothers, infant dopers, infant thieves that's like a disturbed, hateful cry. And that cry is growing louder. Because whites have moved farther and farther away from ghetto blacks and would rather they didn't exist, as Herman Badillo says.

And one night on the news I heard of a black minister, Calvin Butts, who'd supported Badillo in a bid to run against the golem, Ed Koch. The black pols, who feel most embittered about Koch, skewered themselves in the spring of '85. They were hoping to enlist the Latinos in an alliance and smack the mayor with a tough political broom. Herman Badillo should have been that broom. He's as rambunctious as Ed Koch. But the black pols decided on Denny Farrell, an assemblyman from Manhattan, unknown outside his district. A black with Irish blood, he talked of uniting everyone and had no one behind him to unite.

Butts had felt betrayed when the black pols went over to Farrell. I saw him on the tube. He did a kind of snake dance in his chair at the Abyssinian Baptist Church. He was passionate. I admired him. I called the church. He didn't know who the hell I was. "Book," I said, "I'm writing a book." Butts was a gracious man. He agreed to talk.

So I went up to Harlem to meet with the minister. It wasn't unfamiliar ground. I'd lifted weights at the Harlem Y when I attended Music and Art. I was the only white kid in the weightlifting room. But I didn't feel alarmed. I was a lifter, like everybody else, bringing out the worms in my biceps. Twice a week I grunted with Billy Dee Williams, my classmate at Music and Art. He was lithe, and I was gnarled, with little scars from my battles on the roofs around Crotona Park.

But this wasn't the Harlem of 1954. The boulevards

were dead. There was no fabric, no community I could find. One grim bar, the Harlem Moon, and houses with roofs that could have been gnawed by some gigantic rat. The church was glorious, like a Tudor fort, but it sat in a sea of ruin. There were gutted buildings, hulks across the street.

Calvin Butts wore a dark suit. He had lots of diplomas on the wall. He was executive minister of the church, in charge of day-to-day affairs. He counseled the sick and those who were in trouble. He was on the phone when I arrived, trying to calm a woman who was being evicted. I heard him talk about "the police coming in."

He was formal with me, but not unfriendly. He mentioned some *New York* magazine cover of a futuristic Manhattan that was "white, well-to-do, walled in . . . rents will not allow poor people to live on this island."

I didn't want to agree with him. Wasn't a real-estate baron. A "white" Manhattan would bring about its own beatific doom. The ultimate triumph of the grid. A city without a past. The golden grave.

I talked about that distancing I felt between blacks and whites, as if a mutual paranoia had taken hold, a grim gray line, because blacks themselves had become accomplices to a white world's unwillingness to live with them. Some dance was going on that was difficult to tell. I wasn't a bloody sociologist. I couldn't articulate theories of cross-alienation. But I did know that the black middle class had abandoned the poor blacks almost as brutally as the whites had done. To be poor and black in America was something worse than sin—it was not to be at all.

Yet Butts wasn't convinced that there was any deepening distance between blacks and whites. "The same distance has always been there because of race . . . it's a class distance. There's the same distance between whites and whites. The problem is still racism. The whites don't see it. They've been duped. They don't see it because they're doing better than the blacks."

I asked him if a couple of white "pioneers" in Harlem would help.

The minister said no. Whites coming into the community wouldn't improve it.

"But unless whites are present, the City won't cater to the needs of black people." That wasn't my invention. City services always got better when whites were around.

Butts grew angry. "I reject that. The whole system is bankrupt. It needs to be destroyed." The political reality was white on white: blacks had little to say in the machinery of government.

"You have a mayor who's popular and outspoken. The mayor could do more to change this political reality. Instead, he has done more to foster it."

Perhaps, I said. But the mayor doesn't live on his own island. He didn't invent that wall between whites and blacks. I talked about Denny Farrell. Black politicians had sabotaged their own skin.

"A black person can do the same thing a white person can do," Butts declared. "I make no distinction . . . I have to push for those persons who will change the political reality. What I believe as a human being, a citizen, and clergy person is that the racism of whites historically and presently" developed into "a need to keep black people subservient . . . it turned into hatred and distrust for blacks . . . black churches are a phenomenon of white racism."

He'd gone to Atlanta in the sixties, stood together with white ministers, and was "overtly loved" in front of the TV cameras, but as soon as the cameras disappeared, that love was gone. Martin Luther King, Jr., had tried to re-educate America, but there'd been a rejection of his whole movement in the seventies and eighties. A distrust developed among the blacks, "based upon a long history of unfaithfulness, murder . . . blacks never responded to whites out of hatred, greed." Their anger had come from rejection.

"We built your country, we raised your children. Whites have no reason to reject blacks."

We talked about the tension between blacks and Jews. Butts's voice rose from the depths of his chair, as if he were a sad ventriloquist. "The Jewish people seem to have forgotten us."

Ah, I could write a whole rabbinical report on that subject, with variations upon variations in the theme. The Jews had grown conservative, along with the Italians and the Irish. That fantasy of Ellis Island completed itself. A mad, shivering faith had come from the poor Jews, and a sense of fairness. Paranoia. Dreams. A hatred of all pogroms. But those wild beards were gone. Their daughters and sons had moved out of the old dream and into a middle class whose sympathies had created a recent American tribe: the Jewish WASP, conservative and liberal, depending upon the time and the place.

There were also black WASPs running about; a bourgeoisie that had fled Harlem for the suburbs. "The mid-fifties," Butts claimed, "was the beginning of the end. Now we're seeing the end of the end." That ending Butts envisioned was a return to some vitality I couldn't see. Harlem, in my own head, had become like the Lower East Side—a ravaged storage bin, a boneyard. However valuable the real estate, Harlem had no present tense; it existed as a historical artifact. A new black middle class might suddenly appear on St. Nicholas Terrace, but it couldn't re-create the old culture or discover a new one. You can't recycle Strivers Row.

I must have had a gloomy look. The minister smiled. We couldn't have sat together and talked like this sixty years ago, he said. "Even if we did have this conversation in 1925, nobody would publish it."

He was right. But it still wasn't much of a consolation. Blacks had traveled from one form of invisibility to another. Yes, there was Joe Louis and Jackie Robinson. But there hadn't been Claremont Village in 1925—castle-jails in the dunes.

The minister had a Southern lilt to his voice. He'd gone to school in Atlanta, but he wasn't born in the South. He was a kid from Avenue D. Raised in the Lillian Wald Houses that Robert Moses built, "across from tenements filled with Eastern Jews," and competed with blacks and whites at Flushing High School after his family went to

Corona, Queens. "I grew up with whites and Jews and Latinos. I'm not intimidated by them." He'd gone down to Morehouse College and was captivated by "the King mystique." But Butts himself was "a blending of King and Malcolm X, the genteel Southern black culture and the cold crassness of Northern political pragmatism." He'd become another kind of golem. He had the "militancy of Adam [Clayton Powell] and Malcolm juxtaposed with the nonviolent, direct action of King." He felt a need for coalition politics. "I'm not going to be pushed around."

We had to end our talk. Jesse Jackson was in town, and Butts was going to meet him at a noon rally. I liked Jackson, even after he'd talked about "heimies in Heimietown." He was a *schvarze* and I was a "heimie," and what the hell could you do? But he was the only candidate in the '84 Democratic primary who'd had passion and wit and didn't gabble like a wooden man.

I wanted to meet him. But Calvin Butts didn't offer to take me along. We were both one-eyed jacks, looking at each other with all the burdens of American history. Gladiators in an arena that whites *and* blacks had built out of the distortion of a single eye. Even if we could avoid a battle, neutrality wasn't enough. Somewhere, somehow, we'd have to look again and come to love.

twelve

THE DEATH
OF CHARLIE CHAN

[1]

Once upon a time, my Uncle Morris, the only intellectual
in the house of Charyn, took me and my brother to a feast
of Charlie Chan at the Loew's Delancey; a couple of
movies with that master Chinese detective and his
number-one son. Morris was my father's older brother.
He wasn't married then. He must have been forty and
lived at home with my grandparents on Henry Street. He
was a vegetarian. He spoke English like a baron with a
Polish lisp. And he was the only man in my life who read
the *New York Times*. He'd never solved the dynamics of
America. He was much too political to hold a good job. In
an easier world he might have been a lawyer or an om-
budsman. But he couldn't suck needles in a fur shop,
read newspapers, *and* go to college. I loved him, and also

had contempt, because my own crazy father earned more money than Uncle Morris.

But it was Charlie Chan I was getting to. I was six, and that was the peak of my career. Charlie was better than any apotheosis. He'd been given God's face. It wasn't his cleverness that really mattered, or the way he'd put down his number-one son with some aphorism that cut into my heart. It was the mask he wore, a smile so constant it couldn't be periled by pain. In one of the films, *Charlie Chan at Treasure Island* (who can be sure of the title?), the master detective is shot in the sleeve. He doesn't wince. He performs a fat man's ballet, disarms the murderer, and belittles his number-one son, without the slightest tear in that smile. He wouldn't even accept a handkerchief from the murderer's own daughter, to wrap his wound. He was the dad of dads, God playing detective in a fat man's suit. The slanted eyes were apertures, holes in the mask. Being Chinese was one more piece in God's little puzzle. But I solved that puzzle in the dark of the Loew's Delancey. Charlie Chan was Jewish.

What other god could God be?

Never had such a clear picture again. Confusion landed once I left the theater with Morris and my brother. I wasn't so certain of Charlie Chan. We walked up East Broadway, still the psychic heart of the "Jewish Street," with cafeterias, bakeries, political clubs, charities, social alliances, and the Forward Building. It was Morris's world, not my father's. It had all the juice of politics. Morris could dance in the poverty around him. He had that vision of some mysterious link between men. My father had no politics. But he could cut ermine and mink collars with the artistry of a bandit in the days before he went into business for himself and lost every dime, his little bundle in America. Morris's capital was that boiling in his head. He was a wild beard. He believed in some perfectability that was around the corner. My uncle wasn't a golem. He wouldn't concern himself with human greed.

Even then, along that Jewish spine of cafeterias and clubs, there were several Chinese hand laundries: a hint of Chinatown. Morris sang to us about the exploitation of laundrymen—the impossible hours, the impossible life. They had to live in back of the laundries, like gypsies with a hotplate. Couldn't become ermine cutters, like my dad. They had to suffer a laundryman's lot. But they're chinks, I almost said. They'd be lost without their laundries. They loved to iron. Didn't we have hand laundries in the Bronx? I'd jabber in some woeful, invented Chinese when I passed their windows. But I didn't tell this to Morris.

I looked into the window on East Broadway, saw that rooted family of husband, wife, and children in one narrow storefront. They had nothing to do with Charlie Chan.

I was an imbecile, of course. A superior little snot, seething with all the prejudices of Crotona Park. There'd come a time when I'd march to Chinatown every day, eat in restaurants where I was the only "round eye" present. The waiters laughed to see how I'd copied their habit of scooping rice out of a bowl. I loved Chinatown, the bend of its streets. It was utterly outside the grid. Swollen with tourists, yes. A kind of merchants' paradise with poverty locked into the walls. And loneliness. Where do dishwashers retire to? But thank God there were no wine bars and unisex dolls in the crook of Doyers Street.

I still didn't know a goddamn thing about the Chinese in America, or Gam San, as they called it, the Mountain of Gold. Chinatown was my exotic roost. And then that roost began to explode. There were gang wars. The Ghost Shadows and the Flying Dragons. Fiefdoms I couldn't grasp. Territorial disputes. Block associations. Youth gangs with forty-year-old boys from Hong Kong. It seemed like half the constables in the world—the Feds, the Hong Kong Secret Service, the NYPD—came together to cancel the Ghost Shadows and get them off the street.

I found another ghost shadow in the *New York Times*. An article about the death of an institution: the Chinese hand laundry. There'd been five thousand of them in New York when I'd strolled East Broadway with my Uncle Morris. Over three thousand had disappeared. One particular laundryman, David Chin, had arrived in America in 1927 when he was eighteen and wanted to become an artist. He ended up with an eight-pound iron in his fist because he couldn't afford art school. But it wasn't the simple act of working sixteen hours a day, seven days a week. A laundry war began between the Chinese and the Jews. The Chinese were driving the Jewish launderers out with their lower prices. The Jews had done the same thing to the German and Irish launderers—working harder, living in their own stores. And now they put signs in their windows, swearing the Chinese laundrymen ate opium and rats. But the Chinese prevailed, slapping down their irons, supporting wives and children in China. And they'd only been faces in a window. Chinks. I was scribbling about greenhorns, scratching my head off, and there was a whole goddamn immigration I'd missed. What could I do? The Chinese wouldn't reveal themselves to a round eye. And I didn't have a godfather on Doyers Street.

[2]

Henry Stern was my good-luck piece. The unicorn had taken me to lunch at Yankee Stadium and we sat across from a young Chinese commissioner, Rod Chu, the state's number-one tax man. I'd heard of this Chu. He was like a mandarin warrior. He'd investigated his own department of taxation, uncovered sixty-nine employees, some of whom hadn't been paying their taxes for as much as five years. Who the hell knows where the mandarin will strike next? He could investigate the Yankees or Ed Koch. We chatted with knives and forks in our hands. Told him about my book with a certain trepidation. He might dig into my royalty accounts. He didn't have an Irish-Jewish-Italian sense of politics. Only a Chinaman would investigate his own people.

He handed me his card: Roderick G. W. Chu, Commissioner of Taxation and Finance, State of New York. I brooded a couple of weeks and dialed him at his Albany office. I was crafty on the phone.

"Charyn," I said. "Yankee Stadium . . . I was sitting with Henry Stern."

"Yes, I remember you."

And we made an appointment to meet at his *other* office. Rod's people occupied an entire corner of the World Trade Center: Rockefeller's Folly. No pair of twins had ever assaulted New York in such a manner. Ruinous monoliths, they were without romance or play. They seized the sky like some hangman's dream of the twentieth century.

I waltzed down Hudson Street in May to keep my appointment with the Chinese commissioner. I arrived at the monoliths, stood in the central mall. It had no human proportions; people were like ants on a rock floor. But I felt a curious response to the towers themselves. Up close, they were sheathed in a silver skin. Light pierced that skin and traveled out to the Jersey waters.

I got off that rock floor, took an escalator to the underground concourse, and suddenly the whole apparatus made sense. The mall could have been some abstract set out of *Waiting for Godot*. The twins' engine was under the ground. That concourse had all the fury of Times Square—a constant buzz of people, without the three-card monte players, the sex shops, and the mad preachers. I felt like a hillbilly who'd blundered in off the mall, a rube from Hudson Street. There was an entire underground city I hadn't heard about. The different paths took you to subways and shops and plazas. You could have breakfast, lunch, buy a pillow or a pair of socks, and never leave that underground. Its circuitry was absolute.

I rode upstairs to Rod Chu. Had to change elevators. His outpost was on the sixty-ninth floor. I saw the full cut of the harbor from his windows. Ellis Island looked like a tiny toy land, a green dot of decoration in a valley of water. The Statue of Liberty was trapped in a wooden truss. The sea had an incredible skin from the sixty-ninth floor. The track of the ferry boats wasn't a simple churning of water. Each tub left a scar, a whitish wound that wouldn't heal. I still had clay feet. I was as much of a greenhorn as my dad. I lived in a harbor town and had no sense of the sea. Who the hell was I to chronicle New York? Christopher Columbus in knee pants. Henry Hudson's lost son. The Shanghai kid. If my parents had arrived *before* Ellis Island, in one of those English sloops, I might have become a loyalist during the Revolution, a lousy Brit. Or another bug-eyed Benedict Arnold, fiery patriot *and* a rat, with a love of beautiful women.

I sat with Rod and drank red tea. He wasn't Charlie Chan. He looked at you without a mask. Didn't feel I was sipping tea with an inscrutable tax collector. All my prejudices turned to folly. The Yids were a closed and secretive tribe, not the Chinese. All I'd ever seen were laundrymen in a window, a landscape of laundrymen. And there were no eight-pound irons in Rod Chu's office.

His grandfather had "come to the land of the gold mountain" in 1930. He made enough money to bring Rod's dad across the ocean. And Rod's dad served in the army during the war, got his citizenship papers, and "went to China as part of the occupation forces." He met Rod's mom in Shanghai. He was from the provinces, while she came from an upper-class family, but "my mother was enticed and enthralled by this dashing Chinese army man." And so the lady from Shanghai was soon a war bride.

Rod was born in Beth David, "a nice Jewish hospital," and was brought up in Queens. His grandfather would speak only Chinese with him, but Rod admits: "My Chinese is awful." He attended the UN School, which began as "a converted public school built after the Civil War." The school was tiny at the time. "My math class was me." Rod didn't feel oppressed about being Chinese. There were no pogroms in his family, no czars to insist that he was some half-human thing. The Chus were descended from the Sung empire. "There were tens of thousands of us . . . our line of the family goes back three thousand years." And I sprang out of some village nightmare between Warsaw and Kiev. Charyn was an Ellis Island name. Did it come from the word *dark*, like that Russian song, "Dark Eyes"? Ellis was the only castle I could claim.

Rod's grandfather had warned him about commissioners of taxation. "You can't take this job. Everybody will hate you." The Chinese had a traditional disregard for tax collectors. The tax collector was evil, the emperor's money fist. And Rod had been doing well. He was a consultant and senior partner at a big accounting firm. But he decided to become the first Chinese-American tax collector. "Why can't I be a good guy?" he told his grandfather. "Consultants like being loved . . . but I couldn't be an ostrich. I wanted New York tax cheats to know I was deadly serious. Only someone who's driven would be crazy enough to investigate his own people."

Who would the tax man go after next? Teachers? Writers? Musicians? We'd all have to become ghost shadows sooner or later with Rod Chu around.

Rod wasn't a "Chinatown boy." But he had explored those streets with his grandfather, "the youngest man to retire in Chinatown history" (at fifty-five). He'd walk down Mott Street and discover a hundred "uncles." Chinese families are "one degree closer" than families in the West. "First cousins are called sister and brother." And all his grandfather's friends were Rod's "uncles and aunts." The Chus had their own family association, where you "could walk in and never go poor."

But that was the old Cantonese Chinatown. And instant turmoil began after the immigration quotas were lifted in 1965. "You didn't have families coming . . . it wasn't grandfathers sending sons and bringing them in family units. People were coming alone." And they didn't have too many uncles and aunts around. They weren't from a single province near Canton. They were ethnic Chinese from all over the planet, without extended families. They had to look to particular merchant associations for "influence, safety, and power." But the merchants didn't feed them for nothing. "An immigrant comes not speaking the language, he migrates to Chinatown, is enticed by a gang organization" involved in "influence peddling, protection rackets." And now you had a Chinese Mafia in control of every single block, a mob as merchant association, with the new immigrants from Hong Kong and Taiwan as their enforcers and foot soldiers. The associations on Mott and Pell streets were "now headed by rather shady characters."

But Chinatown wasn't simply the romance of war. These gangs didn't have the only cohesion. There was the Chinatown Planning Council, which started up immediately after the lifting of the quotas in '65, and accomplished for the Chinese what the settlement houses did for the Jews eighty and ninety years ago. The planning council helped soften the terror of a new, chaotic immigration. It's a kind of Chinese welfare, funded by Chinese, for the Chinese.

But there's another struggle going on inside New York's Chinese-American community, an attempt to politicize itself. For a hundred years the Chinese in Gam San have kept out of politics. They've rarely formed alliances with other Asian groups. The Chinese still have "bitter feelings toward the Japanese" because of the Sino-Japanese War. But they had a rude awakening in 1982 when "a Chinese guy was clubbed to death in Detroit." Two unemployed automobile workers, disturbed by the growing number of Japanese imports, went after Vincent Chin with a baseball bat "because they thought he was Japanese." No one would dare convict them of murder. It was hard times in Detroit. But they were convicted of "violating the dead man's civil rights." That incident shook up the Chinese and forced them to reconsider their own mandarin posture, their aloofness from the rest of the world. "We're getting blamed for the Japanese," Rod said. "We might as well band together." And the young mandarins of Rod's generation grew "interested in forming coalitions," or "networking," as Rod says.

He doesn't deny the racism that exists among the Chinese themselves. "Everyone who is non-Chinese is a devil . . . there's the white devil and the black devil. Part of that is Chinese snobbery . . . our ancestors were running around in silk brocade while others were running around in loincloths."

But as the Chinese have begun to mingle with whites, blacks, and Hispanics, that image of the "devil" has disintegrated—at least for the younger generation. I didn't get the feeling that Rod was trying to trip any white or black devils on their income tax. And Chinese women seem to prefer those white devils to their own kind. "Virtually all Chinese women marry Americans. My sister says she would never marry a Chinese, because they're real nerds . . . they think of Chinese men as laundry workers."

Ah, we couldn't get away from the poor, beleaguered laundry worker, who'd become a disappearing icon. Yet the laundry worker had supported whole generations of Chinese; he was another one of New York's forgotten tales. Laundrymen seldom graduated to grander things. They're the ghost shadows who sacrificed themselves to build up a small nation of Chinese in America.

I finished my red tea, glanced out at the harbor with its live skin and Liberty in her wooden coat, and said goodbye to the tax collector.

[3]

No one can really name the first Chinese to arrive in New York. It's become another mythical event in a city that loves to narratize every sort of origin. Did Peter Stuyvesant plant the first pear tree in New Amsterdam? It sounds historical. That's enough. And there could have been some "lost" Chinese immigrant who grabbed a bit of Manhattan farmland and fashioned it into Doyers and Pell. Was he a sailor or a priest? One thing is certain. A Chinese junk from Canton landed in New York in the summer of 1847 with a cargo of silk and a crew of thirty-five Chinese sailors. Fifty thousand New Yorkers visited the junk to examine those sailors, who must have seemed like marvels from another planet. The junk didn't return to China with a full crew. "Those who stayed were probably Chinatown's first settlers."

Soon others arrived—stragglers from California's gold

fields and railroad workers without a job. It was a society of bachelors and married men who'd left families behind to seek their fortune in Gam San. There was an active Chinatown by the end of the Civil War, with restaurants, laundries, opium dens, and patriotic societies called tongs; the tong members started as resistance fighters in the wars against the Manchu emperors. There weren't any Manchus in lower Manhattan, and the tongs fought among themselves to claim their different turfs. But they didn't have much to divide: a few square blocks of bachelors.

The Chinese Exclusion Act of 1882 ended the flow of immigrants into Chinatown. The transcontinental railroad had already been built, and Chinese labor wasn't needed anymore. Congress didn't want all those wild Asiatics running around and ruining America. In 1888 it passed the Scott Act, which prevented laborers who'd gone to visit their families in China from returning to the Mountain of Gold. Only scholars, students, merchants, government officials, and travelers could enter. Many of these "scholars" and "students" became laundrymen and grocers.

Chinatown settled into a quiet life of poverty and territorial maneuvers among the tongs—until 1965. Mott was still the tourist mecca, but new Chinatowns appeared in Brooklyn and Queens, dominated by the same secret societies. And the area around Pell Street exploded in every direction. Noodle shops started up in Little Italy. The old, famous Garden Cafeteria, landmark of Jewish intellectuals on East Broadway, turned into a Chinese restaurant. The Forward Building was now a Chinese church. Cash began to flow in from Hong Kong and Taiwan. Chinese landlords owned Jewish bakeries.

It was like any other immigrant "madness." Fortunes were made and lost, crime and prostitution flourished, together with a sense of bewilderment and isolation. Fourteen hundred immigrants were arriving each month. There could be half a million Chinese in New York by 1990, and a million at the start of the next century. Shanghai on the Hudson.

The economics have already gone wild. Banks have failed. Gangs are fighting over the new turf. Poverty is growing, but some degree of order has been maintained by the Chinatown Planning Council. Its president is Hugh Mo, who also happens to be the deputy police commissioner of trials. The tongs like to keep out of his way; he's a tough, determined, passionate man, a street kid like themselves, and not so much of a mandarin, even though his dad had been a law professor in Shanghai who came from a family of farmers and military chiefs.

I met Hugh Mo without the usual hurly-burly of a handshake. Rod organized a dinner for us. But he had to switch restaurants at the last moment. We moved to Division Street. There'd been a gang war around that other restaurant. East Broadway was open turf. New immigrants, ethnic Chinese from Burma, had been testing their muscle out on the street. I sat and ate a ten-course meal with Hugh Mo, Rod, and several young mandarins from the Chinatown History Project, the planning council, and the Human Rights Commission. It was like a Mafia of goodwill. We talked about Old Benny and Young Benny, the lords of Pell Street. No one would be crazy enough to challenge them on their turf. Pell Street was secure.

I wanted to interview Young Benny, but he wouldn't have admired my association with a Chinese tax collector and the police department's own "hanging judge." Who could tell about the tongs? Young Benny might have had his spies on Division Street. I felt an awful lot of silence near our table, as if we were some odd caste of outlaws and social workers, with Hugh Mo as the *good* warlord. He didn't fulfill any picture I had of the Chinese. He wasn't reserved or polite with a round eye he didn't know. He babbled in a slightly flawed English. The hanging judge was a greenhorn from Shanghai. He'd been one of Robert Morgenthau's super assistant district attorneys. A trick Chinaman, a freak. He had a prosecutor's nose for crime in a city where the Chinese had constructed their own invisible wall around One Police Plaza. They took their problems to the lords of Pell, Doyers, and Mott. The tongs were the *police* in Chinatown: enforcers, arbitrators, benefactors, and thugs.

I got along with Hugh Mo; we were secret sharers of some sort—foundlings in America. We'd come from different landscapes, but our pilgrimages had ended in the same spot. Inside that winnowing town, a murderous city that ate its population to bits, we possessed those lunatic ideals, a laundryman's faith in the immigrant—that education was still possible in spite of all the bureaucratic blunders, that the murderous city was also a city of marvels. The anonymous authors of *New York Panorama* understood this fifty years ago. New York loved *and* killed, both were part of its fabric and constitution, its uniqueness among all other cities, because no other city in the world had ever defined itself by the numbers of immigrants it could raise as its very own children, "patient and furious, mad or indestructibly calm. . . . The city is their companion and their mother, their schoolmaster and executioner."

[4]

I went to that beehive brick cave at One Police Plaza to meet with the hanging judge, Hugh Mo. Had to send my shoulder bag through an X-ray machine before I could enter the inner halls. I looked at my bag up on the screen, saw the imprint of my pencil case, notebooks, etc., and felt vulnerable all of a sudden, as if the bones of my life were being exposed in that bag. What is a person's history? An old, heroic pencil case? A bottle of pills? Would the bulls behind the machine confiscate all my Valium?

I passed their little exercise and was given a sticker to wear at police headquarters. I was the guest of Hugh Mo and the NYPD. Pushed number fourteen on the elevator and rode up to the commissioners' floor. Ben Ward had his rooms on the left of the elevator bank and I went right . . . into a line of strange, almost invisible, doors. It was like waltzing in one of Kafka's dreams, without a hint of color. But I found the hangman's door. There was no knob I can remember. I pushed my way into a corridor. I saw secretaries, plainclothesmen, computer consoles.

The hangman was in his office. He had a potted tree in the corner that gave a sense of green to the beehive, those honeycombed ceilings and walls. He was Chinese, after all, in the middle of an Irish mafia that was ruled by a black PC, Benjamin Ward. That was the madness of New York. The Irish were vanishing from the City—the Italians, Jews, and blacks had driven them out of politics—but they still had a rear guard in the NYPD. The greatest functionaries in the world, the Irish were. They ran our subways for sixty years with a beautiful marriage of efficiency and corruption; now the corruption was gone, and the subways grew less and less efficient.

But the Irish hadn't come between the hangman and myself. We were a couple of old-fashioned kids from opposite sides of the map. Hugh's background was much more mysterious than mine. His odyssey was longer and harder. But the street had been our essential home: that bond delivered us from the discrepancies of age, temperament, or skin. We didn't have the old Dutch drive to become rich. We were seekers in New York City, but we couldn't have pronounced what the hell we were seeking. Some golden dust that would reorder things? Turn Claremont Village into the Chrysler Building? Move Trump Tower into Crotona Park? I wasn't that much of a magician. And neither was Hugh.

He was born in tumult, during the communist takeover of China. His father had been with the Kuomintang during the Japanese War. He was the commissioner in charge of wartime rationing and had "the power over people's life and death." He was also a professor of law at Fu Tan University. "He died during the communist liquidation."

And Hugh was a kid from Shanghai. He left China before he was one and lived in Hong Kong with his mother for three years. "She supported herself by writing novels." The family moved to Taiwan and then to Madrid. His mother wanted to get out of that "ideological cesspool of the Far East," with its constant "talk of the Big War" (between China and the U.S.).

He started in a Jesuit school at six. He was now a young man of the West. But he'd come to a "medieval country" with a lot of "begging nuns." And it was like "reliving the Civil War . . . with women shrouded in black, old veterans walking down the street with war medals, so many medals on their chest, their jackets were almost ready to fall off." And Hugh was seen as a schoolboy "from Mars . . . the total Chinese population in Madrid was two hundred." He soon became a madrileño, gesturing with his hands like any other Spaniard. "The Spaniards made me very talkative." Students and pilgrims adopted the talkative Chinese boy. "I was unusual to them. I looked like a white tiger."

But his mother couldn't earn money in Madrid, and she came to New York when Hugh was nine, "took a menial job." The family moved to Chinatown, lived at 149 Elizabeth Street. Hugh "went to school wearing shorts, like European children." He was a wizard in short pants to the Latino kids in his class. "I spoke Castillian Spanish and they spoke Newyorican."

He grew up incredibly poor, with "no sunlight, no pocket money, no money for candy. . . . I ate a lot of chicken and rice. Chicken was the cheapest form of meat. . . . I never tumbled in the grass, but I knew it exists." He remembers having a "Jewish kind of upbringing," where education was almost a Talmudic form of life. "If you learn how to read, no one can take that away from you." He was "following the footsteps of the Jews," who'd come out of the "same old-law tenement buildings."

The white tiger had gone from Shanghai to Hong Kong, from Hong Kong to Taiwan and Madrid, yet however peculiar that path, he was only one more immigrant. "The strength of the immigrant is thirst and hunger. We're not animals. We can't be spoon-fed at school . . . can't pack our gullets with information."

Hugh lives in Queens with his wife and little daughter, who's named Elizabeth, after Elizabeth Street. Those tenements continue to haunt him and shiver inside his head. "That's where I had my beginning . . . if you lose that, you're really adrift." As president of the planning council he's had to deal with Chinatown's "sudden, explosive growth." Earlier immigrants "were more driven. Now people fall behind. There's criminal temptation." Some were "already criminals in the Far East. The family associations involved in gambling rackets turned to the gangs . . . used them as enforcers to keep their membership in line." They "hired tigers, and the tigers get out of hand. . . . Frankenstein tears off his chains and will do some killing in the village."

You have "more and more people in a small area, people are squeezed, opportunities are less, resources dwindle, and there's a gradual breakdown of families" among the Chinese. "It's no different from other poor communities." The good, honest uncles "can't absorb the youngsters." They work for Old Benny, or one of the other lords, and end up on Doyers and Pell, that "hatchet alley," where the tongs "would hack each other to death."

But Hugh has his own style of tong at the planning council. He's not into extortion and drugs. He finds housing and jobs for the newcomers. He's as resourceful as Old Benny, stubborn, gregarious, and his own Frankenstein. He worked "in the trenches" as a prosecutor, a mean little "inscrutable bastard."

And now he's "the man who wears the black hat" at One Police Plaza, a hangman, the guy who can grab a cop's pension away. The police department has its own internal disciplinary system, and Hugh sits at the head of that system as its chief trial judge. The department also has a kind of secret police, the IAD (Internal Affairs Division). Hugh admits that "some IAD guys play their role to the hilt," but "they are there to sniff out wrongdoings." And they sniff far and wide. They're six to seven hundred strong. The cops they catch come before the hangman. Hugh can't sentence a cop to jail. His one authority is the cop's right to employment . . . and his pension. "That's my only clout." A cop "can take two years upstate and say 'I don't give a shit.' His pension is much more important . . . he's worried about his pension. That is the real hit . . . it's tantamount to the death penalty in this department."

Cops can't beat their wives, commit murder, piss on a sidewalk, or smoke marijuana. "Private smoking is no big deal," but it's tragic for a policeman if he's caught. Hugh measured half an inch with his fingers. "A roach this size, they're gone." No wonder cops die early. They have to dance that bitter dance between catching thieves and developing a periscope in the seat of their pants to watch for the IAD.

[5]

Hugh had become my Chinese brother. He'd involved himself in the fate of my book. *His* immigrant story had become mine. He wasn't out to romanticize the Chinese or promote his powers as a judge. "I have no contract here. The mayor can remove me. Ben Ward can remove me." He wanted me to catch the Chinese with all their virtues and their flaws. He got me an introduction to Harriet Tung, "the Chinese Jackie Onassis," and Katherine Wei, a feisty woman of fifty-five, born in Beijing, who was critical of Chinatown, and that didn't bother Hugh. He was trying to tear under that thick net the Chinese had pulled around themselves.

And so I went to Katherine Wei, a one-woman artillery team. Bridge champion, vice president of her husband's shipping firm, author, and ex-nurse. A stunning lady with no reverence for anything or anybody. "I was in Beijing when the Japanese arrived. . . . I was always running from the Japanese." But Katherine ran so hard, she never actually looked upon a Japanese until after the war was over.

We talked about Shanghai, where she'd lived as a girl. Shanghai was a town full of White Russians. The very, very rich went to Europe after the Revolution, but "the second-class royalty came to Shanghai . . . they started beauty parlors." She remembers a lot of English, Russians, French, Portuguese. Living in Shanghai "was like watching *Dynasty*," because of all the "corruption and the glitter." But it was a tale of two cities that had to be told twice. The town was full of intrigue and complications— rich and poor, Chinese and European. The Europeans had their own civil governments, their own armies, their own police. And the Chinese were often "prisoners" in Shanghai. Katherine recalls a park she couldn't enter. The sign at the gate said: "Chinese and dogs not allowed."

She came to New York in 1949, went to nursing school. She's now married to shipowner C. C. Wei and lives in Houston and New York. "Houston tried to copy New York," she says, "and failed. . . . Houston needs an Ed Koch." So do the Chinese in America, according to Katherine Wei. "Koch says, 'I'm Tarzan.'" The Chinese can't do this. "They're always taught to be humble." Katherine began to chide herself. "I'm terrible," she said.

"The Koreans will be a bigger force" in New York City. "They stick together . . . the Chinese are very snobbish. God forbid if your child should not marry a college graduate. It would be most shameful." The mandarins and the old peasant class rarely mingle.

And Katherine didn't find many mandarins on Mott Street. "I feel offended when I walk in Chinatown. Why do they have to be so dirty? . . . I have never got involved with Chinatown. People are going to say, 'She's a snob.'" But Katherine remembers when she "washed people's behinds . . . emptied bedpans. I worked my way up."

She's a fierce, funny woman, fixing herself to box with the entire world. Harriet Tung, whom I was going to see next, "is so Chinese. She's afraid to hurt a fly's feelings. We need people to be more outspoken."

We talked about "Doctor Zhivago," Omar Sharif, who was as much of a bridge fanatic as Katherine Wei. "He's a weird person. I met him in 1972 at the height of his career. He's tiny, small . . . better looking in pictures."

"But what happened to him?" I asked. "He's disappeared."

He'd behaved badly, ignored his fans. "The teenyboppers lined up for Omar. If Omar had a bad match, he wouldn't go out to give autographs."

But a couple of autograph hounds couldn't have killed Doctor Zhivago.

"He was just a big star," Katherine said. "Not a legend. There's a difference. . . ." Then she started to laugh. "I'm so opinionated."

Ah, he was more than a star to me. I wasn't thinking of Zhivago. Or that Arab chief from *Lawrence of Arabia*. It was the gambler in *Funny Girl* who stuck in my head. Barbra Streisand's husband, Nicky Arnstein. He owned horses and camel's-hair coats. And he was the friend and secret partner of Arnold Rothstein. Another Jewish Gatsby, the Egyptian, Omar Sharif.

What could Rothstein have meant to Katherine Wei? She'd have boxed his ears off if he'd been alive. But she wouldn't box with the United States. "I love my adopted country."

She wasn't so kind to Washington, D.C. "I can't stand Washington. Washington people are always hedging. . . . Now I'm fifty-five, and I'm going to say what I think. I'm proud to be a New Yorker . . . my only regret is that people have no place to live. We have AIDS victims nobody wants. New Yorkers have to care a little more."

And she wouldn't hedge on Chinatown. "Chinatown is the pits."

We talked about Ellis Island, how that castle had redefined the psyche of New York . . . and America itself. A hundred million people could trace their line back to someone who's stood in the big hall at Ellis Island.

"I feel so cheated," Katherine said. "I didn't come through Ellis Island. Here I am, getting gypped out of this experience."

[6]

I met with Harriet Tung the next day. Her father-in-law, C. Y. Tung, who'd owned "more ships than Onassis," had been one of the richest men in the world. On my way to her building, I passed the Korean deli at Seventy-fifth and Park that had caused such a fracas in 1984. The owner, Kyung-Sung Choi, had wanted to open an all-night deli at the site of a former flower shop. The community had been in an uproar. Neighborhood residents had marshaled the Landmarks Preservation Commission, the local community board, Friends of the Upper East-side Historic Districts, and Manhattan Borough President Andrew Stein against Mr. Choi. One of the community leaders, Shirley Bernstein, had said a deli wasn't appropriate for Park Avenue. "Flowers might be all right. . . . Or chocolates. Yes, Swiss or Belgian chocolates."

It was like a story out of Jonathan Swift. When I'd asked Arthur Cohen, who lived in the neighborhood, about that furor over the deli, he said, "The rich never run out of milk, so why do they need a grocery on Park Avenue?" And suddenly Mr. Choi wasn't all alone. Jackie Onassis, Dick Cavett, and others had rallied to his cause. You couldn't stop an immigrant from having his dream store on Park Avenue. This was an immigrant town.

I still didn't understand all the hurly-burly and the hullabaloo. The delicatessen was entirely tame. It had the struts of the old flower shop. It was as antique as anything on Park Avenue.

I went up to Harriet Tung. She was a tall, quiet beauty in her late thirties. Harriet had no desire to box with the world. And she'd never played bridge with Omar Sharif. She was born in Hong Kong in 1947, got to California when she was four and a half. She lived in Monterey, where her dad taught at the Army Language School. But he didn't feel it was "dignified . . . for a Chinese-speaking person to teach Chinese." He decided to become an engineer and went back to college in his mid-forties, a man with a Ph.D. And Harriet studied at Barnard during the student and faculty rebellions of 1968. "The Chinese students were not involved in the turmoil. We were curious observers." Harriet Tung, the girl from Hong Kong, followed "the Confucian ethics . . . it's not in good taste to be vociferous or political."

Unlike Katherine Wei, she has become involved with Chinatown, and she doesn't think of it as a filthy place.

The new immigrants "have stirred the imagination of the younger Chinese." The mandarins never mixed with the other classes in old China. "But the tables have turned a bit in the U.S. . . . the poorer classes are succeeding."

Her grandfather was the first Chinese graduate of West Point. He was in the class of 1909, together with George Patton. He took part in the 1911 revolution that broke the Manchu dynasty and established the Republic of China. He fought against the Japanese in 1932 as a general in the Kuomintang. He arrived here after the war, but Chinese generals didn't mean very much in the United States. "He went from a general to working in a laundry . . . he had to support all of us."

Who knows? All the time I was making funny faces in the windows of Chinese laundries, how many generals and scholars and simple poor men did I see? Harriet's grandfather was only one more cut in that sad tale of the laundry worker who couldn't become an artist or remain a general in some phantom army across the sea. Laundryman or not, Harriet's grandfather was buried at West Point.

She mentioned *Year of the Dragon*, Michael Cimino's film about a warlord in Chinatown, which had disturbed the Chinese because it depicted them as a cartel of greedy merchants and stinking little gangsters (male and female) who didn't fight fair. It was a racist fantasy of some dreamland Chinatown, with Mickey Rourke as the Polish-American police captain who is out to destroy the tongs. Harriet hated all the rotten publicity it was giving the Chinese.

"The Chinese always feel it's good to be invisible," she said.

"But you're not." Chinatown was growing like crazy.

"If there's too many of us, we'll be seen as a threat . . . they'll think we'll want to take over everything."

"But people will fear you," I said, talking like the Bronx Machiavelli. "That's not so bad." Even a ghost shadow couldn't stay invisible too long.

Hugh and Harriet had talked about the Chinese following the track of the Jews. They saw New York as a Jewish town. I didn't. That odyssey of Ellis Island was over. The Chinese would have to dance to their own American dream.

[7]

I met with Hugh one more time before he disappeared on a month's trip to China with his mom. He'd gone out to buy a shirt and was late. He took off his old shirt, put on the new, and I saw the holster at his hip. He was with the cops, yes, but he was also a judge, and somehow, the sheer palpability of that gun startled me—not the gun itself, but the small bright leather holster. Ah, *Year of the Dragon*. Hugh could have been Young Benny.

He was angered by Cimino's film. "It's extremely dangerous . . . it perpetrates the myth that the Chinese are violent . . . it took a white man [Mickey Rourke] to tell the Chinese that crime should not flourish."

I disagreed. "It's publicity, Hugh. Bad or good. For the first time the Chinese are entering popular culture. People will think about them. They won't remember the details. They never do. But they'll remember Chinatown."

Then we got back to my old god, that master detective from Honolulu with his fourteen children. "Charlie Chan damaged the Chinese community less. People took it as slapstick."

Not me.

But Charlie Chan was dead. The Chinese had outgrown that image. "We are going to be the Jews of the twenty-first century."

Ah, I thought to myself. Charlie Chan is Jewish. But I didn't tell that to Hugh.

thirteen

RAISSA

[1]

In 1959, when he was ninety-two years old, Frank Lloyd Wright, the greatest, maddest American architect, was asked by a pair of businessmen to design a commercial complex for Ellis Island, which was up for grabs: thirty-three buildings on a twenty-seven-acre sight. The government wanted to get rid of that ghost town, a grass lot with thirty-three caves. Junkmen would sneak onto the island and pick copper off the roofs, like children on a berry hunt, after the station closed in 1954. Ellis had reverted to its eighteenth-century habitat—a windy island cluttered with the bones of forgotten pirates. Perfect for Frank Lloyd Wright.

It was the last commission of his life. He died ten days after accepting it, but Wright had already figured out a new persona for Ellis Island. In fact, he'd been harboring a "perfect city" in his head for over forty years. A city of golden webs, parks, planetary objects, honeycombs and glass spheres—a dreamscape that would undermine the mathematic density of the grid. Wright loved prairies and despised city lots. Ellis Island would become his ultimate prairie town, a futuristic womb, surrounded by water. He would have all the caves leveled and construct a "shimmering crystal city."

But it wasn't some private formula, an old man's selfish wish. Wright "saw the island transformed symbolically from its role as a gateway to the American dream to one fulfilling the dream." His crystal city would be called "The Key," a code name in honor of the island's past. But nothing was to be left of that past except the name itself. The Key would have no interpreters or baggage rooms, no dockside canopies, no men to mark a greenhorn's chest with chalk. It was America as the island of Oz, with moving sidewalks, a magic yacht basin, nightclubs that would exist in a sphere. But all the pirates' bones on the island must have had some particular pull. The more Wright departed from the idea of an immigrant station, the closer he seemed to get. With all its enchantment and golden wire, the Key was a curious inversion of the old Ellis Island. As if the castle of 1900 had grown enormous fanciful ears, and all the immigrants who'd ever landed were frozen onto that island, Americans without ever reaching the shore.

The Key was never built, of course. And now the castle is being restored. Ah, if only they'd leave a little rot. The ruins were powerful when I saw them in 1981. The walls revealed a certain dread. And soon we'll have an oral history show, voices piping out our past. And the immigrant will be looked upon as some nostalgic thing, the great naïf, our lost grandpas and grandmas. Optimistic, innocent, or sad. The rage and the terror will be blasted out of the walls. We'll have little understanding of what those people were really like. We're amnesiacs, and we ignore that odd peristalsis we've *always* had about immigrants, a rhythm that "alternates between hospitality and paranoia . . . between a promiscuous inclusiveness and a nativist recoil."

Perhaps it's a craziness in our blood. Americans are still the most hospitable tribe around. Our xenophobia appears and disappears, but two-thirds of *all* the immigrants on this planet come to the United States. And much of the country sees New York as the pressure point of this "mongrelization" and blames it for its mongrel culture—but New York *is* America at its rawest edge. It's the city as psychopath, energetic, nervous, full of danger, like some hidden heartbeat of the country.

The late Italo Calvino described New York perfectly in *Invisible Cities,* his novel about eternal, endless travel. New York is like Raissa, "city of sadness," in which "there runs an invisible thread that binds one living being to another for a moment, then unravels, then is stretched again between moving points as it draws new and rapid patterns so that at every second the unhappy city contains a happy city unaware of its own existence."

[2]

America and Raissa-New York. A nation and a city that constantly unravel and re-create themselves, with each new mass of immigrants. Perhaps Hugh Mo is right, and the Chinese *will* become the Jews of the twenty-first century, without Charlie Chan. They've kept our public schools alive. There are three hundred thousand Chinese in New York, a bit over four percent of the City's 7,100,000 souls. Yet the Chinese have an incredibly high proportion of students at Bronx Science, Stuyvesant, and Brooklyn Technical High School. "All the Mo brothers graduated from Stuyvesant," Hugh admits. Stuyvesant is practically a Chinese province. The school is "thirty percent Chinese," but it's created problems within Chinatown, an anxiety of expectations. "For every Chinese kid who got into Stuyvesant, many couldn't make it." And the struggle doesn't end at Stuyvesant. There's a fierce competition among Chinese students for openings in the Ivy League, a competition that extends to all other Asian-

Americans. It's become an "Asian-American admissions issue."

The issue exploded at Princeton, where faculty members, students, and alumni began to wonder if a new kind of quota hadn't come to the Ivy League. For example, in 1985 Princeton accepted seventeen percent of *all* applicants, but only fourteen percent of Asian-Americans. Some professors feel that the very best Asian-Americans who didn't make it to the Ivy League are stronger students than "the bottom part" of each entering class.

Ah, it hits upon a bitter string. Jews had a similar problem thirty, forty, fifty, sixty years ago. In Hemingway's *The Sun Also Rises,* Robert Cohn becomes the middleweight boxing champ at Princeton. "He cared nothing for boxing, in fact he disliked it, but he learned it painfully and thoroughly to counteract the feeling of inferiority and shyness he felt on being treated as a Jew at Princeton." And in my graduating class at Music and Art, which was about seventy percent Jewish, only one kid, Nick Cohen, got into Princeton, and he didn't have that acute fever of the "Russian side" of our class. I can't say what's become of Nick Cohen. But I doubt that he was Princeton's middleweight champ. My whole world is like a goddamn Chinese-Jewish parable because I ended up teaching at Princeton over the past six years. And I couldn't avoid stepping on my own tail. All the odd, reclusive kids came to me. . . .

But the Chinese and the other Asian-Americans will win their war with the Ivy League. Their parents have given them that terrible desire for success. How many laundrymen's daughters will graduate from Princeton, Yale, and Penn? But will they grow invisible, as Harriet Tung says? Another generation of ghost shadows? Or will they learn to shout and scream, like the Jews?

Golems and ghost shadows. The Jews can't look back to the Sung empire. We have the dynasty of David, but that is largely myth. I can't recall a Charyn family association. There are hardly enough of us to sit at one table. We're Ellis Islanders. The whole tribe is dwindling in America, German *and* Russian Jews. Paul O'Dwyer remembers with a good deal of fondness the old alliance between the Irish and the Jews. "The Jews and Irish had held sway for fifty years. It was a cozy combination . . . the Jews represented an intellectual level that the Irish admired."

I asked O'Dwyer if New York was still a Jewish town.

"Unfortunately, no," he said, from under a great fist of white hair. And I know what O'Dwyer meant. The screamers were gone. That phalanx of poor Jews, from Ocean Parkway to Essex Street, who dreamt of some perfect island America, their own variation of the Key, have disappeared. Even the richer ones are growing scarce: ". . . the people who were originally told to be fruitful and multiply are doing neither in the United States. . . . Jews are among the least prolific Americans, bearing too few children to replace themselves. . . ."

We're the last of the Mohicans. And the metropolis that's been our cradle will become our grave. Ed Koch is still part of our vanishing tribe—a big part, because he screams louder than the rest of us. But there won't be another screamer after Ed.

And what kind of mark will our little nation leave? Like the Irish before us, and the Italians, we scraped our character upon the surface of the City, and inside its bowels. We weren't bankers. We weren't builders. We didn't put up New York's skyline, create its museums. We were merchants, yes, professors, doctors, furriers, failures, bureaucrats, suicides . . . and thinkers, Galileo without his telescope. The only planets we found were in the five boroughs. And the deepest, darkest thinkers are always criminals of one kind. There's an odd relationship between Jews and cities and the metaphysics of crime.

Robert Warshow touched upon that theme in his book of essays, *The Immediate Experience,* which is about popular culture—often the only culture available to immigrant Jews—and the official culture that surrounded it. Warshow was a movie addict. And his essay, "The Gangster as Tragic Hero," takes on a different tone twenty-eight years after it was written (Warshow died of a heart attack in 1955 at the age of thirty-seven). He was writing about that curious American genre, the gangster film, a genre that seems to have seduced us all. "There is almost nothing we understand better or react to more readily or with quicker intelligence." This was in the days before *Ghostbusters* and *Friday the Thirteenth*. It was also before that mass exodus to the suburbs. The gangster *was* the city, when cities still had a particular charm—dangerous, exciting, without the idea of urban rot. No one had ever stumbled upon gray dunes in the Bronx.

For the moviegoer, at least, the city was white, and the gangster was also white: Bogart, Cagney, Garfield. . . . The gangster expressed "that part of the American psyche which rejects the qualities and the demands of modern life, which rejects 'Americanism' itself." The gangster invariably had some sort of ethnic background. He was Irish, Italian, Jewish—an outsider or a tough immigrant brat. But he was always "the man of the city." Yet the city he inhabited was "not the real city, but the dangerous and sad city of the imagination which is so much more important, which is the modern world." An actual city provides us with actual criminals, and "the imaginary city produces the gangster: he is what we want to be and what we are afraid we may become."

I haven't lost that childhood wish: after forty years of watching movies, I still go to sleep with outlaws in my head, betrayals, codes of honor that have little to do with my waking life. I'm frozen into the gangster film.

And like the immigrant, the gangster is "without culture, without manners, without leisure." But within his specialized work, "he is graceful, moving like a dancer among the crowded dangers of the city." In a very disturbing way, he *is* the immigrant, who sees himself as an outlaw within American culture, greedy and alone. He mocks the immigrant's craving for success. The gangster's own story "is a nightmare inversion of the values of ambition and opportunity."

But if it were only an immigrant's tale, the gangster film would never have had such a wide appeal. Warshow realizes that at some level "the quality of irrational brutality and the quality of rational enterprise become one." The gangster's lawlessness is only another style of law. "In the deeper layers of modern consciousness, *all* means are un-lawful, every attempt to succeed is an act of aggression." And the gangster dies for us like some psychopathic Christ, so that we can mask our aggression and succeed without feeling outlawed and alone.

In New York the actual city and the mythic merge, not out of some romantic notion that crime and business are a single corporation. The Chase Manhattan Bank might have problems, but it hasn't financed any dealerships in Colombian cocaine that I can recall. The Mafia *may* have owned the Chrysler Building at one time or another, and we probably support half a dozen crime families with every piece of meat that goes into our mouths, but that's not really news.

Aggressiveness is a way of life in New York. One has to be an outlaw to survive. We're all gangsters over here, anonymous in that dark outline of the City, no matter what hearths we have. And Ed Koch is the biggest gangster alive. His calling card is quite simple: mess with me, and you'll get hit. He rides in helicopters and speedboats like some prince of the night. He has no political clubhouse, no party machine, and no "culture" at all. He slouches a lot, but he's never slow, and he dances when he has to. He's always nimble in a crisis. He has no children, no heirs, no continuity to his kingdom. He bullies, he enchants, but he hasn't groomed a soul to sit in his chair. His father lived to eighty-seven. Koch will go for a hundred. Our mayor-gangster-golem-king.

[3]

I'd gone to the golem's favorite spot, the South Street Seaport, to have lunch with *Times* reporter Martin Gottlieb. The *Times* was as schizophrenic as the rest of the City. It would rant against rent control and the loss of housing stock and then print tough, compassionate articles about the homeless, the poor, prostitutes, and mad preachers, as if its psyche were split between its own self-

interest, that need to stay alive, and the rude, radical
ghosts of an immigrant town.

New York had become a quilted novel for me in the
pages of the *Times* during the months I researched this
book. I stopped reading sports, and obituaries, and ter-
rorist attacks in the Middle East. I read only New York.
The rise and fall of Anthony Alvarado; Ben Ward getting
stuck in some twilight zone; the tactical maneuvers of
Operation Pressure Point, that war on drugs in the East
Village, and the drug dealers' own survival kit—selling
heroin out of baby carriages, moving their franchises into
subway cars; the creation of Strawberry Fields in Central
Park; the mysterious death of a young black subway
graffiti artist; the madness of AIDS; the politicizing of
corpses by our chief medical examiner; civil war in a Chinese cafeteria; the golem's daily wanderings through his
kingdom . . . news and narratives. It was like reading a
serialized novel in which the characters and landscapes
shifted from day to day—the return of Krazy Kat. And
Martin Gottlieb is the guy I followed with the deepest
pleasure; his articles on the Times Square project and the
tenth anniversary of the fiscal crisis ranged across more
kingdoms than Koch would have dared to tread. I wanted
to meet him.

We planned to have lunch at the Bridge Café on Water
Street. But I was early and I strolled through the seaport.
It was packed. The people I saw couldn't have been tourists. They didn't have that constantly startled and adoring
look of Krazy Kat. They wouldn't pick through merchandise. They sat and drank margueritas. Young Wall Street
wizards, I imagined. I looked at that tiny village with its
reconstructed walls and fashionable shops. It was like coming out of the nineteenth century and into a cookie store.

The seaport was a great success! Captain Hook's and
Parrots, a fake nineteenth-century atmosphere of pirates
and lawlessness in a cardboard setting. South Street isn't a
dream the Dutch would have dreamt for themselves. It's
the fabric of some interior city that's invaded New York,
sat itself down in the metropolis like a merchandise mart
by the sea.

Perhaps I was the old-fashioned pirate who couldn't appreciate the Disneylike wonders of the new port. No matter. I left the neighborhood of Captain Hook's and wandered up Water Street. There were old, peely houses a block away from the seaport restaurants. And now I was in authentic country, an older, crumbling seaport and the trompe l'oeil building at Peck Slip, bridge and streetscape painted on a wall, not with the desire to fool any tourists so they'd disappear into that phantom wall. It was playful, with its own mysterious design, like a teasing answer to South Street itself: a port written onto a wall.

Had my lunch with Martin Gottlieb. He'd grown up on Grand Street, the son of a printer. We chattered about the City we both adored in spite of its murderous problems and that growing "Manhattanization," its universe of projects, the relentless reupholstering of streets, and the loss of older, vital neighborhoods. "Color, folklore, and the fabric of human life take a secondary position to market forces . . . traditions are fragile things. Neighborhood life goes away." Gottlieb recalled the "bitter, vitriolic fights over Lincoln Center" and the dread of another "neighborhood lost. The memory of the old Lincoln Square neighborhood remains in the minds of people. Nobody talks about it. There's an engine in the City, and it chugs, chugs, and chugs, eats up things and spits them out."

We talked about Alphabetland and the rebirth of Avenue B: condos, art galleries, clubs, as if an entire life-style were being woven on the street. "The alphabet blocks are living on a permanent edge, and it's never a static thing. You wonder if real estate doesn't create a flavor in its own right."

And we got onto those sad years of the fiscal crisis. I saw the crisis as some kind of theater that was being acted out in front of our noses, but we couldn't tell too much about the players or the props, except that we were all on the stage somewhere—we were the props.

"Is Nelson Rockefeller the villain of the piece?" I asked. He'd built and built until he bankrupted the Urban Development Corporation, and then an odd sort of domino theory set in; disaster trickled down from the UDC into the metropolis after Rocky abandoned the state to become Ford's vice president. The bankers got scared and began to sell off their City paper.

But Martin Gottlieb wasn't searching for heroes and villains to explain the crisis. "Rockefeller undertook enormous projects." There was "tremendous expansion" under him. "The state used to be a schleppy institution." And the City was operating out of its own private spindle, paying its immediate bills with short-term notes, while the bankers looked around the City and didn't like it at all. The people making the greatest use of services "were now black," and those "representing the City were [white] ethnics." "Cash" Cavanagh, Beame's first deputy, had been an ethnic pet during the Lindsay administration. "He worked off the seat of his pants. He wasn't a white-collar type." Beame's deputies "hadn't forgotten their roots. They cut political corners, worked with the clubhouses," but they had a "sense of legitimate mission. They spent money on hospitals . . . welfare." When the bankers started to demand cuts in City services, "Cavanagh tried to take them around, show them people in straitjackets. But the bankers didn't want to see."

Beame was very bitter because Lindsay's people had shuffled cash around in a similar fashion. But "the bankers wouldn't say a bad word about Lindsay."

"Ah," I said, "the fiscal crisis was a WASP revenge on New York." The WASPs were getting even with a town that had been run by the Irish, the Italians, and the Jews. It was the old hundred-and-fifty-year fight between immigrants and nativists. And now the nativists had won.

Gottlieb laughed but he wouldn't agree. New York had a "hospital system that no white ethnic would walk into in a million years . . . the white ethnics were glad to see the services cut."

And suddenly we had a boomtown again. The golem sat with Ronald Reagan and paid the City's bills. Capital flowed in from Europe, Hong Kong, and Japan. Money clapped hands with art, and New York had become the financial *and* cultural center of the world. Million-dollar

experimental operas were being mounted at the
Brooklyn Academy of Music. An entire satellite of art galleries had opened in the East Village within two years. A row of *serious* theaters had started up on the southern wall of Forty-second Street between Ninth and Tenth. But institutions couldn't make art. They could only package it. And how art sprang up was a very curious business. It had been coming out of certain caves in the Bronx—dancing, scrawling, and rapping that expressed a primitive anger and pride. "You just a bum in the slum . . . but I can shoot piss," I heard a young black man chant on the subway in a kind of machine-gun prose he couldn't have learned at any public school. It was a war cry, and also a cry of acceptance, that distancing between whites and blacks, golden towers and grim dunes.

"The place is in danger of losing its soul," Martin Gottlieb said. "Nobody is willing to find out what it stands for. The City could lose its soul."

[4]

Soul. Is it the dance between a town and its different populations—old, young, rich, poor, black, white, brown, yellow, red? But Manhattan has already become a strange utopia of the childless, the young, and the very old. And the outer boroughs? They're either suburban bedrooms or barracks for recent immigrants: phantom neighborhoods touched with pieces of Manhattan's honky-tonk electric life.

Rudolf, the disco entrepreneur who once ran Underground, Danceteria, Pravda, and other clubs, feels that the metropolis "as a mecca of creativity and craziness is in decline—the city is out." Rio and Hong Kong are in, according to Rudolf. "Rio is definitely happening."

But I'm not in Rio. And Rudolf isn't the only one who laments New York's "decline." George Steiner, who hasn't run Pravda or Underground but has written about Tolstoy and Dostoyevsky, believes Manhattan could be heading for a psychic earthquake. New York "is not the

Federal city, not the national city, but the empire city. . . ." It's where Krazy Kat has come to dream. "It is a capital for and of the refugee." And that power to welcome, to fabulate its own Ellis Island in all five boroughs, has transformed New York into "the capital of the 20th century," an eighty-six-year-old season of outcasts and refugees. Empires have been dismantled. Countries and people have disappeared. And phantoms began arriving from Russia, Poland, Italy, Ireland, Cuba, China, Trinidad, Cambodia, Vietnam . . .

What if the phantoms could no longer afford to come? The tremors would begin. You'd have a haunted house with a lot of cracks in the ceiling. The City's current "boomtown is strictly at the penthouse level." Is New York becoming like a luxurious prison-hotel for the very rich, surrounded by badlands, with no mobility for the young and the poor, and no refugees?

Steiner's both right and wrong. New York is that dream town at the edge. If it cannot school its children or accommodate the young, provide more than penthouses, it will become a ruin with a remodeled face, without energy or remorse, a candied village, like South Street. A painted corpse.

But the phantoms have continued to arrive. Moscovites in Queens. Marielitos in Manhattan. Cambodians in the Bronx. Koreans. Isolated travelers, such as Tadeusz Korzeniewski, a dissident writer from Poland, whose feelings have been so twisted and torn, he stares out at you like young Frankenstein. He was born near the Baltic Sea. Studied electronics in Gdansk, but dropped out of school and started to write poems. Tadeusz needed to find a vocabulary. He wrote a short novel, part of which was published in *Zapis,* an underground literary magazine that the Polish government had tried to chase out of business. The secret police captured Tadeusz after the uprisings in Gdansk, held him in jail for twenty-eight hours. He has nothing but "pathological feelings" toward Poland. Tadeusz "quarreled with everybody." The events in Poland had crazed him. "The new solidarity was a fairy tale," he felt. "It wouldn't survive too long."

He was given a passport "a month before martial law."
He left Poland in three days and went to Paris. "People
didn't want you . . . there were too many immigrants." He
lived in a houseboat on the Seine. He couldn't scribble
words in Paris. "My interior was like ice. I had no ideas. I
was scared about the situation. . . . I'd lost trust with writing. . . . I felt like a lunatic."

He was waiting for an American visa. "Every week I
expected to go to America." That vigil took a year and a
half. He arrived in New York at the beginning of 1983.
Tadeusz felt an odd kind of anchoring here. "America is
the most amazing country in the world . . . and New York
is like a mushroom upon the country." He lived at Mansfield Hall, a beaten-down hotel at Broadway and Fiftieth
Street. There was so much screaming around him, Tadeusz worked in his room "with earplugs" (he was scribbling on a novel). Mansfield Hall was a place "for poor
people, insane people, aspiring Japanese people, displaced people, forgotten people. . . ."

There are strong animals and weak animals, Tadeusz
said, and "New York is a strong animal." He'd never met
"any other such complicated, difficult, live city," where
"human beings are forced, pushed to be more open."

Tadeusz was only one more phantom at Mansfield Hall.
"Immigration is still an important part of New York, especially when the immigration comes from Eastern Europe." He'd moved from "the old capital of the world
[Paris] to the new capital . . . it's easier here." New York
"opens me deeper. I feel an anger close to action. . . ." In
Poland he had to suppress that anger, "put it down." New
York, he says, "liberates my looking at me . . . it opens a
gate in myself. I see so many insane people, so many nice
people. . . ."

Tadeusz was gloomy most of the time. I met him in the
winter, and he wore a huge down coat and a hat with
earflaps that made him look like some fantasy of a Polish
KGB man. I never visited young Frankenstein at Mansfield Hall. He went off to the country to finish his novel
and I didn't see Tadeusz again. But I was taken with him
and all his gloom. His journey out of Gdansk had been a

heroic one. He'd come here utterly alone—a scribbler in
New York. He'd found a magic bow to bend, the City's
maddening cry of love, hate, and ambition, its obsessive
patterning of skyline and streets, like an endless, unsolv-
able puzzle: Raissa, the schizophrenic town that turns sad
just as it's about to discover the riddle of its own hap-
piness.

[5]

I am Krazy Kat, creature of the New World looking for
some Ignatz Mouse to crown him so he can call it love.
Never got to Mansfield Hall, but I did get to the Palladium. I'd never been to a disco in my life. I couldn't
dance. I could hardly swim. My girlfriend, R. (for Raissa),
had tickets to some museum party at the Palladium. R.
loves to dance. I'd known her for twenty-three years.
She'd been a student of mine, my class monitor at Music
and Art. I was substituting for a teacher out with a heart
attack. I entered the class in my baggy pants. R. was sitting in the first row. Couldn't take my eyes off her Egyptian face. A woman among a pack of children. I was
ruined. It was crazy, incurable love, black as blood. R. is
an immigrant girl. She'd come here around the age of
seven, lived at a hotel on the Upper West Side, and taught
herself English by watching the tube. Her dad was in
diamonds. The family moved to Riverdale. I met R. when
she was sixteen. Wanted her to be my monitor for life.
Gave her my Phi Beta Kappa key. R. gave it back. She
studied art at Cooper Union and married a pianist who
worked in a bank. I lost touch with Raissa. Became a
Californian. Returned to New York. My pants were just as
baggy, and I had the same dumb devotion to craft. I was
skinny and hunched. But in my own silvered head I saw
myself as a fat man with a walrus mustache: Flaubert. I
didn't have Flaubert's estates. I would have starved with
my metaphysical mustache if I hadn't crept into college
teaching.

I got gray all of a sudden. Flaubert was aging fast. I had
more and more acidulous theories about art. I was sitting
in a café with Frederic Tuten, my old rival from the
Bronx, when he happened to mention "Raissa," his sweetheart's best friend. I felt a rip in my ear. I knew there
couldn't be another Raissa in town. It had to be my old
monitor from Music and Art. That's how I met Raissa
again, through a simple conversation over a coffee cup.

Dark skin and green eyes, with the aquiline nose of
some pharaoh's daughter. It was love as a battle royal.
Raissa and I couldn't stop fighting. We were like two
hopeless monkeys who kissed and scratched. I was a skeleton with scars. And Raissa was deliciously fat, wearing
my bruises on her body. And that's how we arrived at the
Palladium.

A ten-million-dollar disco stuffed with celebrity art.
Kenny Scharf telephone booths. A Basquiat bar. Keith
Haring's scratches on a wall. Fourteenth Street was the
new heartland of Manhattan. Suddenly, uptown was
dead. The Palladium had established itself at the very
borders of the grid, where the bottom of the island began.
Fourteenth Street was the last road that went from river
to river in a straight line. But I was confused about the
damn thing. The club had opened in May with a terrific
clap of noise. It was attracting everybody: nurses from
across the river, young lawyers, brokers, squash champions, Bianca Jagger, Julian Schnabel. But I couldn't
seem to find the place.

Raissa led me there. No wonder I'd missed the Palladium on my strolls up and down Fourteenth. It was a
ruin on the outside, a hulking marquee that belonged to a
seven-story brick mountain almost sixty years old. Once a
movie theater and a variety house, the Palladium had also
been a rock palace, the home of heavy-metal. But the
punk stars had fled Fourteenth Street. Raissa and I
walked through black velvet ropes under the marquee
and entered the mountain.

The lobby seemed unmolested. Another ruin. The
disco had been built right into the shell of the old movie
theater and variety house. It formed its own crater, like a

magician freezing time into some eternal present that could produce bags and bones without the anxiety and bother of a past. The Palladium had prepared a revolution: the archeology of the new. There were skeletons scattered everywhere, a lacuna of lights, a mannequin corpse under the stairs, animal bones in a cape. We stood on a balcony, watched two video monitors come down from the ceiling like gigantic sledgehammers with a hundred eyes.

Ah, we could have been sailing somewhere. Behind us were balcony after balcony, stairs, closets with pillowcases, bars, old bones, like a ruined ship with a lot of decks. And in the middle was Mickey Mouse, half sculpture, half painting, and who knows what? He presided over the skeleton ship. He was our captain, our leader. I would have preferred Ignatz Mouse. But Mickey would do. He seemed to be melting all the time. The mouse had vertigo. He was a pop-out with paper skin. But he didn't desert the ship.

I was wrong about one thing. The Palladium did have a past. Mickey was the god of America, and the god of Europe too. It was the Dutch all over again. Our skeleton ship was Europe's mad voyage to the New World. The Dutch discovered Mickey Mouse. The Palladium was a dream city floating in the ruins.

Raissa and I got off the balcony and went down to dance. Couldn't stop thinking of *Last Tango in Paris,* with Brando baring his cheeks in the cellars of La Coupole. We had our own cellar here. And Brando was just my age when he took off his pants at La Coupole. Was it time for me to try? Would have been like a christening in the New World, my graduation from Crotona Park. But I couldn't have managed it. You had to dance cheek to jowl in this joint. Besides, I might never have found my pants again in the fray.

I looked up above Raissa and saw a stage set in the ceiling, a replica of Odyssey 2001, the disco in Bay Ridge where John Travolta danced in *Saturday Night Fever.* I whirled around that fake disco in the sky. It was like an archeological dig into the sentimental bones of a city. The

Palladium had resurrected Odyssey 2001 and a piece of Brooklyn in some sort of painted crib.

We were in a spectral village, where future and past swirled next to your knees. I was waiting for Travolta to appear in his white suit and dance around Peter Stuyvesant's leg. It never happened. But I looked into Raissa's eyes and had a vision of New Amsterdam, the mind's New York, with Mickey Mouse as god and the devil. Dancing there, you didn't ever need to die. Hell was right with us. The two video monitors ascended into the ceiling, and suddenly that painted crib started to descend until it captured half the floor, including Raissa and myself. We were stuck inside a painted prison of New York. I didn't see a goddamn door. Blue smoking lights entered the crib, devil lights, and we danced with the Manhattan skyline on the prison walls.

I found a door. We landed in Bay Ridge. There was a sign announcing seven-and-a-half-percent mortgages on the crib's outer wall, mortgages from a Brooklyn bank. Now I understood that crib. It was the battle of the boroughs, with Brooklyn enclosing Manhattan. But Travolta couldn't win. Brooklyn would always remain on the outside of the crib.

Mickey Mouse was the ruler of the West, and Fourteenth Street had become the dividing line of the New World. Above Fourteenth was no-man's-land. And below it was slightly civilized, that's all. Other discos were dying because of "Palladium fallout." Mickey could topple in a couple of seasons, and the Palladium will be one more empty shell, but who cares?

Our Dutch fathers crossed the ocean to build replicas of the world in a town of windmills. The English took that town and turned it into New York, a Tory village that housed redcoats during the Revolution and was loyal to King George. The king's village prospered in the middle of war. It was the home of profiteers and pirates, soldier businessmen, merchants and landlords who squeezed whichever side they could. New York became the fashion capital of British America, with perfumes, periwigs, gold buttons, and gaudy lace. The Brits marched around in

polished leather and danced with loyalist daughters and
wives, waiting for that pest General Washington to fall off
his horse and die in the cornfields somewhere so the silly
patriots would sue for peace and the smartest women
could plan bigger and better balls.

But the general stayed on his horse. And after he
knocked the hell out of Cornwallis, the loyalists scratched
the king's initials, a *G* and an *R* (George Rex), from their
doors. New York fell into a revolutionary fervor and
tossed away its British streets. Crown became Liberty,
King became Pine, and Queen became Pearl. But the
ghosts of King, Queen, and Crown are still there. New
York has always been gaudy and perverse, America's
high-stepping money town. And the Palladium *is* America and money, but with New York's perverse signature.
Mickey Mouse is closer to George Rex than he is to *our*
George. God and puppet, river pilot, he captains the Palladium like a mad, melting king. He has no bricks in his
pants. He bears no malice. He's funny and sweet. He
doesn't have the fears or the drive of an immigrant, never
says "dahlink," like Krazy Kat. He wouldn't have survived
Crotona Park. He has no sense of politics. He lives in that
perfect land of fun; his single want is to wait for Minnie to
bat her eyes at him. The mouse can't resist. He's as se-
duceable as America—the Palladium's pilot and pet.

I left the ruins with Raissa. She batted her eyes like
Minnie. I chased her down the block. Other people were
entering through the Palladium's black velvet ropes. My
breath was short from dancing in a crib. I saw the white
tubing of the Empire State, thought of Lexan sandwiches
and Douglas Leigh. I passed the rebuilt lawns of Union
Square Park. Wasn't a junkie around. The light was peculiar. The park seemed to bathe in the false dawn of a fairy
tale. I couldn't catch Raissa. I ran and ran.

NOTES

ABBREVIATIONS

NYT	New York Times
NYTM	New York Times Magazine
VV	Village Voice

For full citations of the books mentioned only by author and title, please
see the Bibliography, which directly follows the Notes.

1. ELLIS: AN INTRODUCTION

page

12 "I'm not the type to get ulcers. . . ." Edward I. Koch, *Mayor*, p. 39.

18–22 "I don't know who owns this houseboat . . . customer for you."
Ed Koch to J.C., June 13, 1985.

24 "There were sixty or seventy years . . ." Nathan Glazer and Daniel
Patrick Moynihan, *Beyond the Melting Pot*, p. 217.

24 "The Irish came to run . . ." Glazer and Moynihan, p. 219.

26–27 "and parts of New York . . . 'watering place hotel.'" Wilton
Tifft and Thomas Dunne, *Ellis Island*, n.p.

27 "lavish hospitality," Kevin Wolfe, "Island of the Dreams," *Metropolis,* January–February 1985, p. 26
28 "five minutes out of steerage." Cynthia Ozick, *Art & Ardor,* p. 137.
30 ". . . crime was a marginal phenomenon . . ." Irving Howe, *World of Our Fathers,* p. 101.
32 "I can wear what I want . . ." Yannick Noah, quoted in Jane Gross, "Success on the Court Brings Anguish for Yannick Noah," *NYT,* January 9, 1984.
33 "waits every moment . . ." Robert Warshow, *The Immediate Experience,* p. 51.
33 "warped with fancy . . ." Offissa Pup, in Warshow, p. 52.
35 "I hate radicals. . . ." Koch to J.C., June 13, 1985.

2. LAND OF THE SPIDER LADY

39 "Each great capital sits like a spider . . ." Lewis Mumford, *The Culture of Cities,* p. 231.
39 "shapeless giantism." Mumford, p. 233.
39 "megalopolitan growth." Mumford, p. 252.
39 "a Plutonian world . . ." Mumford, p. 255.
39 "A Brief Outline of Hell." Mumford, p. 272.
39 "Nekropolis, city of the dead." Mumford, p. 292.
40 "The tear and noise." Mumford, p. 252.
40 "I like dense cities best . . ." Jane Jacobs, *The Death and Life of Great American Cities,* p. 16.
40 "promenades that go from no place . . ." Jacobs, p. 4.
40 "There is a quality . . ." Jacobs, p. 15.
41 "full of strangers." Jacobs, p. 30.
41 "against predatory strangers . . . peaceable strangers." Jacobs, p. 36.
45 "after 36 years of chain-smoking . . ." Martin Gottlieb, "The Magic Is Faded, But the Ghosts of Broadway Past Still Haunt Times Sq.," *NYT,* August 30, 1984.
47 "society country." William H. Whyte, Introduction to *The WPA Guide to New York,* p. xxviii.
50 "Scattering them is the first shot. . . ." William J. Stern, quoted in Walter Goodman, "Times Sq. Plan: Experts Debate Impact on Crime," *NYT,* February 21, 1984.
50 "The proposal will help to bring back the days of George M. Cohan . . ." Stern, quoted in Gottlieb, *NYT,* August 30, 1984.
50 "may have devised the only conceivable plan . . ." Thomas Bender, "Ruining Times Square," *NYT,* March 3, 1985.
50 "the national cesspool . . ." Whyte, p. xxxi.
55 "You didn't recognize me . . ." Delmore Schwartz, quoted in James Atlas, *Delmore Schwartz: The Life of an American Poet,* p. 353.

3. HAUNCH, PAUNCH AND JOWL

60 "fabricated motherland." Rem Koolhaas, *Delirious New York,* p. 12.
62 "Standing before the kitchen sink . . ." Henry Roth, *Call It Sleep,* p. 17.

63 "one of the vilest characters . . ." Gabriel Miller, in *Dictionary of Literary Biography,* p. 209.

63 ". . . and there was no milk on board." Samuel Ornitz, *Haunch Paunch and Jowl,* p. 23.

63 "a she-goat with udders . . ." Ornitz, p. 23.

64 "A goat manages to get along . . ." Ornitz, p. 20.

64 "I am the cover guy. . . ." Ornitz, p. 30.

64 "our sweet, lawless . . ." Ornitz, p. 31.

64 "Meyer, we've got nothing to look back to. . . ." Ornitz, p. 105.

64 "that hurly-burly time . . ." Ornitz, p. 206.

64 "buxom greenhorn . . ." Ornitz, p. 94.

65 "Control. . . ." Ornitz, p. 250.

65 "'the potatoes we used to bake' . . ." Ornitz, p. 239.

66 "Crime was a source of shame . . ." Irving Howe, *World of Our Fathers,* p. 101.

66 "The Yiddish gangster . . ." Samuel Ornitz, quoted in Miller, p. 209.

67 "more American than the Americans . . ." Miller, p. 212.

68 "lawyers, policemen, and bail bondsmen." Jenna Weissman Joselit, *Our Gang: Jewish Crime and the New York Jewish Community, 1900–1940,* p. 5.

68 "The only thing that interested Jews in Central Park . . ." In Howe, p. 131.

68 "a thousand years behind the times." Ornitz, p. 55.

69 "that certain tenants paid ten times as much . . ." Ornitz, p. 56.

69 "dung upon the Shield of David." Ornitz, p. 57.

70 "physically fit for hard labor." Theodore Bingham, quoted in Joselit, p. 23.

70 "They are burglars, firebugs . . ." Bingham, quoted in Joselit, p. 24.

70 "nursery in crime." Bingham, quoted in Joselit, p. 24.

70 "Whenever we walked into an underworld dive . . ." Abe Schoenfeld, quoted in Joselit, p. 83.

71 "embourgeoisment of New York Jewry." Joselit, p. 158.

71 "Somehow . . ." Joselit, p. 170.

72 "small, flat-nosed Jew." F. Scott Fitzgerald, *The Great Gatsby,* p. 69.

72 "two fine growths of hair . . ." Fitzgerald, pp. 69–70.

72 "for a business gonnegtion." Fitzgerald, p. 71.

72 "he clicked his teeth . . ." Joselit, p. 141.

72 "crumpled against the wall." Donald Henderson Clarke, *In the Reign of Rothstein,* p. 285.

73 "another Jewish boy who had made good." Howe, p. 384.

73 "in accordance with the American requirement . . ." Howe, pp. 99–100.

73 "Arnold was an anomaly . . ." Sidney Zion to J.C., July 20, 1985.

73 "My smart Jew boy." Zion to J.C., July 20, 1985.

73 "loved Harry more . . . wished his brother's death." Zion to J.C., July 20, 1985.

73 "white, womanish hands." Clarke, p. 9.

74 "pantherish quickness." Clarke, p. 20.

74 "Fitzgerald made him look like a bum . . ." Zion to J.C., July 20, 1985.
74 "Arnold was very gay . . ." Clarke, p. 284.
75 "free-fire zone." Zion to J.C., July 20, 1985.
76 "picked out the green light . . . recedes before us." Fitzgerald, p. 182.
78 "Meyer went crazy . . ." Zion to J.C., July 20, 1985.

4. THE MAN WHO SAVED NEW YORK

86 "Forget the epic . . ." Nathanael West, "Some Notes on *Miss Lonelyhearts*," in Jerome Charyn, ed., *The Troubled Vision*, p. ix.
86 "acres of glass." Nathan Silver, *Lost New York*, p. 32.
87 "the regional basket case." Peter C. Goldmark, quoted in Sam Roberts, "'75 Bankruptcy Scare Alters City Plans into 21st Century," *NYT*, July 8, 1985.
87 "The City became . . . like Denmark." Lou Winnick to J.C., May 8, 1985.
87 "bond-crazy . . . worth a yen." Winnick to J.C., May 8, 1985.
87 "Abe, please be careful . . ." Paul O'Dwyer to J.C., March 20, 1985.
88 "be cast across the night sky . . ." E. J. Kahn, Jr., "Lights, Lights, Lights," *The New Yorker*, June 7, 1941, p. 29.
89 "four men to operate the searchlights . . ." Kahn, p. 29.
91 "I was pushing seventy . . ." Douglas Leigh, quoted in "He Lights Up the City Skyline," *Newsday*, January 3, 1984.
91 "the middle of a Lexan sandwich." Douglas Leigh to J.C., July 17, 1985.
91 "we put up the colors . . ." Douglas Leigh, quoted in Susan Schraub Dubin, "The Man Who Lights Up New York," *Town & Country*, September 1984, p. 294.
92 "I began lighting Times Square . . ." Leigh to J.C., July 17, 1985.
92 "The first was a blinking billboard . . ." J. Terry, "Douglas Leigh: The Man Who Lit Up Fifth Avenue," *East Side TV Shopper*, January 5–11, 1985, p. 17.
92 "a few hundred . . ." Kahn, p. 24.
93 "an instantaneous blackout." "Leigh Goes All Out," *The New Yorker*, March 7, 1942, p. 8.
93 "concussion that caused the rings." Leigh to J.C., July 17, 1985.
94 "We're now on a nostalgia kick." Leigh to J.C., July 17, 1985.
95 "I want some buildings . . ." Douglas Leigh, quoted in "New York at Night Is Awash in Light," *Wall Street Journal*, March 21, 1984.
95 "we started out to glorify . . ." Dubin, p. 293.
96 "the roiling, rootless slums." Ben N. Hall, *The Best Remaining Seats*, p. 26.
96 "as a drill sergeant . . ." Hall, p. 27.
96 "magic nickname." Hall, p. 27.
96 "chunky, Napoleonic little man." "Roxy: Auditions Are Held for Radio Comeback This Fall," *Newsweek*, July 28, 1934, p. 22.
97 "glamorize . . ." Hall, p. 36.
97 "I'm going to be . . . and so am I." Roxy, quoted in Hall, p. 30.
97 "dressed the projectionists like brain surgeons." Hall, p. 30.

98 "of satin and rosewood . . ." Hall, p. 38.
99 "Foxy Grandpa." Hall, p. 74.
99 "I'm happy . . . Henry Ford." Hall, p. 12.
100 "rising out of the pit . . ." Hall, p. 257.
101 "a scriptless chorus line . . ." Rem Koolhaas, *Delirious New York*, p. 181.
101 "I would rather die with my boots on." Roxy, quoted in Hall, p. 256.
102 "Death is just a big show . . ." Roxy, quoted in Hall, p. 256.

5. *MATERIAL GIRL*

111 "a great white shark . . ." Carl Arrington, "Madonna," *People*, March 11, 1985, p. 113.
111 "Rather than confining itself . . ." Martin Gottlieb, "A Boom Borough," *NYT*, February 1, 1984.
111 "13th Avenue." Gottlieb, "A Boom Borough."
112 "A great city by the sea . . ." John Russell," Where City Meets Sea to Become Art," *NYT*, December 11, 1983.
113 "mayor for one night . . . a buyer for Bloomingdale's." Lauren Kaye to J.C., May 30, 1985.
113 "She's an intellectual cook." Ann Willen, quoted in *Daily News*, March 7, 1979.
114 "The mayor wanted what he wanted . . . funky, wild neighborhood." Kaye to J.C., May 30, 1985.
116–18 "I grew up . . . the devil up close." Catherine Texier to J.C., April 13, 1985.
118 "When I walk . . ." David Wojnarowicz, quoted in Amy Virshup, "The Night Stuff," *New York*, November 5, 1984, p. 26.
119 "after three days . . . retrieve one of my socks." David Wojnarowicz, "Self Portrait in Twenty-Three Rounds," *Between C And D*, Summer 1984, pp. 3–6.
120–21 "We were street artists . . . drips from the ceiling." Rich Colicchio, quoted in Walter Robinson and Carlo McCormick, "Slouching Toward Avenue D," *Art in America*, Summer 1984, p. 138.
121 "There are . . . the '80s." Peter Nagy, quoted in David Hershkovitz, "Art in Alphabetland," *ARTnews*, September 1983, p. 89.
121 "I wanted a name . . . the right one." Gracie Mansion, quoted in Douglas C. McGill, "Success Stories of Two Galleries in Emerging Art Neighborhoods," *NYT*, February 18, 1985.
121 "All my friends . . ." McGill.
121 "Gracie Mansion proudly . . ." McGill.
122 "the art world's newest monster." Robinson and McCormick, p. 141.
123 "all be forced out . . ." Tom Pollak, quoted in Craig Unger, "The Lower East Side: There Goes the Neighborhood," *New York*, May 28, 1984, p. 41.

126 "I don't want . . . King Kong." Leo Castelli, quoted in Patricia Johnson, "New York's the Place and the Pace for Arts Community," *Houston Chronicle,* December 22, 1984.

127–29 "in the area of Minsk . . . every nine days." Arthur Cohen to J.C., January 21 and February 25, 1985.

129 "They set it up for me . . ." Jean-Michel Basquiat, quoted in Cathleen McGuigan, "New Art, New Money: The Marketing of an American Artist," *NYTM,* February 10, 1985, p. 32.

129 "It's a myth . . ." Mark Kostabi, quoted in Douglas C. McGill, "For Artists, New Paths to Success," *NYT,* April 11, 1985.

129–30 "More Americans go . . . of the American city." Robert Hughes, "On Art and Money," *The New York Review of Books,* December 6, 1984, p. 20.

130 "Art prices are determined . . ." Hughes, "On Art and Money," p. 24.

130 "There is no oblivion. . . ." Hughes, "On Art and Money," p. 25.

131 "painters, sculptors . . . like bluefish." Hughes, "On Art and Money," p. 26.

132 "an art-world Eddie Murphy." Robert Hughes, "Careerism and Hype Amidst the Image Haze," *Time,* June 17, 1985, p. 79.

132 "Montmartre of the Neo . . . like an antelope through a python." Hughes, "Careerism and Hype," p. 78.

132 "In this republic . . ." Hughes, "Careerism and Hype," p. 81.

134 "I think Mary is famous . . ." Julian Schnabel, quoted in Cathleen McGuigan, "Julian Schnabel: 'I Always Knew It Would Be Like This,'" *ARTnews,* Summer 1982, p. 94.

134 "People feel sorry . . ." Mary Boone, quoted in Anthony Haden-Guest, "The New Queen of the Art Scene," *New York,* April 19, 1982, p. 30.

135–36 "I'm not a myth . . . I'm a human being." Mary Boone to J.C., April 5, 1985.

136 "has moved beyond hyping . . ." Thomas Lawson, "The Dark Side of the Bright Light," *Artforum,* November 1982, p. 66.

138 "I take umbrage . . . heroic disease." Sherrie Levine, quoted in Gerald Marzorati, "Julian Schnabel: Plate It as It Lays," *ARTnews,* April 1985, p. 64.

138 "I think people . . ." Schnabel, quoted in Marzorati, p. 69.

138 "Frankenstein presence." Rene Ricard, "Not About Julian Schnabel," *Artforum,* Summer 1981.

138 "The best of Schnabel's paintings . . ." Jeff Perrone, "Boy Do I Love Art or What?" *Arts Magazine,* September 1981, p. 77.

139 "at his brushes like a gorilla . . ." Rene Ricard, quoted in Pepe Karmel, "Art & Exhibitionism," *Vanity Fair,* July 1985, p. 39.

139 "The show was . . . no audience." James Harithas, quoted in McGuigan, p. 88.

140 "And I was tired of cooking." Schnabel, quoted in McGuigan, p. 92.

140 "Painting makes me feel . . ." Schnabel, quoted in Marzorati, p. 69.

140–41 "Agony has many faces . . . to show you does." Julian Schnabel, "The Patients and the Doctors," *Artforum,* February 1984, pp. 55–57.

141 "great father." Frederic Tuten to J.C., May 15, 1985.

141–44 "Promise me . . . They're my favorite ones." Julian Schnabel to J.C., May 15, 1985.

145 "He ordained power . . . instinct for killing." Tuten to J.C., May 15, 1985.

145 "Most kids mess . . . going to throw up." Schnabel to J.C., May 22, 1985.

7. THE PHARAOH AND THE UNICORN

148–52 "It's infantile . . . for grown-ups." Henry Stern to J.C. (all interviews with Henry Stern were conducted during March, April, May, and July 1985).

152 "He took me through . . ." Ed Koch to J.C., June 13, 1985.

152 "I was counting on . . . I would be called." Stern to J.C.

153 "The second morning . . ." Lauren Kaye to J.C., May 30, 1985.

153 "Minor obsessions . . ." Stern to J.C.

154 "significant gamblers . . . your favorite bar." Mickey Mantle, quoted in Tom Callahan, "Willie, Mickey and Nathan Detroit," *Time,* April 1, 1985, p. 86.

155–57 "I'm like Ferdinand . . . trees are leaning down." Stern to J.C.

157 "Muggers would rob you . . ." Jeanette Perez, quoted in William E. Geist, "About New York: The Year the Fish Returned to Crotona Park," *NYT,* May 12, 1984.

158 "postcard blue." Geist.

158 "You get a lot of bank . . . who has to be courted." Adrian Benepe to J.C., May 29, 1985.

158 "larger than a football field." Geist.

159 "The City lost . . . disaster area." Benepe to J.C., May 29, 1985.

160 "was convinced that Negroes . . ." Robert A. Caro, *The Power Broker: Robert Moses and the Fall of New York,* p. 319.

161 "been in government . . ." Ed Koch, quoted in Joe Klein, "Henry Stern Goes to the Park: A Commissioner for All Species," *New York,* August 1, 1983, p. 38.

162 "Hey, I've been dancing . . ." Meade Esposito, quoted in Maurice Carroll, "Esposito Looks Back at the Good Old Days," *NYT,* January 27, 1984.

8. A MAN CALLED ALVARADO

167 "legend of success." Diane Ravitch, *The Great School Wars: New York City, 1805–1973,* p. 310.

168 "saucy to a monitor." Ravitch, p. 15.

169 "One school had . . ." Ravitch, p. 126.

169 "that the first exercise . . ." Ravitch, p. 177.

169 "inferior genetic endowment." Ravitch, p. 311.

170 "More than half . . ." Ravitch, p. 180.

171 "melting pot, the great cauldron of Americanization . . ." Ravitch, p. 243.

172 "throwing erasers . . . dramatic improvements." Herman Badillo to J.C., March 21, 1985.

172 "live in an amputated present tense." Jonathan Kozol, "The Crippling Inheritance," *New York Times Book Review*, March 3, 1985, p. 26.

172 "with a disaster . . . dead in this country." Badillo to J.C., March 21, 1985.

173 "destitute . . . the Public Schools." Ravitch, p. 33.

174 "You walk into a school . . ." Anthony Alvarado, quoted in Nat Hentoff, "The Other Alvarado: A Year of Actually Turning the Schools Around," *VV*, July 10, 1984, p. 32.

174 "he is not religious." Joyce Purnick, "Alvarado Story Moved Fast from Start," *NYT*, March 26, 1984.

176 "Alvarado seemed . . ." Joe Klein, "Tony Alvarado Flunks Math: The Fall of the Schools Chancellor," *New York*, April 2, 1984, p. 41.

176 "great swoops . . ." Purnick, "Alvarado Story Moved Fast."

176 "second-rate services." "Alvarado Wants a Lot More for the Schools," *NYT*, December 18, 1983.

176 "at polar odds . . ." Joyce Purnick, "Alvarado Says His Case Had an Inevitability," *NYT*, April 11, 1984.

176 "an octopus . . ." Anthony Alvarado, quoted in Purnick, "Alvarado Story Moved Fast."

177 "The mayor walks in . . ." Alvarado, quoted in Hentoff, "The Other Alvarado," p. 19.

178 "From the moment . . ." Anthony Alvarado, quoted in Klein, p. 41.

179 "deep quiet." Nat Hentoff, "Do Tony Alvarado's Ideas Have to Be Buried with Him?" *VV*, July 3, 1984, p. 23.

179 "Sargasso Sea . . ." Hentoff, *VV*, July 10, 1984, p. 19.

179 "1,393 quit . . . you're a candidate." Joyce Purnick, "City's Poor Are Hard Hit by a Severe Shortage of Teachers," *NYT*, February 29, 1984.

180 "it cannot police itself . . ." Joyce Purnick, "New York Schools Faulted in Report," *NYT*, September 12, 1984.

180 "Someone like Alvarado . . ." Badillo to J.C., March 21, 1985.

180–81 "at his demise . . . support structure." Franklin Thomas to J.C., May 3, 1985.

182 "I'm old enough . . . traced to that area." Benjamin Ward to J.C., September 11, 1985.

182–83 "The Indians were . . . three or four times." Ward to J.C., September 11, 1985.

9. HOME

185–86 "a country of . . ." Peter Quinn, "In Search of Protestants," *NYT*, March 16, 1985.

188 "Real estate may be . . ." Michael Oreskes, "Tempers Are Rising with Property Values," *NYT*, May 12, 1985.

188 "the most courageous act . . ." Rem Koolhaas, *Delirious New York*, p. 13.

189 "one notch . . ." Oreskes.

189–90 "Children . . . childless." Sidney H. Schanberg, "New York: Home Truth Report," *NYT*, March 16, 1985.

190 "the lowest figure . . .'" Joseph Berger, "Failure of Plan for Homeless Reflects City Housing Crisis," *NYT*, February 19, 1985.

190 "fewer couples . . . solitude." John Vinocur, "Doings at the Louvre and in Chinatown-sur-Seine," *NYT*, March 18, 1985.

191 "We're checking to see . . ." Ed Koch, quoted in Michael Goodwin, "Koch Considers Using Ships as Shelter for the Homeless," *NYT*, April 28, 1984.

192 "He became my guide . . ." Robert Hayes, quoted in Sarah Rimer, "The Other City: New York's Homeless," *NYT*, January 30, 1984.

193 "If we knew the homeless . . ." Hayes, quoted in Rimer.

193–94 "the purge of . . . in terms of government." Robert Hayes to J.C., March 19, 1985.

195 "My home is . . ." Harold, quoted in William E. Geist, "About New York: The Homeless Find 11th St., and a Block Is Upset," *NYT*, January 26, 1985.

195 "There's twenty thousand . . ." Hayes to J.C., March 19, 1985.

195 "briefcase people." Deidre Carmody, "Delivering Dinner to Grand Central, Where the Hungry Homeless Wait," *NYT*, March 2, 1985.

195–97 "But the police . . . wartime period." Hayes to J.C., March 19, 1985.

197 "To make money . . ." Woodrow Gist, quoted in Howard Blum, "Evictions Up, City Marshals Prosper," *NYT*, February 11, 1984.

197 "It's like a ship . . ." David Beseda, quoted in "Downtown Homeless Center Wins Praise," *NYT*, April 20, 1985.

198 "dangerous for . . . safer than the shelters." In George Silberman, "Homeless Shelters Are Dangerous Places," *NYT*, April 8, 1985.

199 "The housing placement . . ." Mark Bullock to J.C., April 4, 1985.

199 "If I stay out late . . ." Sidney Bailey, quoted in Martin Gottlieb, "New York Housing Agency Takes a Bow at 50," *NYT*, June 25, 1984.

199–200 "The first thing . . . help them get out." Bullock to J.C., April 4, 1985.

10. THE WORLD ACCORDING TO KOCH

203 "What Bulgaria has done . . ." Ed Koch, quoted in Joyce Purnick, "Koch Invited to U.N., Assails Russia and Bulgaria," *NYT*, September 20, 1985.

204 "If that's true . . ." Ed Koch, quoted in Joyce Purnick, "Police to Round Up Homeless When a Cold Wave Grips City," *NYT*, January 23, 1985.

204 "the inn is full." Jesse Jackson, quoted in Larry Rohter, "Jackson Brands New York City 'Slum Landlord,'" *NYT*, April 1, 1985.

204 "This is a town . . ." Norman Mailer, at an Executive Board meeting of PEN American Center, September 19, 1985.

204 "*schwarzes.*" Arthur Browne, Dan Collins, and Michael Goodwin, *I, Koch*, p. 199.

206 "incredibly thin skin of politics." Robert Hayes to J.C., March 19, 1985.

206 ". . . I get the bends . . ." Edward I, Koch, *Mayor*, p. 278.

206 "looks like . . . pointy." Ed Koch, quoted in Wayne King, "Howdy Houston! How'm I Doin'?" *NYT*, March 30, 1984.

206 "Every day is dangerous." Koch, p. 347.

207 "poor and Polish." Browne, Collins, and Goodwin, p. 2.

207 "a decorated sergeant." Ken Auletta, "The Mayor—Part I," *The New Yorker,* September 10, 1979, p. 68.

207 "Well, I think . . ." Koch, p. 21.

208 "Other people go . . ." Koch, p. 46.

212 "played the Grieg . . ." Browne, Collins, and Goodwin, p. 127.

219 "Most mayors are . . . difference today." Richard P. Nathan, quoted in Martin Gottlieb, "A Decade After the Cutbacks, New York Is a Different City," *NYT,* June 30, 1985.

220 "the combined debt . . ." Robert A. Caro, *The Power Broker: Robert Moses and the Fall of New York,* p. 326.

220 "The banks had . . . the bankers." Paul O'Dwyer to J.C., March 20, 1985.

220 "with a window . . ." Martin Gottlieb, "New York Housing Agency Takes a Bow at 50," *NYT,* June 25, 1984.

221 "provide him . . ." Caro, p. 463.

221 "Triborough had . . ." Caro, p. 13.

221 "Basically . . . the rich." Herman Badillo to J.C., March 21, 1985.

221–22 "No mayor . . ." Caro, p. 5.

222 "would have been . . ." Caro, p. 688.

222 "unbearable . . . servitude." Roger Starr, *The Rise and Fall of New York City,* p. 200.

222 "cherishes vindictiveness . . ." Browne, Collins, and Goodwin, p. 18.

223 "We wanted . . . subconsciously." O'Dwyer to J.C., March 20, 1985.

223 "Mr. Linsley . . . a boy in short pants." Michael J. Quill, quoted in Woody Klein, *Lindsay's Promise,* p. 59.

223 "He's a most . . ." Ed Koch to J.C., June 13, 1985.

223 "slipping into a tepid bath . . ." Felix Rohatyn, quoted in Martin Gottlieb, "New York's Rescue: The Offstage Dramas," *NYT,* July 2, 1985.

223–24 "The bankruptcy deal . . ." Badillo to J.C., March 21, 1985.

224 "Those of us . . ." Ed Koch, quoted in Michael Goodwin, "Salvation Army Losing City Pacts for Stand on Hiring Homosexuals," *NYT,* March 3, 1984.

224 "that this match . . ." Ed Koch, quoted in "Koch Helps Honor U.N. Anniversary," *NYT,* April 30, 1985.

224 "dangerous people . . ." Ed Koch, quoted in Jesus Rangel, "City Listing Most-Wanted Criminals," *NYT,* March 6, 1985.

225 "This is a thing here . . ." Masselli, quoted in "Tapes on Organized Crime Released," *NYT,* March 7, 1985.

225 "mother——." *East Village Eye,* April 1985, p. 20.

225 "The 'mayor is . . ." O'Dwyer to J.C., March 20, 1985.

225 "He's still my friend." Ed Koch, in Michael Kramer, "The Manes Mess," *New York,* January 27, 1986, p. 12.

226 "I'm gonna be . . . the 800-pound gorilla." Ed Koch, in Michael Kramer, "Manes the Mess and the Mayor," *New York,* February 10, 1986, p. 39.

229–34 "I'm amazed . . . 'such beautiful hair.'" Mary Guerriero to J.C., September 13, 1985.

234 "New York has . . ." Benjamin Ward to J.C., September 11, 1985.

236–39 "the police coming in . . . to be pushed around." Calvin Butts to J.C., April 15, 1985.

12. THE DEATH OF CHARLIE CHAN

246–49 "come to the land . . . laundry workers." Rod Chu to J.C., May 7 and May 16, 1985.

249 "Those who stayed . . ." Fred Ferretti, "A City Within a City Where Old Meets New," *NYT,* February 3, 1985.

252 "patient and furious . . ." *New York Panorama,* p. 422.

253–56 "the power over . . . can remove me." Hugh Mo to J.C., June 26, 1985.

256–58 "I was in Beijing . . . gypped out of this experience." Katherine Wei to J.C., September 4, 1985.

258 "more ships than Onassis." Mo to J.C., July 31, 1985.

259 "Flowers might be . . ." Shirley Bernstein, quoted in William E. Geist, "Park Ave. Residents Want a New Deli to Go," *NYT,* February 28, 1984.

259 "The rich never run . . ." Arthur Cohen to J.C., February 25, 1985.

259–60 "dignified . . . take over everything." Harriet Tung to J.C., September 5, 1985.

261 "It's extremely dangerous . . . twenty-first century." Mo to J.C., September 13, 1985.

13. RAISSA

263–64 "perfect city . . . fulfilling the dream." Kevin Wolfe, "Island of the Dreams," *Metropolis,* January–February 1985, p. 27.

264 "alternates between . . ." Lance Morrow, "Immigrants," *Time,* July 8, 1985, p. 24.

265 "city of sadness . . . its own existence." Italo Calvino, *Invisible Cities,* p. 149.

265 "All the Mo brothers . . . many couldn't make it." Hugh Mo to J.C., June 26, 1985.

266 "Asian-American admissions issue." Michael Winerip, "Asian-Americans Question Ivy League's Entry Policies," *NYT,* May 30, 1985.

266 "the bottom part." Uwe Reinhardt, in Winerip.

266 "He cared nothing . . ." Ernest Hemingway, *The Sun Also Rises,* p. 3.

267 "The Jews and Irish. . . . Unfortunately, no." Paul O'Dwyer to J.C., March 20, 1985.

267 ". . . the people who . . ." Lindsey Gruson, "Jewish Singles Groups Play Matchmakers to Preserve the Future of Judaism," *NYT,* April 1, 1985.

268 "There is almost nothing . . . 'Americanism' itself." Robert Warshow, *The Immediate Experience,* p. 130.

268 "the man of the city . . . afraid we may become." Warshow, p. 131.

268 "without culture . . . dangers of the city." Warshow, p. 136.

268 "is a nightmare inversion . . ." Warshow, p. 137.

268 "the quality of . . ." Warshow, p. 132.

268–69 "In the deeper . . ." Warshow, p. 133.

271–73 "Color, folklore . . . its soul." Martin Gottlieb to J.C., July 23, 1985.

273 "as a mecca . . . definitely happening." Rudolf, quoted in Michael Gross, "The Party Seems to Be Over for Lower Manhattan Clubs," *NYT*, October 26, 1985.

273–74 "is not the Federal city . . . at the penthouse level." George Steiner, quoted in Jo Thomas, "In London, a Warning Sounded About a Declining New York," *NYT*, May 26, 1985.

274–75 "pathological feelings . . . so many nice people." Tadeusz Korzeniewski to J.C., March 16, 1985.

279 "Palladium fallout." Jim Mullen, quoted in Gross.

ACKNOWLEDGMENTS

298 "C'mon, Joe . . ." William Brashler, *Josh Gibson: A Life in the Negro Leagues*, p. 136.

BIBLIOGRAPHY

ABBOTT, BERENICE. *New York in the Thirties.* New York: Dover
    Publications, 1967.
ANDERSON, JERVIS. *This Was Harlem.* New York: Farrar, Straus
    and Giroux, 1983.
ARBUS, DIANE. *Diane Arbus.* New York: Aperture, 1972.
ATLAS, JAMES. *Delmore Schwartz: The Life of an American Poet.* New
    York: Avon Books, Discus, 1977.
BALDWIN, JAMES. *Notes of a Native Son.* Boston: Beacon Press,
    1955.
BELL, DANIEL. *The End of Ideology.* New York: The Free Press,
    1962.
BLACK, MAXINE, ed. *Current Biography: 1940.* New York: H. W.
    Wilson Company, 1940, 1968.
BOSWORTH, PATRICIA. *Diane Arbus.* New York: Alfred A. Knopf,
    1984.

BRASHLER, WILLIAM. *Josh Gibson: A Life in the Negro Leagues*. New York: Harper & Row, 1978.

BROWNE, ARTHUR, DAN COLLINS, and MICHAEL GOODWIN. *I, Koch*. New York: Dodd, Mead & Company, 1985.

CALVINO, ITALO. *Invisible Cities*. New York: Harcourt Brace Jovanovich, 1972.

CARO, ROBERT A. *The Power Broker: Robert Moses and the Fall of New York*. New York: Vintage Books, 1975.

CHARYN, JEROME, ed. *The Troubled Vision*. New York: Collier Books, 1970.

CLARKE, DONALD HENDERSON. *In the Reign of Rothstein*. New York: Vanguard Press, 1929.

COOPER, MARTHA, and HENRY CHALFANT. *Subway Art*. New York: Holt, Rinehart and Winston, 1984.

ELLIS, EDWARD ROBB. *The Epic of New York City*. New York: Coward-McCann, 1966.

FITZGERALD, F. SCOTT. *The Great Gatsby*. New York: Charles Scribner's Sons, 1925.

GLAZER, NATHAN, and DANIEL PATRICK MOYNIHAN. *Beyond the Melting Pot*. Cambridge, Mass.: MIT Press, 1970.

GOLDBERGER, PAUL. *The City Observed: New York*. New York: Vintage Books, 1979.

———. *The Skyscraper*. New York: Alfred A. Knopf, 1982.

GOREN, ARTHUR A. *New York Jews and The Quest for Community*. New York: Columbia University Press, 1970.

HAGENBERG, ROLAND, et al. *East Village*. New York: Pelham Press, n.d.

HALL, BEN N. *The Best Remaining Seats*. New York: Clarkson N. Potter, 1961.

HANDLIN, OSCAR. *The Newcomers*. Cambridge, Mass.: Harvard University Press, 1959.

HEMINGWAY, ERNEST. *The Sun Also Rises*. New York: Charles Scribner's Sons, 1926.

HOWE, IRVING. *World of Our Fathers*. New York: Simon and Schuster, Touchstone Books, 1976.

HUGHES, ROBERT. *The Shock of the New*. New York: Alfred A. Knopf, 1981.

JACOBS, JANE. *The Death and Life of Great American Cities*. New York: Random House, 1961.

JOSELIT, JENNA WEISSMAN. *Our Gang: Jewish Crime and the New York Jewish Community, 1900–1940*. Bloomington: Indiana University Press, 1983.

KLEIN, WOODY. *Lindsay's Promise*. New York: Macmillan Publishing Company, 1970.

KOCH, EDWARD I. *Mayor*. New York: Simon and Schuster, 1984.

KOOLHAAS, REM. *Delirious New York*. New York: Oxford University Press, 1978.

KOUWENHOVEN, JOHN A. *The Columbia Historical Portrait of New York*. New York: Harper & Row, Icon Editions, 1972.

MARK, DIANE MEI LIN, and GINGER CHIH. *A Place Called Chinese America*. Dubuque: Kendall/Hunt Publishing Company, 1982.

MARTIN, JAY. *Nathanael West: The Art of His Life*. New York: Farrar, Straus and Giroux, 1970.

MILLER, GABRIEL. "Samuel Ornitz." In *Dictionary of Literary Biography*, vol. 28, pp. 207–213. Detroit: Gale Research Company, 1984.

MOSCOW, WARREN. *The Last of the Big-Time Bosses*. New York: Stein and Day, 1971.

MUMFORD, LEWIS. *The Culture of Cities*. New York: Harcourt, Brace & Company, 1938.

NEWFIELD, JACK, and PAUL DUBRUL. *The Permanent Government*. New York: Pilgrim Press, 1981.

New York Panorama. New York: Pantheon Books, 1984.

ORNITZ, SAMUEL. *Haunch Paunch and Jowl*. New York: Boni and Liveright, 1923.

OSOFSKY, GILBERT. *Harlem: The Making of a Ghetto*. New York: Harper & Row, 1966.

OZICK, CYNTHIA. *Art and Ardor*. New York: Alfred A. Knopf, 1983.

PACE GALLERY. *Julian Schnabel*. New York: Pace Gallery, 1984.

PATERSON, VIRGIL W. *The Mob: 200 Years of Organized Crime in New York*. Ottawa, Ill.: Green Hill Publishers, 1983.

RAVITCH, DIANE. *The Great School Wars: New York City, 1805–1973*. New York: Basic Books, 1974.

REYNOLDS, DONALD MARTIN. *The Architecture of New York City*. New York: Macmillan Publishing Company, 1984.

ROHATYN, FELIX G. *The Twenty-Year Century*. New York: Random House, 1983.

ROTH, HENRY. *Call It Sleep*. 1934. Reprint. New York: Avon, Bard Books, 1964.

SANDERS, RONALD, and EDMUND V. GILLON, JR. *The Lower East Side*. New York: Dover Publications, 1979.

SCHOENER, ALLON, ed. *Portal to America: The Lower East Side,*

1870–1925. New York: Holt, Rinehart and Winston, 1967.

SCHWAM, KEITH. *Shopping Bag Ladies: Homeless Women*. New York: Manhattan Bowery Corporation, 1979.

SILBERMAN, CHARLES E. *Criminal Violence, Criminal Justice*. New York: Random House, 1978.

SILVER, NATHAN. *Lost New York*. New York: Schocken Books, 1967.

Souvenir Journal to 107th Washington Square Outdoor Art Exhibit. New York, 1985.

STARR, ROGER. *The Rise and Fall of New York City*. New York: Basic Books, 1985.

TAUBER, GILBERT, and SAMUEL KAPLAN. *The New York City Handbook*. Garden City, N.Y.: Doubleday & Company, 1968.

TAURANAC, JOHN. *Essential New York*. New York: Holt, Rinehart and Winston, 1979.

TEXIER, CATHERINE, ed. *New York Creation*. Paris: Autrement, 1984.

TIFFT, WILTON, and THOMAS DUNNE. *Ellis Island*. New York: W. W. Norton & Company, 1971.

TUCILLE, JEROME. *Trump*. New York: Donald I. Fine, 1985.

TUCKER, KERRY. *Greetings from New York*. New York: Delilah, 1981.

UNIVERSITY ART MUSEUM, *Neo York*. Santa Barbara: University Art Museum, 1984.

WARSHOW, ROBERT. *The Immediate Experience*. Garden City, N.Y.: Doubleday & Company, 1962.

WHITE, E. B. "Here Is New York." In *Essays of E. B. White*. New York: Harper and Brothers, 1949.

WHITE, NORVAL, and ELLIOT WILLENSKY, eds. *AIA Guide to New York City*. Rev. ed. New York: Macmillan Publishing Company, 1978.

WPA Guide to New York City, The. 1939. Reprint. New York: Pantheon Books, 1982.

ZION, SIDNEY. *Read All About It*. New York: Berkley Books, 1984.

ACKNOWLEDGMENTS

Been writing this book since I was five, storing up memories in my fur like a Bronx grizzly bear. Something was wrong. I was a predator, and I couldn't say why. Had no instincts toward family and human kindness. I loved baseball, movies, and little else. I was insane about the New York Giants. Ah, I could give you a whole battery of facts and feelings about the '46 Giants, who lived in last place. They had the sweetest shortstop, Buddy Kerr, and a Jewish third baseman, Sid Gordon, but those Giants just couldn't jell. And then, sometime in '47, the year of Jackie Robinson, I heard of a black Babe Ruth, and I hoped to God the Giants would grab him. His name was Josh Gibson. But Gibson was dead. He'd died that January, an old man of thirty-five, haunted by Joe DiMaggio. He'd stare out his window and have conversations with Joe. "C'mon, Joe, you know me. You ain' gonna answer me?"

Gibson wasn't a New Yorker. He may never have visited the Bronx. But he was my hero, a rebel catcher in the Negro Leagues (I didn't know he was dead). All my heroes were outcasts, cave children. Spinoza. King Kong. Josh Gibson. DiMaggio himself, who seemed utterly alone in his perfection, Bartleby with a baseball bat.

I'm forty-eight years old, twice the child I was at ten. I still admire cave children like Koch and Herman Badillo, who can't stop battling. I couldn't have completed this book if Koch hadn't married New York and become our hundred and fifth mayor. It's hard to think of a hundred and four mayors earlier than Ed Koch. He's the end point—dream and song—of the village I've been carrying in my furry head all these years.

I owe a debt to him and Herman Badillo, Arthur Cohen, Don Sohn, Tadeusz Korzeniewski, Frederic Tuten, Robert Hayes, Paul O'Dwyer, John Simon, Andrew Fenrich, Henry Stern, Harvey Charyn, Mark Bullock, Mary Boone, Catherine Texier, the Reverend Calvin Butts, Franklin Thomas, Roderick Chu, Louis Winnick, Miguel Algarin, Julian Schnabel, Rachel Horovitz, Lauren Kaye, Dan and Rhoda Wolf, Harold Brodkey, Hugh Mo, Douglas Leigh, Martin Gottlieb, Sidney Zion, Kirkpatrick Sale, Glen Kau-Lee, Douglas Century, Matthew Affron, Neal Hirschfeld, Suzanne Sekey, Benjamin Ward, Katherine Wei, Harriet Tung, Adrian Benepe, Norman Wikler, Mary Guerriero, Raissa, and Faith Sale.

INDEX